The Book of Business Anecdotes

Peter Hay

WINGS BOOKS
New York • Avenel, New Jersey

This 1993 edition is published by Wings Books,
distributed by Outlet Book Company, Inc., a Random House Company,
40 Engelhard Avenue, Avenel, New Jersey 07001,
by arrangement with Facts On File, Inc.

Random House
New York • Toronto • London • Sydney • Auckland

Printed and bound in the United States of America

Library of Congress Cataloging-in-Publication Data

Hay, Peter, 1944-
    The book of business anecdotes / Peter Hay.
        p.   cm.
    Originally published: New York: Facts on File, c1988.
    Includes bibliographical references and index.
    ISBN 0-517-09376-6
    1. Business—Anecdotes. I. Title.
  [HF5351.H34 1993]
  650'.0207—dc20   93-4347
                                                              CIP

8 7 6 5 4 3 2 1

CONTENTS

ACKNOWLEDGMENTS

I owe a great deal to the late Ralph Carson, whose friendship and unique class in entrepreneurship at the University of Southern California helped me to understand the human dimensions and humane values of business.

I salute all those friends, associates and acquaintances in the business world whose achievements and entrepreneurial struggles have moved and inspired me, and in particular: Bill and Sandy Adler; Jytte Allen; John Arrowsmith; Keith Atwater; Lia Benedetti; Dr. Gerd Bucerius; Gautam Dasgupta; Cordelia Dunlaevy; Maureen and Conner Everts; Bella and Clément Feinsilber; Mira Friedlander; Hermine Fuerst-Garcia; Deirdre Gainor; Marilyn Gross; Thomas Hegedus; Peter Huber; Bill Ilminen; Uta Jeron; Eva, Judy and Paul Kolosvary; Steve Kovacs; Nancy Lee; Walter Leonard; Arlene Levin; Bonnie Marranca; the Miller family (Ethel, Howard, Barry, Steve and Wendy); Hilda Mortimer; Cora Seiler Muirhead; Wendy Newman; Renee Paris; Nacho Ramirez; Deborah Reed; David Robinson; Don Rubin; Norma and George Ryga; Nicholas Siegel; Christine Skube; Harold Spector; Martin Squire; Ron Stern; David Tempest; Roy Wallace; Art Warshaw; and Cindy White.

I deeply appreciate the guidance, advice and support given by my editor, Gerard Helferich. My thanks to Alice Misiewicz for copyediting the manuscript. Richard Kahlenberg, my friend and agent, has kept me going through the rough patches. Oliver Muirhead, David Parrish and John Sarantos gave valuable assistance in researching this book. Librarian Anthony Anderson has kept me from being jailed for overdue books.

As always, I am happy to acknowledge my debts to my mother, Eva Hay, for her constant encouragement and research, and to my wife,

Dorthea, consumer expert, author of several computer books, and managing editor for a major software company. Through her I have been able to experience, if vicariously, the ins and outs, and ups and downs, of American business at its leading edge.

PREFACE

The origin of this book goes back to my early addiction to books in general: reading them, buying them, publishing them, and now writing them. When I was a teenager in England, I would spend much of my school vacation among the stalls of second-hand booksellers on Charing Cross Road. There I found odd volumes of the Percy Anecdotes—published in the 1820s—a vast collection of stories on every subject. Some of these volumes bear the headings of "Commerce," "Industry," and "Enterprise." My collection of anecdote books grew over the years, and, having filled an entire room with them, it became logical (and financially unavoidable) to increase my holdings by writing my own.

The last anecdote collection devoted exclusively to the present topic was an American compilation in two volumes by a man writing under the pseudonym of Frazar Kirkland. The work had a rather fulsome title: *Cyclopaedia of Commercial and Business Anecdotes; comprising Interesting Reminiscences and Facts, Remarkable Traits and Humors, and Notable Sayings, Dealings, Experiences, and Witticisms of Merchants, Traders, Bankers, Mercantile Celebrities, Millionaires, Bargain Makers, etc. etc. in all Ages and Countries; Designed to Exhibit, by Nearly Three Thousand Illustrative Anecdotes and Incidents the Piquancies and Pleasantries of Trade, Commerce, and General Business Pursuits.* This useful book was published during the Civil War in 1864. Clearly, much has happened in the intervening years. It is time for an update.

Anecdotes are often confused with jokes and humorous stories with which board chairmen like to pepper their speeches at annual meetings and dull banquets. The stories are usually taken from books with the word *Toastmaster* somewhere in the title, and they are rarely about real people. A genuine anecdote, however, is not "one about the boss and the secretary"; it is, in Webster's definition, a "biographical incident" about somebody who actually lived and did or said something worth remembering. It may end with a witticism and make one smile, but it can also be instructive, descriptive, inspiring, or poignant.

Analysis of an event in the past may trigger a solution in the present. The mysteries of business success and failure are rarely found in formulae, but rather in the struggles of entrepreneurs and the exemplars of companies they founded. That is why they teach the case method at the Harvard Business School and why *In Search of Excellence* is about specific corporations. My purpose in compiling this collection of mostly true stories about the many worlds of business is primarily to entertain and to inspire. But if businessmen and businesswomen get ideas from this book that might help them, or if a millionaire is inspired by an example of philanthropy, so much the better.

This book is organized by topics, some of which have general appeal (e.g., money or politics), and others that will guide a manager, a banker, or an employee into subjects of professional interest. I am not a specialist in business. This work reflects a generalist concern with what is the dominant culture of the age. Business is no longer just the business of America; it has become the culture of the late twentieth century. Increasingly, business thinking, practice, philosophy, and ethics dominate the educational system and the media, including publishing and entertainment. We talk not only about the "movie business" and the "television industry," we see also hospitals and prisons run as businesses. Indeed, governments are selling shares in public services.

George Bernard Shaw was listening once to a long flowery sales pitch by Samuel Goldwyn, who went on and on about his intent to turn *Pygmalion* into an artistic film. The dramatist finally interrupted the mogul: "The reason we won't make a deal, Mr. Goldwyn, is because you are mainly interested in art, whereas I am only concerned with money." There has always been a connection between commerce and art, and many an artist has looked in the mirror and found a corporation staring back. But even I was startled a short time ago, while quietly tending my little corner of the academic grove, when the recently appointed chairman of my department tried to explain the university's new policy that professors should consider themselves individual profit centers. Corporate culture has become simply *the* culture, and I hope this book will provide a perspective on what that means.

Peter Hay
Los Angeles, California
November 1, 1987

· 1 ·

ABOUT MONEY

LEGAL TENDER

Wears Well

The Roman emperor Vespasian is still famous for his saying that money does not smell. Oil billionaire J. Paul Getty, who built the imitation of a Roman emperor's villa in Malibu, California, was of a different opinion. He said: "Money is like manure. You have to spread it around or it smells."

I have not found the origin of the phrase *stinking rich*. But my favorite comment about money is Myron Cohen's quote about a model's remark to garment maker Al Rosenstein of Roseweb Frocks: "The nicest thing about money is that it never clashes with anything I wear."

Filthy Lucre

Sándor Ferenczi, the Hungarian disciple of Sigmund Freud, once wrote an article with the title "On the Ontogenesis of the Interest in Money." Anticipating some of the attitudes of the 1960s, the doctor compared coins with body wastes: "It is nothing but odorless dehydrated filth that has been made to shine."

1

Every Business Needs One

One of Andrew Carnegie's boyhood playmates was Henry Phipps, who spent the rest of his life working for Carnegie. They were utterly unlike. Phipps had also come of a wretchedly poor background, but he had none of the dash and sparkle of Carnegie. He was the plodder, the bookkeeper, the economizer, the man who had an eye for microscopic details. His abilities consisted mainly in smoothing the ruffled feelings of creditors, in cutting out unnecessary expenditures, and in shaving prices. Carnegie used him to keep the bankers complaisant.

"What we most admired about young Phipps," a Pittsburgh banker once remarked, "is the way in which he could keep a check in the air for three or four days."

Making Money

A wholesale forger of bank notes, whose operations in the middle of the eighteenth century caused nothing less than consternation in the Bank of England, was the notorious Charles Price, commonly called "Old Patch."

His skill as an engraver was equalled only by his cleverness in putting paper into circulation. As regards manufacture he did everything himself—made his own paper with the proper watermark, engraved his own plates, and manufactured his own ink. His plans for disposing of the forged notes were laid with great astuteness, and he took extraordinary precautions to avoid discovery: he had three homes, with a different name and a different wife at each. He was so expert in disguises that none of his agents or instruments ever saw him in his own person, that of a compact, middle-aged, not-bad-looking man, inclined to stoutness, but erect and active in figure, with a beaky nose, clear gray eyes, and a nutcracker chin. Sometimes he went about with his mouth covered up in red flannel and his gouty legs swathed in bandages. At another, he was an infirm old man wearing a long black camlet cloak with a broad cape fastening close to his chin. He victimized numbers of tradesmen, passing, under various disguises, bank notes of large value for which he would take the change. The lottery offices suffered greatly at his hands. He bought up tickets in large quantities with his forged notes, always requiring change.

When Price's depredations were at their height, it was supposed that they were the work of a gang, but he really worked single-handedly. His disguise as "Old Patch" was known, and he was frequently advertised as such, without result. For a long time the Bow Street officers were hopelessly ineffectual, and in the end Price was caught only by accident. One of his many endorsements of a forged note was traced to a pawnbroker, who remembered to have gotten it from one Powel. "Powel" imprudently returned to the pawnbroker's, was arrested, and was found to be no other than Charles Price. Price was known to the authorities for he had been in trouble before, chiefly for defrauding the famous actor and dramatist Samuel Foote, in a brewery partnership, for which he had been sent to Newgate Prison. Price, immediately after his arrest, smuggled a hasty note to one of his wives with the brief words, "Destroy everything," which she did, burning his disguises, smashing up the engraving tools, and destroying the copper plates. Still, the case seemed strong against Price: he could not deny his identity, and feeling that all was over, he hanged himself in his cell.

Real Worth

Clint Murchison, one of the Texan oil magnates, said that he calculated a man's real worth about twice what he owned.

Ask Me Another

"How can I ever repay your troubles?" asked a client of Clarence Darrow, after he won her case.

"Madam," replied the attorney, "ever since the ancient Phoenicians invented money, there has been an easy answer to that question.

LENDERS

The Royal Pawnbroker

George Heriot was an Edinburgh goldsmith whose fortune was founded on the patronage of Anne of Denmark, queen to James VI of Scotland, who ascended to the English throne as James I in 1603. Heriot first became Goldsmith in Ordinary to H℞ Royal Highness and then, a little later was appointed to the King, who gave him a small apartment in Holyrood Palace. Heriot's clientele grew as a result of this royal patronage, but he found his royal customers poor payers. So he charged them stiff interest, and, just to make sure that his loans would not go sour, he also became the royal pawnbroker.

A story from this warm, if sometimes prickly relationship tells of Heriot going to see the king, who was sitting by a cozy fire that smelled of sweet scented woods imported from the East.

"The fragrance is sweet," the goldsmith remarked, to which the king replied: "Aye, and is costly."

"I will show you one more costly still," and Heriot invited his king to his public booth next to Saint Giles's Kirk, where James saw a small fire in the forge used to melt gold.

"Is this then your fine fire?" asked the king in scorn.

"If you would wait a little, your Majesty, till I get the fuel." Then Heriot opened his strong box and took from it a bond for £2,000 that he had lent to the king and threw it upon the burning coals: "Now, which is more costly, your Majesty's fire or mine?" The king graciously acknowledged losing the argument and yet ending as the winner.

Later, when the court moved from Edinburgh to London, George Heriot expanded his banking services and became an important figure in London, where he died in 1624. Two centuries later, Sir Walter Scott based the character Jingling Geordie in *The Fortunes of Nigel* on George Heriot.

The Secret of Long Life

Voltaire, the French philosopher of the enlightenment, became rich enough to retire by the time he was 40. He achieved self-sufficiency not from his prolific pen, but by investing his earned income in young noblemen who had yet to receive their inheritance. Voltaire charged 10 percent a year—*for life*. The young men were too eager to obtain the loans to worry about the long years ahead. Besides, the philosopher looked so pale and sickly, as if he could pass on at any moment. He died at 82, a very rich man.

Poor Relations

As Charles Lamb once said, there is nothing so purely irrelevant in nature as poor relations. Ben Franklin found it so when one of his poor relatives borrowed $50 and then asked for a sheet of paper to give him a promissory note. "What," asked the irritated Franklin, "you want to waste my stationery as well as my money?"

The Importance of Being Seen

Around the turn of the century a speculator by the name of Charles Flint got into financial difficulties. He had a slight acquaintance with J. P. Morgan, Sr., and decided to touch him for a loan. Morgan asked him to come for a stroll around the Battery in lower Manhattan. The two men discussed the weather in some detail, and other pressing matters, when finally, after about an hour or so, the exasperated Flint burst out: "But Mr. Morgan, how about the million dollars I need to borrow?"

Morgan held out his hand to say goodbye: "Oh, I don't think you'll have any trouble getting it now that we have been seen together."

Disappointment

Arsène Houssaye, director of the Comédie Française in the middle of the nineteenth century, told this story about Baron Rothschild being approached for a loan by one of his acquaintances. The man needed 2,000 francs until the end of the month.

"Here it is," said the baron, "but remember: as a rule I only lend to crowned heads." M. de Rothschild never dreamed of seeing his money again, but at the end of the month, the borrower returned with the whole sum. The baron could scarcely believe his eyes, but he also sensed that this would not be the end of their relationship. Sure enough, a month later, the acquaintance reappeared, asking this time for a loan of 4,000 francs.

"No, no, my friend," the baron declined ingeniously, "you have disappointed me once already when you repaid me that last sum. I do not wish to be disappointed again."

Stratagem

A moneylender complained to Baron Rothschild that he had lent 10,000 francs to a man who had gone off to Constantinople without a written acknowledgment of his debt.

"Write to him and demand back 50,000 francs," advised the baron.

"But he only owes me 10,000," said the moneylender.

"Exactly, and he will write and tell you so in a hurry. And that's how you will have acknowledgment of his debt."

BORROWERS

The Advantages of Being in Debt

Samuel Foote, the eighteenth-century comic actor and writer who is often called the "British Aristophanes," developed a philosophy about being in debt that would qualify him for today's cashless society. He gave the following arguments for living on credit:

It saves the trouble and expense of keeping accounts.
It makes other people work in order to give ourselves repose.
It prevents the cares and embarrassments of riches.
It checks avarice and encourages generosity as people are more commonly liberal with others' goods than with their own.
It possesses that genuine spark of primitive Christianity that would inculcate a constant communion of all property.

In short, Foote concluded, it draws on us the inquiries and attentions of the world while we live and makes us sincerely regretted when we die.

Principles

The eighteenth-century playwright and politician Richard Brinsley Sheridan was always hard up for cash. A friend once remarked: "Being from an illustrious Irish family, is it not strange that your name has no O' prefixed to it?"

"It is strange," replied the amiable Sheridan, "because no family has a better right to it. We owe everybody."

At another time, Sheridan was being pressed by his tailor to pay at least the interest on what he owed. The wit put him off with, "It is not my interest to pay the principal, nor my principle to pay the interest."

Sleep

Charles Fox, one of Richard Brinsley Sheridan's contemporaries, piled up huge debts for gambling and other extravagant habits. His aristocratic father reproached him more than once: "I do not know, sir, how you can sleep and enjoy the comforts of life, thinking about the vast sums you owe everyone in town."

"I do not know, sir," replied the young man, "how my creditors sleep."

Another story is about one of those sleepless creditors who kept dunning Fox for a small debt: "I beg your pardon, Mr. Fox," said the dunner, "but you know I have waited for a long while. Still, I don't want to make the time of payment inconvenient to you. I only desire you will fix upon some day in the future when you promise to pay."

"With pleasure, my good man," Charles Fox replied. "Suppose we name the Day of Judgment. But stop! that will be a very busy day for you; suppose we say the day after."

He Would Rather Not Be in Philadelphia

In late life William Penn, the father of Pennsylvania, suffered great financial reverses and was constantly plagued by creditors. He had a peephole made in his front door, where he could identify visitors before letting them in. One day a creditor had knocked repeatedly on Penn's door without success when one of the servants happened to be returning to the house.

"What's the matter," asked the tradesman, "won't your master see me?"

"Friend," the servant replied looking at the door, "my master has seen thee, and does not like your looks."

A New Way to Pay Old Debts

The poet Ben Jonson, Shakespeare's younger contemporary, owed a vintner some money, for which reason he avoided his own house. But one day by chance he met in the street his creditor, who demanded to be paid. However, the tradesman offered an alternative: if Jonson accompanied him back to his house and answered four questions, the vintner would forgive the debt. The author agreed most willingly, and went at the time appointed, asked for a bottle of claret, and drank to the vintner, praising the wine greatly.

"This is not our business;" said the creditor. "Mr. Jonson, answer me my four questions, or pay me my money, or go to jail."

"Pray," said Ben, "propose them."

"Tell me first, what pleases God? Secondly, what pleases the Devil? Thirdly, what pleases the world? And lastly, what best pleases me?"

"Well, then, Ben thought for a moment and lapsed into verse:

God is best pleased when man forsakes his sin;
The devil's best pleased when man delights therein;
The world's best pleased when you do draw good wine;
And you'll be pleased, when I do pay for mine.

The vintner was satisfied, gave Ben a receipt in full, and a bottle of claret into the bargain.

Reassurance

And another story to drink to is about the painter James McNeill Whistler, who treated his creditors with the utmost geniality. One of them was at Whistler's home to discuss a long-outstanding bill when the artist offered him a glass of champagne.

"How could you afford champagne," asked the outraged tradesman, "when you cannot even pay my bill?"

"My dear man, let me assure you," said the painter with champagne in hand, "I haven't paid for this either."

INTEREST

The Greatest Invention

Sam Bronfman was once asked what he considered the most significant invention by the human mind.

"Interest," replied the founder of the House of Seagram without a moment's hesitation.

Insight runs in the family. Edgar Bronfman, who now controls the largest liquor company in the world, once remarked: "To turn $100 into $110 is work. But to turn $100 million into $110 million is inevitable."

Interesting Interest

Few things affect so many of us as the cost of money: the interest charged when we borrow, or paid to us when we lend. Here are some highlights in the brief history of interest rates, culled from various antiquarian sources:

> In the thirteenth century the Lombards (in Italy) frequently demanded 20 percent for the use of money. About 1200 the countess of Flanders was obliged to borrow money in order to pay her husband's ransom. She procured the necessary sum from Italian and Jewish merchants. The lowest interest she paid was 20 percent, and some lenders exacted 30. In the beginning of the fourteenth century, Philip IV fixed the legal rate to be used at the fairs of Champagne at 20 percent: James I of Spain lowered it to 18. As late as the year 1400 it appears that the interest rate in Placentia was at the rate of 40 percent. This is the more extraordinary because at that time the commerce of Italian states was considerable.

The first mention of a rate of interest in England is in the reign of Richard I, when it was 10 percent. The word *interest* was first defined in an act of the British Parliament in 1623, where it was made to signify "a lawful increase by way of compensation for money lent." The rate fixed by the act was £8 for the use of £100 for a year, in place of the previous usurous rate of £100. The rate was lowered to £6 in 1650, and by an act of 1713 it was reduced to 5 percent. However, the restraint was found prejudicial to commerce, and it was totally removed in 1854.

The Pound of Flesh

It may come as a surprise to some that Shakespeare's model for Shylock, the archetypal usurer, was Catholic, not Jewish. In Gregorio Leti's biography of Pope Sixtus V it is stated:

In the year of 1587, ten years before the probable date of the production of Shakespeare's play, a Roman merchant named Paul Maria Secchi, a good Catholic Christian, learned that Sir Francis Drake had conquered San Domingo. He imparted his news to a Jewish trader, Simson Ceneda, who either disbelieved it or had an interest in making it appear so. He obstinately contested the truth of the statement, and to emphasize his contradiction added that he would stake a pound weight of his flesh on the contrary. The Christian took him at his word, staking one thousand scudi against the pound of flesh, and the bet was attested by two witnesses. On the truth of Drake's conquest being confirmed, the Christian demanded the fulfillment of the wager. In vain the Jew appealed to the governor, and the governor to the Pope, who sentenced them both to the galleys—a punishment they were allowed to make up for by a payment of two thousand scudi each to the Hospital of the Sixtine Bridge.

The First Pawnshop

As Venice became the world center for trade and banking during the thirteenth century, the cities of the Lombard League began to deposit their money with Venetian bankers. They also got some interesting collaterals deposited, such as the Crown of Thorns, reputed to have been worn by Christ on the cross (it was estimated to be worth about $35,000 in a 1933 book), while the last Latin emperor of Constantinople pawned his son.

Thirty years before Columbus sailed for the New World, a Franciscan friar of Perugia by the name of Bernardino de Feltre won exemption for a charitable institution that allowed a needy person to borrow money by leaving a valuable object as collateral. In redeeming the article, an additional 15 percent was tacked on toward the expense of running the service. This public pawnshop became a venerable institution that continues to flourish half a millennium later, under the name of Banco di Credito e Pegno (Bank of Credit and Pledge). It is thought to be the oldest continuous banking service still in operation.

How to Please a Customer

Child's Bank was one of London's oldest and most distinguished financial houses, going back to the seventeenth century, until it was absorbed about sixty years ago. It made money for itself in a way that has become time-honored: during most of its existence, Child's never paid any interest for money on deposit. According to a story, a wealthy customer in the early nineteenth century went around shopping to various banks. They were all anxious to accommodate him by offering competitive rates of interest. But the reply at Child's was, "We shall be happy to take care of your money for you, but we shall not give you any interest at all upon it," and this reply seems to have pleased this customer so thoroughly that he opened an account immediately, and all his descendants continued to bank at Child's well into this century.

Compound Interest

From a speech in Congress more than 100 years ago:

> It has been supposed here that had America been purchased in 1607 for $1, and payment secured by bond, payable, with interest annually compounded, in 1876 at ten percent, the amount would be—I have not verified the calculation—the very snug little sum of $136,000,000,000; five times as much as the country will sell for today. It is very much like supposing that if Adam and Eve had continued to multiply and replenish once in two years until the present time, and all their descendants had lived and had been equally prolific, then, saying nothing about twins and triplets, there would now be actually alive upon the earth a quantity of human beings in solid measure more than thirteen and one-fourth time the bulk of the entire planet; and if all these people had been thrifty, and saved one cent a year and invested it at 10 percent, compound interest, the amount of currency at eighty-eight cents in gold would buy not only all the real estate there is in this world, but ten times as much as there is in the universe, at double the government price for public lands, and leave enough to do the entire sewerage for the main streets connecting the fixed stars, and to pave the Milky Way with well-cut diamonds of the first water, nine feet cube, three

thousand miles wide (including sidewalks to be made of condensed rainbows, three billions to the square yard) and a distance of 996,834,329,648,196,314,983 thousand million billion trillion miles long. And I believe there would be considerable left in the bank even then.

Value

George Eastman was planning to build a large theater for the city of Rochester, where Kodak has its headquarters. He was going over the blueprints for the 6,000-seat house.

"We could probably get another two seats into the orchestra here," he told the architect, who was surprised that Eastman would be bothered with such detail.

"Let's say that each seat would bring in 30 cents per performance," the businessman replied, "or 60 cents for the two. With six performances that would come to $3.60 a week. In a year that might amount to $187.20—which, by the way, is the interest on $3,120 for a year."

Belief System

Ben Franklin was showing foreign visitors around Philadelphia, when a strangely dressed group of people walked by.

"Who are these people?' asked one of the visitors.

"They belong to a religious sect and they're called Quakers," said their guide.

"What do they believe?"

"They believe in six percent compound interest," Franklin replied.

YES, WE HAVE NO MONEY

Making Change

From the reign of Queen Elizabeth I to that of Charles II, according to an old source,

> so much inconvenience was felt in trade for the want of small change that the tradesmen and victuallers coined small money or tokens for the benefit of trade. This small money, halfpence and farthings, was coined by the

corporations of cities and boroughs by several of the companies there, and even by the tradesmen in country villages.

At the borough of Chester, in Derbyshire, Mr. Edward Wood, and afterwards his son, Richard Wood, coined money. Both were apothecaries, and on their death, the dies and the press were found in the house, with the device *Apollo Opifer*. The Woods coined only halfpennies, and there were two set of dies, one for the father and the other for the son's money.

This practice continued until the year 1672, when Charles the Second coined a sufficient sum of money for the purposes of commercial intercourse.

Eggnest

When Dr. Johnson and James Boswell were touring the Hebrides, they were informed on the island of Skye that eggs were only fourpence a score. The learned doctor, who was rarely lost for an explanation, deduced "not that eggs in your wretched island are plentiful, but that pence are scarce."

Which brings to mind another story about eggs and money:

George I of England, who was also still prince of Hanover, often traveled among his dominions, usually making one of his stops at the Dutch town of Helvoetsluys. But because of the high prices charged by the rapacious merchants of the town, the king was determined to avoid buying a whole meal. So while his servants were changing horses, he went into the inn and asked for three fresh eggs. After they were prepared and eaten, the king asked how much he would have to pay for the eggs.

"Two hundred florins," came the reply.

"How so?" cried the astonished monarch. "Eggs cannot be so scarce in this republic."

"No," said the innkeeper, "but kings are."

Quarters and Bits

Frederick Law Olmsted, while he was traveling in the southern Cotton States from 1853 to 1854, heard of isolated communities where people had never seen a dollar in their entire lives. It seems that in some areas of the South, the only silver known was the Spanish dollar, and the people used hammer and chisel to cut the dollar into halves and quarters. The latter was broken further into "bits" and then again into "picayunes."

Greenback

European paper money apparently originated in the Middle Ages, when travelers, afraid of being robbed on the highway, deposited their coins with goldsmiths, who issued a paper receipt. This was then accepted instead of real money by various establishments for food and lodgings, rather as credit cards became common in recent years. Apart from the discredited "continental," paper money was practically unknown in the United States until the Civil War, when Abraham Lincoln ran out of real money with which to pay his troops. He sent some of his advisers to ask Salmon P. Chase, secretary of the treasury, about printing paper money, a suggestion that was rejected by the secretary as unconstitutional. Lincoln wrote back to Chase: "If you take care of the money in the Treasury, I will take care of the Constitution." And so the "greenback" was born.

Lincoln gave credit to Colonel Edmond Dick Taylor for suggesting the new kind of money, at least according to a letter that appeared in the *New York Tribune* on December 6, 1891 after the colonel's death. Lincoln's solution seems a bit close to "voodoo economics" as is being practiced today, and the letter may be worth quoting for other recent parallels involving a president and a colonel, and the way they bypassed the responsible cabinet secretary. This is what Lincoln is supposed to have written:

My dear Colonel Dick—I have long determined to make public the origin of the greenback, and tell the world that it is of Dick Taylor's creation. You had always been friendly to me, and when troubled times fell on us, and my shoulders, though broad and willing, were weak, and myself surrounded by such circumstances and such people that I knew not whom to trust. Then said I in my extremity, I will send for Colonel Taylor; he will know what to do. I think it was in January, 1862, on or about the 16th, that I did so. You came and I said to you, "What can we do?" Said you, "Why, issue Treasury notes bearing no interest, printed on the best banking paper. Issue enough to pay off the army expenses, and declare it legal tender."

Chase thought it a hazardous thing, but we finally accomplished it, and gave to the people of this republic the greatest blessing they ever had—their own paper to pay their own debts. It is due to you, the father of the present greenback, that the people should know it, and I take great pleasure in making it known. How many times have I laughed at you telling me plainly that I was too lazy to be anything but a lawyer!

Yours truly,

A. Lincoln

Frogs

Soon after the appearance of the greenback the first jokes began to circulate. One went: "Frogs were the original greenbacks, and since they first drew breath there have been inflationists."

Frankly, My Dear

One of the very first acts of the Continental Congress after the American Revolution broke out was to authorize the printing of paper money. It began innocently enough, with only $2 million printed, but by 1779 there were $240 million circulating to finance the war—all credit advanced by the people of the United States in good faith that a dollar made of paper was worth that in "real money."

However, in an all-too-familiar way, prices began to rise, and the value of the paper dropped precipitously, despite Congress's various appeals and sanctions. There was even an attempt to outlaw inflation, as in this act passed in January 1776: "Resolved, therefore, that any person who shall hereafter be so lost to all virtue and regard for his country as to refuse said bills in payment, or obstruct or discourage the currency or circulation thereof shall be deemed, published and treated as an enemy in this country and precluded from all trade or intercourse with the inhabitants of these Colonies."

The laws of economics being higher than those of government, within three years a paper dollar was worth between two and three cents in specie. "The attempts to regulate its value had been absolutely futile"; wrote one historian, "to this day there is no term in the American vocabulary so expressive of contempt as 'not worth a continental.'"

Washington's Dollar

Senator William M. Evarts of New York took a distinguished Englishman to visit Mount Vernon. They stood on the high bank overlooking the Potomac, and the English visitor recalled the story that Washington had been able to throw a silver dollar across the river from that point.

"I wonder if that was really possible," he mused.

"Why, I don't know about that," the senator replied. "You must remember that in Washington's day a dollar could go farther than it does now; and what is more, that would not be such a feat to perform by a man who threw a crown across the Atlantic Ocean."

Down Looks Like Up Sometimes

After Germany lost the World War I and faced impossible reparation payments to the Allies, her industries were destroyed and her treasury stood empty. The German mark plunged into a steep decline, but one peculiarity of the situation was that the Germans themselves seemed to be the last to notice it. Irving Fisher, an American economist, was on his way to visit Germany in 1922. He stopped in London to talk to Lord D'Abernon, then British ambassador to Germany, who warned him: "Professor Fisher, you will find that very few Germans think of the mark as having fallen."

"That seems incredible," Fisher replied. "Every schoolboy in the United States knows it."

But the professor found the ambassador right. Everybody he met in Germany thought not of the currency falling, but in terms of commodities rising.

Bad News for Gold Bugs

Economist Irving Fisher, in his book *Money Illusion* (1928), recalls asking his dentist how much the cost of gold had gone up, given that everybody was complaining about galloping prices. The doctor asked his assistant to look up the invoices for the gold he had been buying for fillings, and she came back with the information that the price of gold had remained pretty much the same.

"Isn't that surprising? Gold must be a very steady commodity," said the dentist to Fisher, who replied: "It's about as surprising as that a quart of milk is always worth two pints of milk."

· 2 ·

BANKS AND BANKERS

HISTORY

Lombard Street

The word *bank* is derived from the Italian word *banco*, a bench erected in the marketplace for the exchange of money. (In Greek, on the other hand, a *bank* is still called a *table*.) The first of these benches was supposed to have been established by Jews living in Lombardy around the year 808. Much later, some left Italy and settled in Lombard Street, still the heart of London's financial district. The mint in the Tower of London was in ancient times the depository for merchants' cash, until Charles I laid his hands upon the money and destroyed the credit of the mint in 1640. The traders were driven to some other place of security for their gold to prevent their apprentices from absconding with it. In 1645 they consented to lodge it with the goldsmiths in Lombard Street, who were provided with strong chests for their own valuable wares. Thus was born the English banking system.

There are several reminders in English of the Italian origins of banking. The word *bankrupt* owes its origin to *banco rotto*, because when a money-changer could not pay his way, his bench was broken. The use of the letters "L.s.d." to denote English currency until very recently came from the precursor of Italian, the Latin words *Libra*, *Solidus* and

Denarius. Passbooks are so called because customers in the old days examined their own accounts regularly and allowed them to continue, or to pass. The word came from the Italian *passare*, which is still used to denote current money. In the records of Child's Bank, going back three hundred years, the phrase appears at the end of many of several entries: "I allow, or pass, this account."

Checks

In the early days of English banking, a deposit was recorded by putting a notch on a stick, which was split in half. The customer would take home one end and the bank keep the other. Money could only be withdrawn when the depositor matched his piece, called a *bank stock*, with the other half, which was called a *check*.

On the other hand, the great etymologist Walter Skeat connects the word "cheque" to the game of chess, which goes back thousands of years. The squares of the game became known as "checkers," and we retain the use of the word "exchequer" because of the chequered board, or cloth in patterns of chequers, which were originally helpful for computation. Checkers were used in counting and reckoning, and Skeat believed that they implied an order for which we have a check, or stop, just as in the game of chess "checkmate" is derived from the Persian "Shah mat," meaning "the king is dead." The cheque then became a counterfoil, by which, if necessary, one could stop payment, referring not to the slip of paper given to someone, but to the stub in the cheque-book, which is retained for such an eventuality.

The National Debt

The first European bank was probably the one established by the Republic of Venice in the twelfth century. Venice was the leading mercantile state at that time, but it was war and its concomitant evil—the income tax—that led to the introduction of a banking system. A levy was raised on the richest citizens, in return for which the republic undertook to pay an annual interest of 4 percent. The lenders established an office for the accounting and disbursement of this interest. Eventually, as the interest on the national debt was always paid promptly, every registered loan came to be considered productive capital and could be transferred for other loans. So, gradually, this office became a deposit bank; its chief depositor being the government of Venice. The demise of this venerable institution came with the French invasion of 1797, when in the words of a contemporary observer, "the freedom of the city and the independence of the state being lost, the guarantee, and consequently the credit, of this ancient bank vanished like a dream."

Saving England

The defeat of the Spanish Armada in the English Channel in 1588 is traditionally seen as the beginning of the rise of the British Empire and the decline of the Spanish. But the real battle was fought a year earlier behind the scenes by an anonymous banker who came to the help of Queen Elizabeth. When the queen heard of the designs of Spain, she had no ships capable of opposing their fleet; it would take twelve months to build and ready those vessels that stood in various ports and docks. A banker who was well acquainted with the state of Spanish finances knew that their fleet had to be financed through bills drawn on the Bank of Genoa. Without the bills, the armada could not set sail. The financier as chronicled, then

> conceived the idea of buying up all the paper or bills that could be met with in every commercial town in Europe, and to deposit them in the bank of Genoa, that by his large remittances he might have the bank so in his power as to incapacitate it, whenever he chose, from giving any aid to the Spaniards. Being well aware that it only required those remittances be so long in Genoa until the season should obstruct the sailing of the fleet, he calculated that these exchange operations would cost about £40,000 sterling, and he proposed to the queen to extricate her at this price from the dilemma. The proposal was accepted and carried into effect with so much secrecy that King Philip's hands were tied, and he could not send out the fleet till the following year.

The Merchant Banker

Sir Thomas Gresham, who later founded the London Stock Exchange, originally had a store on Lombard Street. Over his door hung his crest, a grasshopper, by way of a sign. Gresham was both a banker and merchant. According to the nineteenth-century antiquarian John Timbs:

> A banker in early times pursued a very different trade from that which occupies the attention of the opulent and influential class so called at the present day. It is well known that the latter derive their profits from the employment of fluctuating sums of money deposited in their hands for convenience and safety by the public; and for the security of which, the respectability of the banker is a sufficient guarantee. But this is a

refinement of comparatively recent introduction, with which our forefathers were wholly unacquainted. As late as the time of Swift, bankers gave and took a bond on receiving and lending money, and made their profit by obtaining a higher rate of interest, or usury, as it was called, on the latter operation than they allowed on the former. Ten or twelve percent was the customary rate of interest during the reign of Queen Elizabeth; at which period, we mean no disrespect to the banker when we say that he united in his person the trades of the usurer, the pawnbroker, the money-scrivener, the goldsmith, and the dealer in bullion. A German traveler, called Hentzner, who visited England in 1593 says that he saw in Lombard Street "all sorts of gold and silver vessels exposed to sale, as well as ancient and modern coins, in such quantities as must surprise a man the first time he sees and considers them."

Defaced

The bank of Amsterdam was founded in 1609 to assist the thriving commercial activity in that city. Amsterdam was then a perpetual fair that brought in coins from all over the world. But the gold and silver coins were often worn and defaced, losing as much as 10 or 15 percent of their face value. The merchants could never find enough new coins for their transactions, and the value of bills became variable to a great degree of fluctuation when the worn coins were weighed. It was to remedy this problem and to fix the par value of the currency that the merchants of Amsterdam established a bank on the model of that of Venice. Ironically, its first capital was formed with Spanish ducats, a silver coin that Spain had struck to finance its war against Holland, and which, as one writer put it, "the tide of commerce had caused to overflow in the very country which it was formed to overthrow."

The Old Lady

The Bank of England was given a Royal Charter in 1694. It was the brainchild of William Paterson, who had tried and failed to establish a Bank of Scotland. Paterson, a grand visionary, was also the first with the idea of joining the Pacific and Atlantic oceans at the Isthmus of Darien, more than 200 years before the Panama Canal was built.

The first governor of the bank was Sir George Houblon, whose house was conveniently built on the present site of the bank in Threadneedle Street. Sir George is remembered another way: the messengers still wear pink frock coats and scarlet waistcoats based on the liveries of his household.

The first deputy governor was Michael Godfrey, the man most intimately involved in formulating the plan with Paterson. Unfortunately, he was killed by a cannonball while inspecting a trench at Namur, where he was seeking an interview with William of Orange. This incident was recalled by a later governor of the bank while touring France during World War I in the company of Lloyd George. When they were invited to visit the battlefield at Bethune, Lord Cunliffe was reported to have said to the Prime Minister, "When poor Godfrey fell at his King's side they acclaimed him a hero, but if I die in your company, the comment may be less flattering."

Scottish Peril

Just as the Jews, dispossessed of their country during two millennia, built a power base through commerce and finance, the Scots, too, after they lost independence, spread out all over the world.

Despite the fact that its founder was a Scotsman, the Bank of England later tended to exclude any Scots from its management, adopting perhaps the view of an anonymous Irishman who waxed indignant over the influence of the Scots in his own country, remarking that "if ever a Scotch plebeian succeeded in acquiring a fortune in China, he would end by becoming prime minister there; and if the Chinese emperor would let him go on, there would not be a single ecclesiastical, civil or military situation in the whole empire that in the course of ten years would not be filled by Scotsmen."

This recalls a story B. C. Forbes told almost 300 years later, about the Glasgow chamber of commerce sending one of its prominent members on a fact-finding tour of English factories, hoping that the Scots might benefit from their examples.

"Weel, what kind o' lads did ye find the Englishers?" they asked him on his return.

"As I met only with the heids o' businesses," replied the emissary, "I didna meet ony o' thim. They were a' Scotsmen."

Rocky Start

The exclusive firm of Coutts Company has served the banking needs of the British royal family since the eighteenth century. It began with James and Thomas, the sons of an Edinburgh merchant, who founded the bank when they settled in London. After James's death, Thomas put the stamp of his personality on this great institution. As an illustration of his character, there is a story of how he acquired and almost lost his first royal customer.

Thomas Coutts was entertaining fellow bankers at his house one evening when one of them related that a certain nobleman had applied to him for a loan of £30,000 and had been refused. Coutts said nothing, but after his guests left at ten o'clock, he took a stroll over to the noblemen's house and left a message with his steward: "Tell his lordship that if he calls on me in the morning, he may have what he requires."

On the following morning the nobleman went to the bank. Mr. Coutts received him with great politeness, and taking £31,000 notes from a drawer, presented them to his lordship, who was most agreeably surprised and asked: "What security am I to give you?"

I shall be satisfied with your lordship's note of hand," was the reply. This was instantly given.

Mr. Coutts's generosity was not forgotten. A few months later, his lordship sold an estate and deposited £200,000 with Coutts. He recommended the bank to several members of the nobility and told George III of the helpful banker, whereupon the king opened a sizable account. However, when his majesty learned that Coutts had advanced the huge sum of £100,000 to help the parliamentary election campaign of Sir Francis Burdett, whom the king disliked, he closed his account and transferred this money to a local bank at Windsor. King George, whose financial judgment seemed to match his political acumen, subsequently lost much of that money when his Windsor Bank failed. And that is how Thomas Coutts received again the patent of Royal Banker.

The Napoléon of Finance

Gabriel Julien Ouvrard was the dominant French financier in the early part of the nineteenth century; following the French Revolution he was empowered to issue his own paper currency. During the reign of Napoléon, Ouvrard became the business partner of Charles IV of Spain, enjoying a monopoly of commerce with the Spanish possessions in America during the war with Great Britain. When Napoléon read this contract, he crumpled it in his hand, and admonished Ouvrard in the presence of the council of his ministers: "You have lowered royalty to the level of commerce."

Whereupon, M. Ouvrard, to the surprise of all present, respectfully but boldly replied: "Sire, commerce is the life-blood of states; sovereigns cannot do without commerce, but it can do very well without sovereigns." Napoléon's answer, if any, is not preserved. But Ouvrard had the last word anyway: after the emperor's fall, he became known as the "Napoléon of finance."

A Good Place to Make Money

At one time Ouvrard chose debtor's jail rather than pay five million francs he owed a creditor. He lived like a prince, spending extravagant sums on food and his lodgings in jail. Since the financier also held the post of the contractor-general, the government of France was anxious to avoid the scandal of having one of its own appointees in prison. But when M. de Villele, the finance minister, came to dinner expressly to ask him to pay his debt, the banker replied: "Parbleu, Monsieur, it is easy for you to suggest this, but I must serve five years here for the five millions I owe. I gain, therefore, by my imprisonment, one million francs a year. If you know of any speculation that is more lucrative and sure, I am not obstinately wedded to this—I'd pay and come out tomorrow."

The Bank Always Wins in the End

During one of the many Irish rebellions, some of the rebels decided to get even with a powerful banker against whom they had many grievances. This was in the days when banks issued demand notes that they were obliged to redeem with gold. So when the rebels decided to burn the banker's notes, they forgot that they were actually destroying his debts, and that for every note that went into the flames, a corresponding value went into the banker's pocket and out of their own. Which goes to show that the bank, like the casinos, usually wins, even if it is a Pyrrhic victory.

Xenophobia

Some believe that America's chronically unbalanced trade with foreign nations is at least partly due to a lack of desire to trade abroad. The domestic market in the United States, the largest in the world, had for a long time satisfied most American manufacturers. The other reason is the kind of banks we have. As anyone knows who has tried to cash an out-of-town check or obtain foreign currency in New York or Los Angeles, the U.S. banking system is perhaps the most parochial and undeveloped among Western nations. Joseph Wechsberg, in his book about merchant bankers, recalls visiting a prominent investment banker on Wall Street. On his desk, in beautiful leather binding, was a volume he had prepared with the title *What I Know About Foreign Securities*. He handed it to Wechsberg with a smile. Inside, all the pages were blank.

PANICS

The Past Is But Prologue

Charles II, the pleasure-loving monarch of England, had little patience for the details of running the country. Between pleasing his mistresses and rewarding his friends, there was not much money left to fight the Dutch, who were paying a visit with an armed flotilla. Wrote a later historian:

> The government had suffered a succession of humiliating disasters. The extravagance of the court had dissipated all the means which Parliament had supplied for the purpose of carrying on offensive hostilities. It was determined only to wage defensive war; but even for defensive war the vast resources of England were found insufficient. The Dutch insulted the British coast, sailed up the Thames and carried their ravages to Chatham. The blaze of ships burning in the river could be seen in London; it was rumored that a foreign army had landed at Gravesend. The people, accustomed to the secure reign of Cromwell, were in utter consternation. The moneyed portion of the community were seized with panic. The country was in danger. London itself might be invaded. What security was there, then, for the money advanced to the government? The people flocked to their debtors; they demanded their deposits; and London now witnessed the first run upon the bankers. The fears of the people, however, proved fallacious, for the goldsmiths—as the bankers were then called—met all demands made upon them. Confidence was restored by a proclamation from the king, stating that the demands on the exchequer should be met as usual; and the run ceased.

Blood in the Streets

Sampson Gideon, a great Jewish banker in the eighteenth century, was the most famous financier of his day. Economic advisor to Sir Robert Walpole, the prime minister of England, he was known for his humor. Gideon's shrewdness combined with experience gave rise to such comments as, "Never grant a life annuity to old women: they wither, but they never die."

Gideon's greatest coup was during the failed rebellion of Bonnie Prince Charlie in 1745. As the Pretender's army approached London, the king and his government were trembling, and stock prices fell precipitously. Gideon unhesitatingly spent ever penny he had, mortgaged and borrowed to the hilt, until he bought up more than half the stocks in the market.

When the Pretender retreated, the stocks rose, and Gideon made another fortune, illustrating the dictum (attributed to Bernard Baruch) that the best buy signal is blood actually running in the streets.

A Way to Deal with Panic

Bonnie Prince Charlie's rebellion caused a financial panic in the City of London. As the Pretender marched from Scotland to Derby, there was a run on the Bank of England. The clerks evolved a dual strategy for facing the crisis. First, they worked to rule and paid out very slowly with the smallest coins available. Because of the amounts involved and the distractions caused by hysterical people waiting their turn, the tellers frequently were forced to check their calculations and start counting out the coins all over again. The directors of the bank were also smart enough to plant their own agents in the line, with instructions to immediately return the money that had just been withdrawn. By such means the panic of real customers was gradually reduced or turned into miserable weariness.

Post-Haste

Up to about 1775 almost anybody in England could start a bank, even if he did not have money: "Every grocer, draper, tailor and haberdasher who chose might flood the country with his 'miserable rags.'" Every country banker had a London agent who flooded tradespeople in the city with so many country banknotes that they became completely discredited. In the crisis of 1793, about 100 country banks stopped payment and 300 were seriously shaken. There was the story of Jonathan Backhouse, banker, driving from London to Darlington in a chaise full of gold to meet a threatened run on his bank in Darlington. One of the wheels came off the carriage, so Backhouse piled the gold at the back of the chaise, thus "balancing the cash" and made it into Darlington on three wheels. According to Maberly Phillips (in his *History of Banks, Bankers and Banking*), the threatened run was deliberately organized by Lord Darlington in retaliation for a disagreement.

The Panic of 1832

One of the more extraordinary panics in history caused a run on the Bank of England and was said to have been caused by placards appearing all over London with this instruction: "To stop the duke, go for gold." The duke of Wellington was very unpopular at the time of the Reform Bill of 1832, and was considered leader of the old guard. Rumor spread on May 14 that he had formed a cabinet. "The run upon the Bank of England for gold coin was so incessant, that in a few hours upwards of half a million was carried off," according to a contemporary historian. The graffiti were "the device of four gentlemen, two of whom were elected members of the reformed Parliament. Each put down twenty pounds, and the sum thus clubbed was expended in printing thousands of these terrible missives, which were eagerly circulated, and were speedily seen upon every wall in London. The effect was electric."

Main Street

Although speculators and brokers are the most immediately affected in a market crash, the much wider tragedy of a financial crisis is felt on Main Street. This extract is from an anonymous New York merchant's diary as he was going under during the Panic of 1857:

August 18th, 1857—Refused discounts at bank. Couldn't raise money to pay duties, and obliged to make over a valuable importation of goods. Cashier says come again next offering day.

21st—Went and saw matters ten times worse. Saw the bank president who told me I *deserved* to be "pinched" for importing so heavily, and that I needn't come there again for six weeks. Couldn't discount a dollar. Concluded to call on B. and borrow a few thousands. Found a note on my desk from B., begging me to lend him some money, or he would break. Tried C. Same luck.

22nd—Pitched out at another bank. Customer in, wanting to see that fresh importation. Spent three hours trying to borrow enough to pay the duties. No success.

24th—Ohio Life and Trust Company failed. Tried to sell paper in the street at three percent a month. No buyers. Fortunate remittance from the West—know the post-mark—Jones is a good fellow. Draft for $5,000—drawn on the Ohio Life and Trust Company!

25th—Loan called in. Begin to feel choky in the throat. No appetite. Tried to sell out my importation of dry goods at twenty percent less. Nobody with any money to buy. Went home sick.

27th—Resolved never to put myself in the power of the banks again. Miserable institutions. Spent the whole day trying to borrow, and barely escaped protest. My own notes stuck in my face at three percent a month. Overheard broker say: "You're a gone man if you can't take your own paper at that price." Feel very much so, but got to keep a stiff upper lip.

28th—Four brokers failed. Times worse than in 1837. Feet sore with running about to raise money. Can't collect a dollar from the country. Everybody out on the same business—all borrowers, no lenders. Desk full of bills receivable, perfectly useless. Wish I'd never seen a piece of dry goods. Would have been as easy as an old shoe if I had not imported. I had no business to build that new house; the old one was good enough. Ought to have been content with the moderate things, and lived on half the money. Store rent too high. Obliged to spread out too much on credit to pay expenses.

29th—Neighbor failed. Bank failed. Friends call to ask if the rumor of my failure be true. Air black with foul reports. Half past two P.M., account withdrawn, and—*notes unpaid.*

The rest is silence.

Perfect harmony

In later years Congressman Francis Cushman of Washington State used to dine out on how hungry he went during the panic and depression years of 1893 to 1895: "It was fortunate for me that I lived in Tacoma then, for Tacoma is on the seacoast, and on the seacoast there is always an abundance of clams. When the tide is out the table is set. I assure you that I ate clams and ate clams and ate clams until my stomach rose and fell in perfect harmony with the ebb and flow of the tide.

Shrug

George Washington Carver, the great agriculturist, lost his entire life savings during the Great Depression, due to the failure of an Alabama bank. "I guess somebody found a use for it," the septuagenarian remarked philosophically, "'cause I wasn't using it myself."

His Last Stand

When the Ohio Home State Savings failed in the early 1980s, its owner, Marvin Warner, unburdened himself. As *Fortune* quoted him: "I feel like Custer being shot at from all sides. Maybe it's because I'm flamboyant, maybe it's because I'm a Democrat, maybe it's because I was a bachelor for a long time, maybe it's because I'm Jewish. . . . I have no idea."

Failure of the bank or the consequent losses to thousands of individuals and businesses obviously had nothing to do with it.

CUSTOMERS

Identification

These days when we carry a wallet full of licenses, credit cards, and other identification, it is hard to imagine what it must have been like in the days before these existed. In the nineteenth century, an American bank cashier named Foster was presented with a check by a strange man.

"I wished him to be identified," the teller recounted, "and he said it was impossible, as he had no acquaintances in the city, and the man seemed quite disappointed. Suddenly a happy thought presented itself to him, and he began to unbutton his vest and pull up his shirt, remarking that it was all right, he had got his name on his shirt flap. It was such a novel idea, and the check being for a small amount, I concluded to pay, and he went away happy."

Red Tape

That anonymous man, who kept his name to himself, might have taken comfort from what happened to another bank customer, whose name was practically synonymous with money. When Nathan Meyer Rothschild, on a trip back from Scotland, stopped in Montrose, he found he needed some money. He went to the local bank and requested cash for a draft of £100 on his agent in London. He was, however, much surprised at the refusal of the bank manager to honor his check, without (as that functionary said) having the genuineness of the signature—which he was utterly unable to read—previously accredited. The manager insisted that it must first be forwarded to London. To this arrangement Mr. Rothschild was compelled to submit; and as at that time it took six days before an answer could be received from London, he was detained until the reply came, which, of course, proving favorable, he was able to pursue his journey.

Revenge

In the early days of the Rothschild empire, the Bank of England refused to discount a large bill drawn by Amschel Rothschild of Frankfurt on Nathan Rothschild of London. The bank officials claimed that "they discounted only their own bills, and not those of private persons."

"Private persons!" Nathan Rothschild exclaimed, "I will make those gentlemen see what sort of private persons we are!"

He spent the following three weeks gathering all the five-pound notes he could find in England and on the Continent. Then he presented himself at the Bank of England at the opening hour. He drew from his pocket a five pound note, and they naturally counted out five gold sovereigns, at the same time looking quite astonished that the Baron Rothschild should have personally troubled himself for such a trifle. The baron examined the coins one by one and put them into a little canvas bag, then drew out another note—then a third—a tenth—then a hundredth. He never put the pieces of gold into the bag without scrupulously examining them, and, in some instances, weighing them in the balance, as he asserted that "the law gave him the right to do." The first pocket book being emptied and the first bag full, he passed them to his clerk, and received a second, and thus continued, till the bank closed.

The baron took seven hours to change £21,000. But as he also had nine employees engaged in the same manner, the House of Rothschild had drawn £210,000 in gold from the bank, and he had so occupied the tellers that no other person could change a single note.

The bank officials were amused, in their own English way, at this little pique of Baron Rothschild. They laughed less when they saw him return the next day at the opening of the bank, flanked by his nine clerks. And they stopped laughing altogether when the king of bankers announced: "These gentlemen refuse to pay my bills, so I have sworn not to keep theirs. Only they should know that I have enough to employ them for two months."

"Two months! Eleven million pounds in gold drawn from the Bank of England—more than we possess!" The next morning a notice appeared in the financial journals that henceforth the Bank of England would honor Rothschild's bills the same as their own.

Mother's Name

The practice of asking a customer's mother's maiden name goes back more than a century. In *Our Cashier's Scrap-Book* (published in 1879), H. C. Percy, tells the story of a young woman who opened a deposit account with the Mariners' Saving Bank in New London, Connecticut. Asked what her mother's maiden name, she replied: "Which one? For she had been married twice."

Irony

Percy also tells the story of J. B. Smith, one of Boston's mid-19th century black entrepreneurs, who catered many society functions, presenting a check at his local bank. The teller asked for identification.

"Young man, don't you know me?" asked the astonished customer. The teller confessed that he did not.

"Then it is evident," said Mr. Smith, "that you have not moved in the first circles of society."

Needs No I.D.

Herb Hatch, one of the more colorful Canadian distillers (he ran Gooderham & Worts) was once visiting Calgary on business, when he suddenly needed $10,000. He went into a branch office of the Bank of Toronto, but found that he had no identification. This was in the days before credit cards, and according to Peter Newman (in his book *the Bronfman Dynasty*), the manager was forced to call Toronto.

"Describe him to me," asked his superior.

"He's the most foul-mouthed man I've ever heard. He's called me every four-letter name in the book."

"That's him." The man in the head-office needed to know nothing more. "Give him all the money he wants."

Lineage by Coinage

An aristocratic British diplomat once tried to impress Calvin Coolidge. He took out an old coin from his pocket and said: "The king on this shilling is the one who made my great-great grandfather a lord."

Coolidge was unimpressed. He reached for a nickel and told the Englishman: "My great-great grandfather was made into an angel by the Indian on this coin.

Noisy Deposit

Calvin Coolidge, when governor of Massachussets, was asked to open an account at a Boston bank as a gesture toward the local banking industry. The governor made a deposit and, not long afterward when he walked by the bank with a friend a terrific noise could be heard from inside the building.

"What in heaven's name do you suppose that is?" the friend exclaimed.

Coolidge, a man of few words, many of which were witty ones, replied: "Oh, that's that deposit of mine drawing interest."

Mind Your Own

James Thurber had overdrawn his bank account and was invited by his bank manager to come in and discuss the problem. During the interview, the manager was appalled to discover that Thurber had no idea about the state of his account since he did not keep track of checks he wrote.

"How do you know, then, how much money you have in your account?" asked the exasperated manager.

"I thought that was your business," the humorist replied.

Cochon

The Pereire brothers were Jewish bankers in Paris during the nineteenth century. One of their customers, the manager of a large concern that was deeply indebted to the bank, resented the conditions and interference by the bankers in his business. Exasperated at one of their meetings, the manager flung the question at one of the brothers: "Do you mean to eat me up?"

"My religion forbids me to do that," replied the banker, referring to the Jewish dietary laws, which forbid the eating of pig meat.

A Small Business Loan

Canadians have often been called "hewers of wood, and pitchers of water" because of the country's heavy dependence on primary resources. Constant efforts to change the country's economy to a wider manufacturing base are frustrated by a deep-seated conservatism in the banking system, which is a cosy oligarchy: the whole of Canada has fewer that ten major banks. This true story about Canadian banking is from the author's personal experience.

I was director of a small literary publishing company in Vancouver, British Columbia, called Talon Books. Each spring our cash flow dried up, as we waited for bookstores to pay for shipments of Christmas past and as our government subsidy grants were always in the proverbial mail. Each spring my partners and I had to go to our local branch of the Bank of

Montreal and get a loan of $10,000 to tide us over. The company had been doing this for seven or eight years with clockwork regularity, taking as security a $10,000 savings bond deposited each time by one of my partners' mother.

This particular spring in the late 1970s, our printing bills were heavier and our deficit yawned wider than usual, so the company needed $15,000. But our security bond was still only $10,000. We thought that the bank manager, who saw our steadily increasing sales figures year in and year out, would let us have it. We were wrong. He shifted uneasily in his leather chair and waited to see if one of our parents would come up with the family jewels. Finally one of my partners had an inspiration: "What about our inventory? Why can't we borrow against our inventory?"

"What inventory?" The man seemed mildly interested.

"Well, we have a quarter million dollars worth of books. That's why we have all these printing bills—we publish books."

"So these books," the banker proceeded cautiously, "have printing in them?"

"Yes, that's what we manufacture."

"I cannot give you the loan," he said with an air of finality. "The paper would have been worth something, but you've spoiled it by printing on it."

A couple of years later, partly as a result of this incident, I decided to leave Canada. My wife and I started a small publishing house of our own in Los Angeles. We were new in town, with no track record, but we had one manuscript we needed to get printed. We went to see the loan officer at City National Bank on Sunset Boulevard, where we had opened an account. We presented our project and outlined our prospects. We asked for $15,000 and got it—on our signature.

The Man Who Saved

Ferenc Molnár, the Hungarian playwright and coffeehouse wit, told this story about Bleichröder, a great Berlin banker in the early decades of the century.

A man went to see Bleichröder to beg for a few hundred marks. The banker asked him why he needed the money. The man explained abjectly: "I had a business, which I spent years in cultivating, so that it finally brought in more than enough for me to live on. Then, when it began to prosper, I managed to save up fifty thousand marks. I had a book-keeper. The book-keeper stole the money. Then he disappeared. I went bankrupt."

The man began to sob. Bleichröder watched him for a while.

"My poor friend," said the banker finally with great paternal benevolence that made the man hopeful. But then Bleichröder continued: "I won't give you a penny, not one penny!"

"Why not?" asked the bankrupt businessman.

"Why not? Because a smart man would have taken the fifty thousand and run off long before his book-keeper even got the idea."

INSIDERS

Rich Sinner

Lewis Lloyd, one of the founders of the successful banking firm of Jones Lloyd and Company toward the end of the eighteenth century, began his career as a Unitarian minister in Manchester, England. He soon became tired of that vocation because, he used to remark at dinner, he found it "much more profitable and agreeable to spend my time in turning over bank notes, than in turning up the whites of my eyes." However, Mr. Jones retained some of the flavor of his religious training in his remarks. When Frys and Chapman, the Quaker bankers, failed, a member of the society took his account to Mr. Lloyd, who welcomed the new customer: "How right you are, my friend; it is wiser to put thy money with a rich sinner than a poor saint."

Trivial Pursuit

How did people who worked in banks a hundred years ago amuse themselves before there was electronic mail? I found this:

The cashier of the First National Bank of St. Paul, Minnesota, had occasion to notify the cashier of a bank in a different part of the state that his account was overdrawn. He received the following telegram in reply:

June 13, 1871

See Matthew 15:29

To which the following was telegraphed back promptly:

June 13, 1871

Examine Matthew 5:25-26

In case the reader lacks a Bible at hand, here is the solution. Matthew 15:29: "And his fellow servant fell down at his feet, and besought him, saying, Have patience with me, and I will pay thee all." And Matthew 5:25-26 reads: "Agree with thine adversary quickly, whilst thou art in the way with him; lest at any time the adversary deliver thee to the judge, and the judge deliver thee to the officer, and thou be cast into prison. Verily I say unto thee, thou shalt by no means come out thence, till thou has paid the uttermost farthing."

Given the length of these quotations, and that telegrams were charged by the word, the cashiers should have been commended for thrift as well as for their knowledge of the scriptures.

Double Entendre

J. Pierpont Morgan attended a diocesan convention in New York and entertained the assembled clerics with the story of an unworldly clergyman.

"This good man was as ignorant of financial matters," narrated the tycoon, "as the average financier is of matters ecclesiastical. He once received a check—the first in his life—and took it to a bank for payment. 'But you must endorse the check,' said the teller. 'Endorse it?' asked the old minister in a puzzled tone. 'Yes, of course; it must be endorsed on the back.' 'I see,' said the man of the cloth. And turning the check over he wrote across the back of it: 'I heartily endorse this check.'"

Partners

Two of the most famous firms in investment banking grew out of petty quarrel between the partners: J. Pierpoint Morgan and Joseph W. Drexel. Even when their bank was small, Morgan went about his deals in a curiously secretive manner. In the middle of negotiating a major purchase, he would leave a slip of paper in the cashbox, reading simply "$10,000,000—J.P.M.," and that is all that the bank would know about it until the deal was consummated.

The firm was so small that Drexel and Morgan occupied a single partner's desk, measuring perhaps no more than five feet square. One day Morgan came to work as usual, took off his high hat, and laid it on Drexel's side of the desk.

"John," said Mr. Drexel, a man of genteel demeanor and aristocratic bearing, "I want you to keep your hat on your side of the table. If you don't, I'll take my cane and knock the top of it off." Morgan never said a word, but he rose, put on his hat, walked into the bank, and came back. As he returned he put his hat away over on Drexel's side of the table and sat down. Drexel got up, took his cane, and, as good as his word, knocked the top off the hat.

The two men started to clinch. Both were in a fighting mood. Each weighed close to 300 pounds. Before damage could be done, Anthony J. Drexel, brother of Joseph, who happened to be in the bank, noted the disturbance of the generally quiet atmosphere, rushed in and separated them, and ordered the two "children" to sit down.

"Don't you think I was right?" Joseph asked his brother, telling him the cause of the trouble.

"I do not," was the reply. Whereupon Joseph rose and said:

"I close up my interest in this bank today at three o'clock. I will leave what money I have in the bank as a special, but I am through with this banking firm." And he put on his hat and walked out, never to return.

Breeding

Investment banking, as practiced until recently, was the domain of a few distinguished families. A story from the 1920s has a Chicago banking house writing to the Boston investment firm of Lee, Higginson and Company for a letter of recommendation about a young Bostonian they were considering for a job. The letter came back stating that the young man's father was a Cabot, his mother a Lowell; further back there were the Saltonstalls, Appletons, Peabodys, and others from Boston's First Families.

A few days later, Chicago sent a curt letter acknowledging Lee, Higginson and Company for its trouble. Unfortunately, the material was not helpful. "We are not," the letter went on, "contemplating using the young man for breeding purposes."

Which brings to mind another story about the same kind of proper Bostonians visiting Chicago. At a dinner in their honor, one socialite remarked: "In Boston, we place all our emphasis on breeding," referring to her distinguished lineage. Her host could not refrain from coming back with: "In Chicago, we too think that's a lot of fun, but we also have a great many other interests."

Prolific Reason

There used to be a rule at the Bank of England that every employee had to sign in upon arrival at work, and, if late, to give a reason. The chief cause of delay in those days was the terrible fog. So, on foggy days, the first man to arrive wrote "fog" opposite his name. Those who followed wrote "ditto." One day, however, the first man gave as his reason "wife had twins." Twenty other late men, of course, automatically wrote "ditto" underneath.

Complaints

The Bank of England, being a central bank, deals mainly with other banks, seldom with the public. But in the summer of 1932, the government offered holders of War Stock a choice of redeeming these bonds or having the unusually high interest (5 percent!) reduced. The bank was immediately under siege by hordes of ordinary customers, waiting in queues, as only the British can. However, there were many complaints addressed to the chief accountant's office, which according to banker John Parry, "was invariably devoted to charges of incompetence by the staff."

Each complaint was scrupulously looked into and, in the huge majority of cases, error or confusion on the part of the correspondent was found. In spite of this it was the custom to answer all such letters with courtesy and patient explanation. The only exception I can recall was brought about by an inhabitant of Birmingham who wound up a letter of vituperation with the words: "It is clear that you employ a lot of damned fools at the Bank for the purpose of misleading us stockholders." To which the Chief Accountant answered: "It is my experience that total rudeness is invariably the outcome of total ignorance."

Mistakes

But John Parry admits that mistakes were made at the Bank of England:

I remember an unhappy instance when the misreading of a first name resulted in a change of the stockholder's sex. Incredibly, the mistake was repeated on the envelope containing the letter of regret. At this the recipient wrote: "Once and for all, my name is James. This may be funny but it isn't Fanny."

I was not always innocent myself. On one occasion a lady returned a letter of mine requesting an explanation of the opening sentence. To my dismay I found I had written: "Madam, I beg to accompany the returning form."

Parry left the Bank of England soon after.

· 3 ·

TAKING STOCK

THE STOCK EXCHANGE

Let Me Try and Explain

In the old days in Hungary, when it was still a capitalist country, a group of people at a party were arguing for and against the institution of the stock exchange. An aristocrat was all for abolishing it, having lost as much money there as playing cards or ponies. Two financial types however, were enumerating all the benefits the stock exchange provided for raising capital, for encouraging investment, for the smart to make money. A gentleman who had been listening silently finally wanted to know: "I've heard you argue for the past half an hour, but I can't make out what a stock exchange really is."

"Let me explain it to you," one of the financiers volunteered. "The Exchange is a blessed place where millions are lying on the floor: in gold, in bonds, in readily convertible cash."

"I see," said the gentlemen, trying to visualize it all.

"And all you have to do," the financier continued, "is bend down and reach for it."

"Really?"

"There are hundreds of people crammed on the floor of the exchange and all are trying to bend down and pick up all this money."

"It sounds wonderful," sighed the innocent.

"It is wonderful, and there is only one small problem."

"What's that?"

"It's true that all you have to do is bend down and scoop. But when you do, your own wallet usually falls from your pocket and spills everything you've got onto the floor."

La Bourse

Stock exchanges originally were real markets for merchants to exchange goods. Such markets existed in the Middle Ages, especially in the trading centers of northern Europe, the cities of the Hanseatic League. Later, such a place came to be known as *La Bourse,* as the stock exchange is still called in French and most languages other than English. The term originates from a square in the center of Bruges, where, according to an antiquarian, stood a large building that had been erected by the whole family of La Bourse, whose coat of arms, representing three purses, was painted on the walls. The merchants of Bruges made this old house the place of their daily assemblies; and, when afterwards they went to the fairs in Antwerp and Mons, they called the places they found there for the assembling of merchants by the name of La Bourse, or the Bourse.

The Royal Exchange

The Royal Exchange in London dates back to the reign of Elizabeth I. Sir Thomas Gresham, a prominent merchant, purchased the site and laid the first stone on June 7, 1566. He was acting on the instigation of his father, Sir Richard, who thought that it would benefit the dignity and efficiency of the City to have a proper marketplace, instead of trading in the open on Lombard Street. His proposal was first turned down, and it took another thirty years for the Court of Aldermen to accept his son's offer.

The first building of the stock exchange in London cost £6,000. When it was finished, Queen Elizabeth proceeded from Somerset House on January 23, 1570, accompanied by a train of nobility and attendants, to Sir Thomas Gresham's magnificent mansion, where a sumptuous dinner was provided for her whole court. Then the party went to the new building, where every shop and every tenant was exhibited to the utmost advantage. After gratifying her curiosity, the queen commanded to proclaim it by trumpet, the Royal Exchange.

The original Royal Exchange perished in the Great Fire of 1666. Charles II laid the first stone of the New Exchange, which bore the emblem of a grasshopper, in memory of Sir Thomas Gresham. According to legend, Gresham was the son of a poor woman who left him exposed in a field, but the chirping of grasshoppers led a boy to the spot and saved the infant's life. When he was knighted, Sir Thomas had the grasshopper incorporated in his crest of arms. (This story, however, seems inconsistent with the fact that his father was already a knight.) The New Exchange opened in 1670 and burned down again in 1838. The present building was opened by Queen Victoria in 1844.

Wall Street

The New York Stock Exchange was started on May 17, 1792, when twenty-four brokers met informally under a buttonwood (sometimes called sycamore) tree on the site of present-day 68 Wall Street. There they agreed on a uniform rate of commissions on the sale of stocks and bonds. By 1816, a permanent organization existed, consisting of twenty-eight members. As early as 1837 the organization had grown to be a power, according to a jaundiced observer a generation later,

> but a power for evil rather than good, since it stimulated in the community a thirst for speculation. In that year, too, fell the great banking and brokerage firm of J. L. & S. Josephs, agents of the Rothschilds, and rated at $5,000,000, involving multitudes in a widespread ruin. The successors and assigns of the twenty-eight brokers of 1816 have, indeed, fed on strong food and waxed exceeding great. They number [in 1870] between ten and eleven hundred, and own, or control wealth which is counted by the ten million. The old sycamore has decayed and fallen beneath the storm, and they meet no longer under "the greenwood tree," though there is a poetic fitness in such a place of meeting for the taurine and ursine herd; but in marble temples dedicated to Mammon, the God of riches, the ponderous iron doors whereof turn like the Miltonic gates of the celestial city on golden hinges.

Menagerie

Like many of the money marts in Europe, Wall Street began as a market for animals other than bulls and bears. This is a snapshot from the middle of the nineteenth century:

> It is a good dog market, cow market, and bird market. If you want a pair of horses, and any description of new or secondhand carriage, wait a little, and they will be paraded before you. You will find there the best fruit, and

the finest flowers in their season. If you would have a donkey, a Shetland pony, or a Newfoundland dog, a good milch cow and calf, a Berkshire pig, a terrier, white mice, a monkey or parroquets, they are to be had in Wall Street.

On Sunday or early in the morning during the week it is like the street of a deserted city. About ten o'clock it begins to show signs of extraordinary animation. Through the day the turmoil increases, people rush to and fro, and literally stagger 'like drunken men.' Toward three o'clock the street appears undergoing a series of desperate throes. Men rush madly past each other with bank books in their hands, uncurrent money, notes, drafts, checks, specie. Occasionally, you may see an individual on the steps of a building, evidently waiting for something, with an air of forced calmness. From time to time he turns his eyes anxiously to the great dial-plate which is displayed from the church, and then up and down the street. The minute-hand has marked five into the last quarter. In ten more minutes it will be three o'clock. Occasionally an acquaintance passes; the man attempts as he bows to smile pleasantly; he can't do it, he only makes a grimace. What is he waiting for? That individual has a note to pay, or a check to make good before three. He has worked hard, but the fates are against him. One friend is out of town, a second is short, a third can't use his paper: he has sent to the last possible place. Look! the young man is coming. Yes? No? He runs eagerly up, thrusts the welcome little slip, a check for the desired amount into the hands of the now agitated principal; it is rapidly endorsed, and on flies the youth to the bank.

Breaking the Rules

Recently there have been a number of scandals on Wall Street in which people have been jailed or fined as much as $100 million for insider trading. A 100 years ago or so, the rules were broken much more often, but the penalties were also a good deal easier to bear, as this description (published in 1870) of the New York Stock Exchange shows:

The Roll-Keeper records the fines, and no body of men are to all appearance more fond of breaking over minor rules, and promptly meeting the penalty, than New York stockbrokers. The annual dues of the Exchange are only fifty dollars, but the fines of individual members not seldom mount up to nearly ten times that sum. Any interruption of the presiding officer while calling stocks renders a broker liable to penalty—"not less than twenty-five cents"—for each offence. To smoke a cigar within the Exchange costs five dollars. Non-attendance at special meetings subjects one to a fine of anything under five dollars. A broker cannot stand on a table or chair without paying a dollar; or innocently fling a paper dart at a neighbor without being amerced ten dollars. It costs twelve and a half cents to call up a stock not on the Regular List, and all the way from one to five dollars to do anything not enumerated in these offences which may be deemed indecorous by the Presiding Officer.

Bestiary

I found this nineteenth-century explanation for the familiar animal metaphors used in stock market jargon:

A speculator is called a "bull" or a "bear," according to his interest in the market. A bull buys stock for a rise, and the term may be derived from his likeness to the animal of the bovine genus who tosses upwards with his horns. He is said to be "long" of stocks, because he is presumed to always hold his stock ready for their delivery on sale.

A "bear" is one who sells stocks for future delivery, which he does not own at the time of sale. The name "bear" is said to have been first given at the time of the South Sea Bubble to such persons as were operating to depress stocks, because they were acting the part of a man who would kill a bear for the sake of his skin. As a bull is said to be "long" of stocks, so a bear is said to be "short of funds."

Glad You Asked

The following explanation of bears is attributed to Dean Jonathan Swift, the acerbic author of *Gulliver's Travels*, who lived through the South Sea Bubble:

He who sells that of which he is not possessed, is said, proverbially, to sell the *bear's skin*, while the bear still runs in the woods; and it being common for stock-jobbers to make contracts for transfering stock at a future time, though they were not possessed of the stock to be transferred, they were called sellers of bear-skins, or *bears*. Another interpretation arises from the general character for *trampling under-foot*, which agrees with their department of business, viz. to keep down the stocks.

Geography

H. L. Mencken once defined Wall Street as a "thoroughfare that begins in a graveyard and ends in a river."

BROKERS

The Virtues of Hard Work

R. Foster Winans, convicted in 1985 for trading secrets from his "Heard on the Street" column in the *Wall Street Journal*, made only $10,000 from the illegal profits of $700,000 garnered by his insider traders. He claims to have told his stockbroker: "I don't want to know if we make a bundle on my tips. I might get lazy."

Butcher and Broker

Dishonest brokers are not of recent origin. One rogue during the middle of the eighteenth century began his career as a butcher in London, before going after bigger prizes. James Bolland was described by a contemporary as

> a man of low extraction, but of great mind, of immense impudence, and unrivaled crime. There was nothing at which he would hesitate to obtain money with which to carry on his stock dealings; and, having once commenced, he soon found that the legitimate wants of his trade—that of butcher—were not sufficient to support him. He formed, therefore, a wooden weight, which, resembling one of fifty pounds, weighed only seven, and thus, in his capacity of tradesman to one of the public institutions, practised his roguery with great success. From butcher he turned sheriff's officer, revived every past iniquity, invented new frauds, and employed his money in buying lottery tickets, to which pursuit he was occasionally attached. He robbed the broker with whom he dealt, alike of his mistress and of his money; and with the latter bought the place of city marshal. The citizens, however, discovered that his integrity was equal to his impudence, and refused to maintain their bargain.
>
> Every moment he could spare was passed at the stock market, where his schemes were marked by a singularly bad fortune. Every speculation went against him; he never drew a prize in the lottery; and, finding there was a chance of his becoming penniless, he added forgery to his long list of crimes. The fraud was discovered and he paid the penalty of his life.

A Broker Is Hung

In the wake of recent inside trading scandals, a number of formerly highly placed members of the financial community have been barred from the stock exchange. The following cautionary tale from eighteenth-century England may cheer up ex-stockbrokers about the relative lightness of their punishment, as well as comfort their victims, who may have fantasized revenge of a different kind upon their current brokers.

John Rice, a London broker, induced his customers to give him complete power to receive dividends and to sell their interests in stocks, and often used the proceeds from one sale to cover his losses in another transaction. One of his female clients, whom he had thus robbed, wrote to him of her intent to come up to London from the country. Unable to restore the principal, Rice became alarmed and fled to Holland leaving with his wife £5000 of the misappropriated property. Ignorant of his deeds, and anxious to join him, the broker's wife also embarked for Holland. The weather was rough and the vessel was driven back, and a bailiff sent in search of the husband apprehended the wife, who yielded all the money in her possession. The search continued for Rice, and being at last found, he was made to suffer the stringent penalty of the law: In 1762 he was taken to a place of execution and hung by the neck until dead.

Brokers of Misfortune

The broker is the connecting link between buyers and sellers. He is a middleman, one who negotiates sales or contracts as an agent. According to an old book, Sereno Pratt's *The Work of Wall Street*, "the word *broker* is old. The early English form was *broceur*. By some it is believed to be derived from the Saxon word *broc*, which meant misfortune, and the first brokers indeed appear to have been men who had failed in business as principals and been compelled to pick up a precarious living as agents."

Wall Street Spectacles

"The broker is narrow in the sense that he looks at everything through Wall Street spectacles," wrote an observer at the turn of the century.

A thing is good or bad, wise and foolish, just as it happens to affect the immediate interest of the Street. If, for instance, the market is depending upon a United States Supreme Court decision, the broker cannot see why the decision is delayed. If there is a strike in the coal fields, he cannot see why the operators and miners should be so inconsiderate as to disturb the prices of stocks. He is impatient of any consideration other than that of his own interest. But the broker is broad in another sense. The Wall Street horizon is almost as wide as the world itself.

How this peculiar view of the world affected Main Street then and now was also put into verse by Wilbur D. Nesbit in the early 1900s. He called his satire

A Cry from the Consumer

Grasshoppers roam the Kansas fields and eat the tender grass—
A trivial affair, indeed, but what then comes to pass?
You go to buy a panama, or any other hat;
You learn the price has been advanced a lot because of that.
A glacier up in Canada has slipped a mile or two—
A little thing like this can boost the selling price of glue.
Occurrences so tragic always thrill me to the core;
I hope and pray that nothing ever happens any more.

Last week the peaceful Indians went a-searching after scalps,
And there was an avalanche 'way over in the Alps;
These diametric happenings seem nothing much, but look—
We had to add a dollar to the wages of the cook.
The bean-crop down at Boston has grown measurably less,
And so the dealer charges more for goods to make a dress.
Each day there is some incident to make a man feel sore,
I'm on my knees to ask that nothing happens any more.

It didn't rain in Utah and it did in old Vermont—
Result: it costs you fifty more to take a summer's jaunt;
Upon the plains of Tibet some tornadoes took a roll—
Therefore the barons have to charge a higher price for coal.
A street-car strike in Omaha has cumulative shocks—
It boosted huckleberries up to twenty cents a box.
No matter what is happening it always finds your door—
Give us a rest! Let nothing ever happen any more.

Mosquitoes in New Jersey bite a magnate on the wing—
Result: the poor consumer feels that fierce mosquito's sting;
The skeeter's song is silenced, but in something like an hour
The grocers understand that it requires a raise in flour.
A house burns down in Texas and a stove blows up in Maine,
Ten minutes later breakfast foods in prices show a gain.
Effects must follow causes-which is what I most deplore;
I hope and pray that nothing ever happens any more.

Overtime

Today's stockbrokers tend to be rather hurried and harried. The complexity of urban life is compounded by the enormous volume and variety of trading crammed into a few hours. In the more freewheeling days of the nineteenth century, the days were longer:

> In the feverish days of the Civil War, night brought no rest to the stockbrokers. Scarcely was dinner well-through than up at Madison Square, first in a cellar beneath the Fifth Avenue Hotel, afterward in Gallaher's Exchange at the Broadway corner of Twenty-third Street, the members came together anew, and carried on their hoarse and frantic biddings into the small hours. Even at present [in 1870], during every access of speculative excitement, throngs gather in the corridors of the Fifth Avenue Hotel, and country guests can hear on every side the confusing street slang, with its subdued but significant utterances of "Take em!" "A thousand more!" "Closed at a quarter!"

Tepid Affair

In 1971 a book appeared called *Confessions of a Stockbroker—Wall Street Diary*. It was published under the pseudonym of "Brutus." An insider's account of how brokers think and operate, the book is full of frank and irreverent advice for the small investor. Brutus advises communicating with your broker regularly once a month (preferably during the full moon), and getting into this habit "like a Pap-test." For the really small investor, the one who buys 20-share lots, Brutus has this advice: "Play your stockbroker as you would a neighbor you were having an affair with—once a month will keep you *both* interested."

Revolutionary Tactics

"Brutus," the pseudonymous author of the 1971 book *Confessions of a Stockbroker*, one morning got a call from the member of a revolutionary cell that claimed it was planning to blow up Kodak's headquarters in Rochester, New York. The young anarchist wanted to short on the stock. Brutus told him that he needed to have a minimum of $2000 in his account. The man counteroffered with some hash and a carload of amphetamines he had parked in a Trenton, N.J., lot. The deal was never made, but Brutus came to believe that revolutionary zeal could be diverted into playing the market.

Pressure

One court recently awarded Helen Aldrich of New York $1.7 million when she sued the firm of Thomson McKinnon, claiming that she and her invalid mother had lost their entire investment of over $400,000. Their broker, according to *Newsweek*, traded in their utility bonds for volatile stock options, netting his firm $143,000 in commissions. Justice Kevin Thomas Duffy remarked on the pressure he felt the brokerage firm had exerted on its brokers, which drove them to act improperly: "I have heard of people perspiring when they were forced to lie," the judge concluded, "but one of the Thomson McKinnon managers sweated so profusely in the cool courtroom that his glasses fogged up."

Santa's Revenge

Complaints about brokerage houses (there were 16,000 filed with the Securities Exchange Commission in 1986) are usually handled by an arbitration process run by brokers or settled in private. Many fleeced clients feel only more frustrated when legal suits against brokers drag on for years and transfer the remainder of their earthly goods into lawyers' pockets. It was perhaps that thought that prompted a doctor in Pittsburgh, Pennsylvania, to an act of desperation. Grover Phillippi later claimed that his commodities broker, Robert Haye, had diminished his winnings by hedging his positions in the market. Haye counterclaimed that his strategy had actually prevented Phillippi from taking losses; in fact, the client made money through this strategy. The aggrieved doctor, getting nowhere in his case against the firm of A. G. Edwards, turned up at the brokerage house's 1983 Christmas party dressed as Santa Claus. Afterward, he offered Haye a ride, then kidnapped him and tortured him for twelve days, trying to get the broker to admit that he had deliberately robbed him. In this he did not succeed, but the doctor got caught in another scheme to kidnap a Paine Webber broker, which brought a sentence of several years.

Fish Story

Warren Buffett, one of the legendary investors of our times, made his immense fortune by staying as far away from the financial markets as possible. From his perspective in Omaha, Nebraska, the man who recently bought the ABC network likes to use the story of a sports fisherman who goes into a store to buy a lure, to describe what goes on on Wall Street. The salesman offers the fisherman a wide variety of ingenious, colorful, and expensive gizmos. Unable to choose, the sportsman asks: "Do fish really like this sort of thing?"

To which the salesman replies curtly: "I don't sell to fish."

PLAYING THE MARKET

Speculation

The difference between speculation and real gold was once explained by Baldwin Bane, the first administrator of the Securities Act, introduced after the Great Depression to regulate the stock market.

A stock promoter came to see Mr. Bane in Washington, D. C. and raised hell because the Securities Commission was holding up the registration statement of his stock, which described in rosy terms the amount of gold waiting to be harvested on a certain hill out West. The proposed prospectus was full of expert opinions by geologists, engineers, and surveyors, whom the commission's own experts did not wholly believe. Mr. Bane knew from his own experience that a man with a real, honest-to-God gold mine would not have to come East but could raise capital by selling shares to his neighbors. In the middle of the scene with the promoter, who was yelling and cursing at government interference, a secretary brought in a telegram, addressed to the promoter, care of Baldwin Bane. The wire had come from the promoter's partner on the mine site and it read: "CANCEL REGISTRATION. HAVE FOUND GOLD."

A Dream as Wide as the Continent

When Jay Gould was 13 years old his one dream was to build a transcontinental railroad. Later he figured out that one could simply buy one that somebody else had built. Cornelius Vanderbilt had just about consolidated his iron grip across the United States and was missing just one link: the Erie Railroad. Gould, with the aid of Daniel Drew and James Fisk, sold the old Commodore more than $7 million worth of illegal stock. The three unholy conspirators then escaped from Wall Street to Jersey City, just ahead of the law. From across the water, Gould bribed the New York legislature to declare the fraudulent stock legal and to outlaw the union of the Erie with Vanderbilt's New York Central. Then he relentlessly proceeded to buy up a number of trunk lines that he had earlier helped into bankruptcy.

Gould's favorite method of speculation was "the corner"—forcing his enemies into a box where they had no choice but to buy his stocks high and sell theirs low. His most notorious exploit was trying to corner the gold market by misrepresenting that he had President Grant's approval for the scheme, which resulted in the 1869 crash. At his death, Gould's vast fortune and railroad companies passed on to his son, George Jay Gould, who was outsmarted in competition by the Western railway magnate Edward H. Harriman. The original dream went up in steam during the panic of 1907.

Right and Wrong

Henry Adams, a contemporary who wrote about Jay Gould's giant speculations in the period following the Civil War, might, some would say, just as well have been commenting on Wall Street today:

> He was a broker, and a broker is almost by nature a gambler, perhaps the very last profession suitable for a railway manager. In speaking of this class of men it must be fairly assumed at the outset that they do not and can not understand how there can be a distinction between right and wrong in matters of speculation, so long as the daily settlements are punctually effected. In this respect, Mr. Gould was probably as honest as the mass of his fellows, according to the moral standard of the Street, but without entering upon technical questions of roguery, it is enough to say that he was an uncommonly fine and unscrupulous intriguer, skilled in all the processes of stock gambling, and passably indifferent to the praise or censure of society.

Good Deeds

Jay Gould was generally known as the "Devil of Wall Street," yet there is at least one story that points toward the other direction. Once when Gould was attending his local church, the minister asked the financier how to invest $30,000. Gould advised him confidentially to buy shares in Missouri Pacific. The stock did rise for a while, but then spent itself in a speculative fever and collapsed. The minister, who held on for too long, was all but wiped out. He poured out his woes to Gould, and the financier there and then wrote out a check to cover his entire losses. Then the minister confessed that despite Gould's request to the contrary he had given the tip to buy Missouri Pacific to many other members of the congregation. "Oh, I guessed that," Gould replied merrily, "and they were the ones I was after."

Triangle

James Fisk, one of the archetypal speculators on Wall Street, began life as a Yankee trader. During the Civil War he enriched himself from both sides: he sold contraband cotton and Confederate bonds in the North, while unloading blankets to the Union army at enormous profit. His deceptively open manner and good humor brought him early to the attention of Jay Gould and Daniel Drew, the railroad speculator, who used young Fisk as front man for a number of questionable deals. However, the unholy alliance was brought to a dramatic end soon after the attempt to corner the gold market. Fisk had left his wife for Josie Mansfield, a well-known actress, who was secretly in love with Edward Stokes, Fisk's business partner. Josie turned over much of the money Fisk lavished on her to Stokes, which broke up the two men's partnership. Then his mentor, Jay Gould, fearing the unfavorable publicity from the affair with Josie Mansfield, asked Fisk to remove himself from the Erie's board. As the young speculator was planning his next move, his former partner, Edward Stokes, shot him to death on the staircase of the Grand Central Hotel in 1872.

Ever More Livermore

The most mysterious man on Wall Street in this century was undoubtedly Jesse Livermore. The son of a poor Massachusetts farmer, he was a teenager when he started working at a Boston brokerage firm as a boardboy. In the days before electronic tapes, boys climbed on chairs and ladders to chalk up the changing stock prices on a giant board. After a few weeks young Jesse noticed that he could guess which direction the next change in each stock's price would take, and as a sort of game, he marked it with an arrow pointing either up or down. One day in 1893 he drew his arrows next to fifteen stock quotations, and he turned out to be right on every one of them. His employers did not wish to see their image as a respectable investment firm tarnished and asked young Jesse to stop dabbling in the occult.

Borrowing $10, Livermore started to play his hunches in bucketshops, pure gambling dens, where one could bet on market movements and usually quickly lose one's money. But by the time he was 21, Jesse Livermore had made enough to quit his job in Boston and become a full-time speculator in New York. In April 1906 he asked one of his brokers to sell short several thousand shares of Union Pacific, one of the blue chips that was leading up the rest of the market in a major bull rally. When the broker implored him not to commit financial suicide, Livermore bought several thousand shares more.

"According to observers who were hanging around the broker's office at the time," writes Max Gunther, "Livermore had a vaguely puzzled air about him, as though he didn't quite understand his own actions. And yet, as he walked out of the office, he seemed oddly serene." Two days later San Francisco was leveled by an earthquake, taking with it a vast amount of Union Pacific track and property. The stock crashed, and Livermore made about $300,000 in less than a week.

Boredom

Commodity traders, along with air traffic controllers, suffer from the highest incidence of stress, ulcers, and burnout. Stanley Kroll, an expert on commodities, finally quit in 1974 and moved to Switzerland. Trading in commodities is for the highest rollers in the investment game, where fortunes can be made or lost in a very short time. In the long run, just as in the casinos, most players either lose to the market or get wiped out by commissions. The hardest thing to do in the commodities market is to sit tight and live with one's decisions. Stanley Kroll used to have a maxim by Jesse Livermore taped on to his telephone, which he read each time he reached for the receiver: "Money is made by sitting, not trading."

Unlike the brokers, the customers suffer from a different kind of strain. Stanley Kroll had a customer who worked in the merchant marine as a radio operator. Whenever he got shore leave, he would take his accumulated salary and gamble it away. Kroll gave him a desk in his office, where he would watch the man plotting the movement of prices on charts with different colored pencils. As John Train tells it in his highly readable book, *The Money Masters:*

> One day, he sat down and for four days did not enter a single order.
> "Maybe the guy's getting good after all," Kroll said to himself. Then one morning Kroll's clerk announced in a loud voice, "Bunge (a large trading house) is buying wheat." The radio operator almost broke his leg getting across the room to the order clerk to enter a buy order. Wheat declined, and as usual the man lost his savings. Later on Kroll asked him, "Why did you do that?"
> "I don't know," the operator answered. "Maybe I was bored."

Women Speculators

Although one hears little about women speculators (except for the legendary Hetty Green), they have been playing the markets for centuries. We find them as active players in the Mississippi Scheme in France and the South Sea Bubble in England. Today, of course, women are working as brokers, analysts, and senior executives in major brokerages. William Fowler, the ascerbic chronicler of Wall Street in the middle of the nineteenth century, describes the women speculators in the patronizing and sexist tone of the period:

> On almost any bright day, when stocks are rising, a dozen or more showy carriages may be seen drawn up in front of the offices of prominent brokerage houses, waiting for the gorgeous dames who ride in them to come out, when they have transacted their business with their brokers. Most of these speculative ladies are dowagers with large bank accounts, for which they, perhaps, thank their departed husbands, or fathers, or uncles, and which they are now using as margins in stock-speculation, and almost always for a rise, for it seems to them an incomprehensible thing that any money can be made by a fall in stocks. Like so many Magdalens, they roll their fine eyes, not repentantly, but avariciously upwards, towards the towering heights of Rock Island, or New York Central, where they hope to make their profits. . . . At Saratoga, in July, 1863, three young ladies, possessed of a will and several thousand dollars of their own, made up a pool in Harlem on their individual account, and bought two thousand shares in a neighborhood of 100. Within four weeks the rise to 181 showed them to be winners to the amount of $75,000. This seemed to justify them in going into the wardrobe line. Consequently, they might have been seen every day sitting on cushioned stools at Stewart's and Arnold, Constable & Company's palaces, and making heavy investments in moire antique, Mechlin lace, and India shawls. But alas for the vanity of human expectations; they did not sell their Harlem, and six or eight weeks from that time they received, not a billet-doux, but a call for more margin, for Harlem had sold down to 75, and instead of making $75,000, they would, if they sold, now lose $25,000.
>
> Fortunately all of these young ladies belonged to the heroic mould, and instead of going into hysterics or sitting down and having a good cry, they went manfully, or rather womanfully, to work and raised money, furnished the necessary margin to their broker and vowed by Nemesis that they would hold their Harlem until they could make their $75,000 once again. Brave girls! Their heroism in six months was rewarded, for the latter part of April, 1864, while the Commodore was hoisting Harlem, they drew $80,000 out of their broker's hands.

The Lady Brokers

In his mid-seventies Cornelius Vanderbilt fell under the spell of two of the most remarkable and unusual women ever to hit New York. In January 1870 the *New York Herald* described the sudden appearance of the two fashionably dressed lady speculators who set up a brokerage office on Wall Street under the name Woodhull, Claflin & Company. Mrs. Victoria Woodhull was soon to become politically notorious as the first female candidate to run for president of the United States—long before women even had the vote. Her running mate in the Equal Rights Party was the first black to run for vice-president, Frederick Douglass.

But it was Victoria's sister, Tennessee Celeste Claflin, notorious even in her teens as a clairvoyant and miracle worker in a medicine show traveling throughout the Midwest, who captivated the aging Commodore, who distrusted doctors and believed that diseases could be cured by spells and chants. There was a great fad about something called "magnetic healing." Practitioners claimed to create and transmit electricity through the laying on of hands, and Vanderbilt liked Tennessee's hand well enough to ask for it in marriage. However, when he heard the rest of her reputation—that she often liked to dress as a man and that the two sisters advocated free love—the Commodore, who had spent a lifetime to achieve some degree of respectability, got cold feet and quickly married a more traditional Southern belle.

When a reporter from the *New York Herald* went to the offices of the lady brokers, he did not find it difficult to deduce who might lurk behind their statement, "We have the counsel of those who have more experience than we have, and we are endorsed by the best backers in the city." Amid the Victorian furnishings of the office there was a photograph of Cornelius Vanderbilt on the piano, and nearby hung a framed motto: "Simply to Thy cross I cling."

Never Sell What You Haven't Got

Cornelius Vanderbilt had several maxims regarding business in general and the stock market in particular. "I bide my time," he used to say. Here is a contemporary account of his willingness to impart advice:

> In 1864, during the memorable rise in Harlem stocks, a son of the late Dean Richmond, president of the New York Central Railroad, who had been selling Harlem at low figures, found himself likely to be several thousand dollars out of pocket, in consequence of the upward movement of the stock. In his extremity, he went to Vanderbilt, introduced himself as the son of his old friend, told him his situation, and asked his advice. "Never sell what you haven't got," the Commodore grimly responded. Upon this hint young Richmond covered his short contracts, and went long, and in a few weeks recovered what he had lost.

After the Fall

Joe Hirshhorn was 6 years old, the twelfth of thirteen children, when his widowed mother emigrated from Latvia to Brooklyn. He sold newspapers as a boy, and once on a school outing to Lower Manhattan he was fascinated by the traders on the Curb (now the American Exchange) conducting their incomprehensible business literally on the street. Joe left school at 14 in order to help support his family, but working as a clerk in a jewelry store did not satisfy him. The street urchin remembered the excitement of the Curb and found himself two jobs: charting stocks for the *Magazine of Wall Street* all day and an extra shift till 2 A.M. as a telegraph messenger. Young Joe managed to save up $255, with which he set himself up as a broker on the Curb at the time America was entering World War I. Within a year his stake grew to $168,000, most of which he lost when peace broke out. Undaunted, Hirshhorn took his remaining $4,000 back into the market, and not one to repeat the same mistake twice, he became one of the wealthiest stock and mining speculators of the century. He was an unabashed gambler, who once declared, "I am not interested in the blue chip stocks and their dividends. I've always wanted the sort of proposition that costs a dime and pays $10."

In 1929 J. H. Hirshhorn and company applied for a seat on the New York Stock Exchange, which at the height of the speculative fever cost half a million dollars. But he got cold feet and withdrew the application, and by August he had pulled out of the market altogether. He came through the crash with $4 million.

Two Commandments

The stock market operates on rumors and tips, most of which are like Samuel Goldwyn's verbal contract: "not worth the paper it's written on." Bernard Baruch, one of the legends of Wall Street, had about ten rules he said he followed. But pressed, he once honed it down to two commandments: First, never pay the slightest attention to what a company president ever says about his stock. And second, when good news about the market hits the front page of the *New York Times*, sell.

The Horse's Mouth

Financiers are always scanning the news to see what might affect the stock market. There is an old story about a broker who tried to go to the source. At a reception, he asked the French statesman Talleyrand whether there was any truth to the rumor that George III had suddenly died. The politician replied in confidential tones, "I shall be delighted, of course, if the information I have to give you can be of any use to you." The financier nodded vigorously while Talleyrand continued with a mysterious air, "Some say that the king of England is dead, others that he is not dead; but for my own part, I believe neither the one nor the other. I tell you this in confidence," the statesman cautioned, "so do not commit me."

The Real Dope

J. P. Morgan, Sr. had a similar if more direct way of imparting tips. Asked by someone what the market was about to do, he is reported to have replied: "It will fluctuate."

Tip

Hetty Green, known as the "Witch of Wall Street," spent most of her life around brokerage offices, and was often asked by all and sundry to give out financial tips. When someone pressed her to suggest where to invest money, Mrs. Green replied: "The other world."

Conundrum

B. C. Forbes one day received a letter from Will Rogers commenting on Forbes's stock advice column. It read: "I hope some day, brother Forbes, to be rich enough to be able to act on some of your stock market advice." At first Forbes took this as a compliment. Rereading it, he wasn't sure.

Check the Color of Your Parachute

When Jack Kapp was head of Decca Records he had a butler who liked to play the stock market. Naturally, he wanted the boss's advice about stock in Decca, which then stood at fifteen.

"It's probably a good buy," said Kapp.

"And you're probably right," said the butler, "but I think I'll wait to pick it up when it reaches to ten."

"If it ever reaches to ten," his employer replied, "you'll be out looking for another job."

Timeliness

One of the French Rothschilds was asked the familiar question: "How did all the members of your family manage to amass such a vast fortune?" The old baron smiled faintly and answered: "By always selling out too soon."

The Golden Rule

Warren Buffet, generally considered the savviest investor in the United States, is a follower of Benjamin Graham's conservative and long-term strategy of buying only shares that are deeply undervalued. The principle is that though it may take time, others will discover those values and the shares will inevitably rise; on the other hand, no emotional see-saws in the market will affect stocks that are based on solid value. With this philosophy Warren Buffet has become one of the richest men in the world. Often asked for his secrets of investing, he usually gives two rules: "The first rule is not to lose money. The second rule is not to forget the first rule."

On Sleeping Well

During the great financial panic of 1857 Daniel Drew, legendary speculator, had risked $1.5 million endorsing the acceptances of his Erie Railroad Company. Asked if he could sleep at night with such large interests at stake, Drew replied calmly: "Sir, I have never lost a night's rest on account of business in my life."

On the other hand, Dickson G. Watt, speculator at the turn of the century, used to tell a story about the man who was so nervous that a concerned friend asked him what was the matter.
"I can't sleep."
"Why not?" the friend asked.
"I'm carrying so much cotton in future contracts that I can't help thinking about it all night. What can I do?"
"Sell down to the sleeping point," the friend advised.

The Public Is Always Wrong

There are countless theories about playing the market, but they all seem to agree on this one point. Thomas F. Woodlock defined the principles of successful stock speculation as based "on the supposition that people will continue in the future to make the mistakes that they have made in the past." There is also the oddlot theory. When the oddlotters sell more than they buy over a period of time, the traders assume that the market has got to go up, because the little guys, who can afford to buy only lots of less than hundred shares, are always wrong.

One explanation for why the public is usually wrong may have to do with ignorance. In 1959 the New York Stock Exchange conducted a survey and discovered that 40 percent of those who owned stock could not say what exactly a common stock was. That was 10 percent fewer than those who were on the verge of purchasing stock. At the very time that the poll was taken, a man named Otis T. Carr was conning hundreds of New Yorkers into buying shares in O. T. C. Enterprises, which claimed to have developed a flying saucer. He promised a select few who bought in at the ground floor the moon, literally—Carr would take them up there on his aircraft, which conveniently could operate indefinitely without fuel.

Get Out of Town

In the 1950s, Nicholas Darvas, a Hungarian-born economist-turned-professional dancer, made $2 million using a system to play the stock market. He described his experiences as a Wall Street outsider in a sensational bestseller *How I Made $2,000,000 in the Stock Market.* One of his techniques for making money was to keep as far away as possible from New York, financial newsletters, or any kind of advice. While he was constantly touring the world, his broker was permitted only to airmail to him a copy of the stock tables in *Barron's* (no articles) and to wire him specific quotes of stock prices on request.

Even Bernard Baruch, who was very much an insider, adopted a habit of salting down his profits in cash or bonds—"where it won't forget who owns it"—then leave New York and "soar off like an eagle, circle high above men to look things over."

You've Got a Problem?

Jack Dreyfus, founder of the group of funds that bear his name, first picked stocks using his sensibilities as a first-rate bridge player. Then, recognizing that the stock market is driven more by mass psychology than economic factors, he began consulting a psychologist. After a while Dreyfus put the shrink on the payroll, with his own office, and encouraged his money managers to take regular consultations. Occasionally, it was the psychiatrist who got anxious and would summon the money manager, as it happened one day to a friend of the financial writer "Adam Smith," who reported their conversation in his book *The Money Game*:

"Polaroid," said the psychiatrist.

"Polaroid," repeated the portfolio manager.

"It's awfully high here, don't you think?" suggested the psychiatrist.

The portfolio manager mulled over the possible unconscious implications of this.

"I have a lot of Polaroid, personally," said the psychiatrist.

"It's come up awfully fast. Should I hold it?"

The portfolio manager sat up. "It's going to be all right," he said, in soothing tones. "It's going to work out just fine."

The psychiatrist slid into a more relaxed position. "I worry about Polaroid," he confessed.

"Let's examine this," said the portfolio manager, "and see why you're so worried. I think I can be of some help . . ."

Witchcraft

Like every place and human preoccupation where fortune is counted in coins, the stock market has always attracted its share of system players, mystics, and astrologers. At times the line dividing the analytical experts with their charts, and the fortune-tellers who read palms and act on hunches is too thin to be distinguishable. As in the casino, anybody with too good a record of steady successes in moneymaking is invested with an aura of the supernatural. In 1971, a journalist by the name of Max Gunther investigated some of the past and living legends who claimed that they could outsmart the market, in an entertaining book called *Wall Street and Witchcraft*. During his research, Gunther tracked down a colorful bunch of people ranging from scientists investigating ESP to apparent nuts.

There was the little old man, T. O. Tully, who took his life savings upon retirement from the plumbing supply business and in fifteen years turned $3,000 into $800,000. Tulley modestly claimed to know what the market was going to do the next day. Max Gunther interviewed him at Delmonico's: "I walk around and feel the—well, the aura, I suppose you'd call it." Although Mr. Tulley could not quite explain the nature of the aura, he had developed a theory about his prescience:

> My theory is that what I've got here is some kind of mass telepathy. You see, anything that's going to happen on the market tomorrow is pretty well decided now in people's minds . . . . The market is a kind of psychological engine, you see. The numbers that come out on the tape every day are the result of what people have been thinking the previous day, the previous week and month . . . . My head seems to be a kind of receiving station for all those millions of thoughts. I can tell when optimism is rising and when it's waning.

Just in case this sounded too vague, Mr. Tulley told his interviewer that he had a feeling that the market would do well the next day, but then run out of steam. The following day the Dow rose eleven points and drifted around for the rest of the week.

Newsletters

Among the hundreds of financial newsletters that investors use to anticipate market movements, quite a few use astrology, tidal tables, and other forms of ancient divination. Some of the best-known market experts employ color graphs and charts, based on historical analysis and long-range economic theories, to predict the future. It has also been demonstrated that choosing stocks by throwing random darts at the stock pages could produce as good as or better results than some rather expensive expert advice. *Esquire* in 1985 mentioned a newsletter put out by a well-known astrologer, *Jack Gillen Predicts,* which sells for $150 a year. Gillen casts his horoscope based on the birth data of a company or the individuals involved in speculation. When a New York couple reportedly followed his advice and lost their entire investment on pork belly futures, they simply switched to another astrologer who charges $215 for his newsletters.

Bill Foster advises his customers to make their trades almost to the minute. He reads the horoscopes of commodities through a computer. "I take what's happening in the sky," he explained to Donald Katz in *Esquire,* "and then I apply thirty thousand 'aspects' to draw a comparison to prices in history. If 'Sun squared Saturn' means that 75 percent of the time soybeans with certain birth signs will fall in price, then I tell my customers the price of beans will fall."

Uncannily, Foster's predictions record was ranked third in accuracy by the *Commodity Traders Consumer Report.* He was right 62 percent of the time, and since even some of the greatest speculators have asserted that 40 percent was sufficient to become rich, some of Bill Foster's customers—many of whom are farmers (because they "understand the power of the sky")—must be quite content.

Chutzpah

John Templeton, one of the most respected investors of the present era, began as a poor but brilliant student at Yale, then went to Oxford as a Rhodes scholar. As a trainee at Fenner & Beane, one of the brokerage companies that later merged with Merrill Lynch, Templeton believed that the outbreak of war in Europe would end the Great Depression, starting with the stock market. By this time, young Templeton was working for a seismic exploration company. He called on his former boss at Fenner & Beane and asked him to buy $100 worth of every stock on the New York and American Stock Exchanges selling for under one dollar a share. The broker balked and tried to talk him out of it, but Templeton ended up as the proud owner of a portfolio consisting of stock in 104 companies, one third of which were bankrupt. The bill came to about $10,000, which Templeton did not have. With the chutzpah of youth, he asked his former boss to advance the money to him. Within a few years, Templeton's portfolio of dogs and turkeys had realized $40,000 and his career as a money fund manager was launched.

Chartist

John Templeton, the money fund manager, once had a partner named Vance, who, according to John Train,

> used to enjoy lecturing about investments. Part of his kit was a huge chart plotted on a roll of wrapping paper. It was so big that during his lectures he would have to get a volunteer from the audience to help him unroll it and put it on the wall. This chart plotted the market for the previous twenty years. Then there were different squiggly lines representing the various factors that influence it—industrial production, money supply, and so on. Year after year if you had followed it you could have known where the market was headed and made a killing. When the audience, fascinated, demanded to know what it represented, Mr. Vance told them. It was the rate his hens were laying in the chicken coop in back of his house.

How to Lose Your Shirt

As Joseph Kennedy once told a class at the Harvard Business School: "Almost anybody can lose his shirt on Wall Street if he's got enough capital to start with and the proper inside information."

MANIAS, BUBBLES, CRASHES

Tulips, Anyone?

"The crowd always loses," according to Fred C. Kelly, an expert on the stock market during the Great Depression, "because the crowd is always wrong." Almost everyone knows this piece of market wisdom, but Kelly gave a reason for it: "It is wrong because if behaves normally." Bernard Baruch attributed his fortune in the stock market in part to David Mackay's classic book, *Extraordinary Popular Delusions and the Madness of Crowds*, first published in 1841 and still in print. It deals with such phenomena as the Dutch tulipmania of the seventeenth century.

The most famous and perhaps least explicable speculative fever in history swept Holland for three years in the seventeenth century. As the industrious and usually sober Dutch became wealthy, the desire grew to find ways of showing off that wealth. But rather than finding the usual outlets—larger houses, expensive clothes, jewelry, perhaps commissioning another family portrait from Rembrandt—the Dutch caught a virus known as the tulip craze. In 1634, according to one account,

> The chief cities of the Netherlands engaged in a traffic which destroyed commerce and encouraged gambling, which enlisted the greediness of the rich and the desire of the poor, which raised the value of a flower to infinitely more than its weight in gold, and which ended in wild and wretched despair. The many were ruined, the few were enriched. Bargains were made for the delivery of autumn roots, and when in one case there were but two in the market, lordship and land, horses and oxen were sold to pay the deficiency. Contracts were made, and thousands of florins paid for tulips which were never seen by broker, by buyer, or by seller. For a time, as usual, all won and no one lost. Poor persons became wealthy. High and low traded in flowers; sumptuous entertainments confirmed their bargains; notaries grew rich, and even the unimaginative Dutchman fancied he saw a sure and certain prosperity before him.
>
> People of all professions turned their property into cash; houses and furniture were offered at ruinous prices; the idea spread throughout the country that the passion for tulips would last forever; and when it was known that foreigners were seized with the fever, it was believed that the wealth of the world would concentrate on the shores of the Zuyder Zee, and that poverty would become a memory in Holland. That they were honest in their belief is proven by the prices they paid. Goods to the value of thousands of florins were given for one root; another species commonly fetched two thousand florins; a third was valued at a new carriage, two gray horses, and a complete harness; twelve acres of land were paid for a fourth, and sixty thousand florins were made by one dealer in a few weeks. Merchants possessed a vast or limited capital, in proportion to the magnitude or insignificance of their tulip roots. Daughters were portioned with a few ounces magnificently, and noblemen of the highest consideration and family importance vested their possessions in a perishable vegetable that could be carried in a teacup.
>
> When the bubble burst and the roots suddenly fell in public estimation, abject poverty stared the nation in the face. Confidence vanished; contracts

were void; defaulters were announced in every town of Holland; dreams of wealth were dissipated; and they who a week before rejoiced in the possession of a few tulips which would have realized a princely fortune, looked stupefied and aghast on the miserable bulbs before them, valueless in themselves and unsalable at any price.

It Can't Happen Here

A mania of almost equal magnitude swept the young United States: this time the object of speculative attention was not homegrown flowers but imported merino sheep. It began in 1815 or 1816 when a gentleman in Boston imported half a dozen sheep from Spain. Following the War of 1812 with England, the Americans thought they could take on the British in producing superior woolen fabrics for the world market. The first merino sheep, which cost a $1 in Andalusia, fetched $50 in America. Before long, a whole fleet of private vessels left for the Mediterranean. By the end of 1816 there were about 1,000 merino sheep in the United States, but, defying the law of demand and supply, the price per head reached $1,200. The merino mania grew more rabid still, according to one source:

In the fall of 1817, what was then deemed a very fine merino buck and ewe were sold to a gentleman in the western country for the sum of eight thousand dollars; and even that was deemed a very small price for the animals. They were purchased by a Mr. Samuel Long, a housebuilder and contractor, who fancied he had by the transaction secured an immense fortune. There also resided in Lexington a wealthy gentleman named Samuel Trotter, who was known as the money-king of Kentucky, and who to a very great extent controlled the branch of the Bank of the United States. He had two sheep—a buck and a ewe—and Mr. Long was very anxious to possess them. Mr. Long repeatedly importuned Mr. Trotter to obtain this pair of sheep from him, but without success. One day, however, the latter said to the former:

"If you will build me such a house, on a certain lot of land, as I shall describe, you shall have the merinos."

"Draw your plans for the buildings," replied Long instantly, "and let me see them; I will then decide."

The plans were soon submitted and Long eagerly accepted the proposal, and forthwith engaged in the undertaking. He built for Trotter a four-story brick house, about fifty feet by seventy, on the middle of an acre of land; he finished it in the most approved modern style, enclosed it with a costly fence, and finally handed it over to Trotter for the two merino sheep. The establishment must have cost, at the very least, fifteen thousand dollars.

But, alas! A long while before this beautiful and costly estate was fully completed, the price of merinos declined gradually; and six months had not passed before they would not command twenty dollars each, even in Kentucky. Mr. Long was thereafter a wiser but a poorer man. He held on to this pair until their price reached the par value of any other sheep; and then he killed the buck and the ewe and invited all his friends to a princely barbecue.

The Schemer and the Economist

The years 1718 to 1720 saw two of the most ruinous speculations of modern times: the Mississippi Scheme, which drove Paris into a frenzy, and the South Sea Bubble, which had the same effect on London. In each case, shares in exotic foreign ventures were inflated by rumor and greed, and when their prices crashed, thousands of speculators were wiped out.

The man behind the Mississippi scheme was John Law, a colorful adventurer who might have qualified in our own days for the Nobel Prize in economics. The son of an Edinburgh goldsmith, Law was noted for his early genius for solving the most intricate problems in arithmetic. Later, the handsome young man (he was known as Beau Law) moved to London, where he started gambling, and eventually killed a man in a duel. After he was tried, sentenced to death, then pardoned, Law decided on a change of air, and his gambling won him a fortune in Paris. He took his hurried leave from that city by eloping with Lady Catherine, the third daughter of Nicholas, Lord Banbury. Lady Catherine happened to be married to a Mr. Semour.

Enter John Law, serious economist. Returning to Scotland, he began publishing tracts on ways to stimulate economic activity, principally by increasing the money supply. Like William Paterson, he proposed the idea of establishing a national bank, but was turned down by the Scottish Legislature. So Law went back to Paris, where he saw a government drowning in debt piled up by Louis XIV's wars and extravagance. Based on rumors of untold riches newly discovered in the American colonies of Mississippi and Louisiana, Law again proposed a bank to support vast trading companies, profits from which would pay off the national debt. (He first offered his plan to the king of Sardinia, who told him he was not powerful enough to ruin himself.) In 1716 Law opened a bank under the protection of the duke of Orléans, the regent of France.

In 1718 Law's was declared a royal bank and the shares rose to upward of twentyfold the original value, so that in 1719 they were worth more than eighty times the amount of all the currency circulating in France. A shortage of shares caused a frenzied speculation, bidding up shares in both the bank and John Law's East India and Mississippi companies, bringing wrenching changes in France's essentially feudal class structure. Wrote an English observer:

> Most of the people of property of every rank in that kingdom, seduced by the prospects of immense gains, subscribed both in the banks and in the companies. At the height of the Mississippi scheme, when John Law issued another fifty thousand shares at 550 livres each, the Rue Quincampoix, the dirty little street where he resided became almost impassable. People of the highest rank clustered about his dwelling to learn their destiny, and delicate women braved all weathers with the hope of enriching themselves. Prelates, marshals and peers cringed at the lackeys and swarmed in the anti-chamber of the Scottish adventurer. A rumor of his indisposition sent the stock down nearly two hundred percent, and the announcement of his recovery sent it up in the same proportion. The frenzy became general. A rage for shares infatuated every rank; from six in the morning until eight in the evening the street was filled with fervent worshippers of the scheme. The dissolute courtiers of the yet more dissolute Regent shared in this spoil. The princes of the blood were not too proud to participate. The ante-chamber of Law was crowded by women of rank and beauty—his mistress was flattered by ladies as irreproachable as the court of the Regent would allow them to be—and interviews with Law were sought with so much assiduity that one lady caused her carriage to be upset to attract his attention and another stopped before his hotel and ordered her servant to raise the cry of "Fire!" The people emulated one another in luxury. Equipages more remarkable for splendor than for taste rolled about the streets. Footmen got up behind their own carriages, so accustomed were they to that position. One of those who had done so recollected himself in time to cover his mortifying mistake by saying he wished to see if room could be made for two or three more lackeys whom he was resolved to hire. The son of a baker, wishing a service of plate, sent the contents of a jeweller's shop to his wife with directions to arrange the articles properly for supper. The Opera was crowded with cooks, ladies' maids and *grisettes*, dressed in the superbest styles of fashion, having fallen from a garret into a carriage.

As Law issued another 300,000 shares, by now at 500 livres each, his original purpose was temporarily achieved: the Regent took advantage of the popular excitement to pay off the national debt.

There was only one slight problem: France was on the verge of economic collapse. Finally, the stupendous fabric of false credit fell to the ground. The shares sank in value as rapidly as they had risen, reducing the government to bankruptcy and ruining tens of thousands of families. It was clearly time to put the fox completely in charge of the chicken coop, so John Law, whose companies already controlled the whole of French foreign trade, was now appointed comptroller-general of finance, which in effect elevated him to the premiership of France. However, he lasted just five months, when he had to leave town a second time to save his life, rescuing only 800 louis d'or from his immense paper fortune. The great economist died in poverty in Venice, in 1729, "occupied to the last in vast schemes of finance, and fully convinced of the solidity of his system, the signal failure of which he attributed to panic."

The Law of Physics

The word *bubble*, in reference to any ruinous speculation, was first applied to the transactions of the South Sea Company, created, curiously, in 1720 with the pretext of paying off the British national debt. With a monopoly over new trade routes to the South Seas, the company was touted to become the richest the world ever saw, promising to multiply investments many times over each year. Innumerable bubble companies started up, most of them patently absurd: one prospectus promised to start "a company for carrying on an undertaking of great advantage, but nobody to know where it is." Exchange Alley was the seat of the gambling fever; it was blocked up every day by crowds, as were Cornhill and Lombard Street with carriages. Shares in the same bubble were sold, at the same instant, 10 percent higher at one end of the Alley than the other. When Sir Isaac Newton was asked whether the South Sea stock would likely continue to rise, he answered that he could not calculate the madness of the people. Jonathan Swift wrote a ballad:

> There is a gulf where thousands fell,
> There all the bold adventurers came;
> A narrow sound, though deep as hell,
> 'Change Alley is the dreadful name.

South Sea stock was quoted at 550, and in four days it rose to 890, then fell to 600; but was finally raised up to 1,000 percent, and then fell to 700. The alarm now increased, and in a few days the price fell to 400. Among the victims was John Gay, the poet, who, having had some South Sea stock presented to him, supposed himself to be the master of £20,000; his friends importuned him to sell, but he refused, and profit and principal were lost.

Insurance Mania

During the eighteenth century England was gripped with all kinds of speculative fevers, which included insurance. To those who believe that getting a Lloyd's policy on a movie star's legs or bust is something new, here are some curiosities from those early days.

A certain William Helmes of London's Exchange Alley offered insurance on female chastity. Other companies insured baptism, marriage, and increasing children's fortunes. Long before automobile insurance, the Crown Tavern in Smithfield offered horse owners a policy against the possibility of their animal being stolen, injured or—something that would be nice for car manufacturers—dying a natural death. One could get insurance against highwaymen and against being cheated or lied to. A company by the name of Plummer & Petty offered insurance for death caused by drinking rum.

After a time insurance "wagers" became the rage. Policies were openly laid on the lives of public men. When George II fought at the battle of Dettingen, 25 percent was paid against his safe return. Following the defeat of the Pretender in 1745, thousands of pounds were laid against his whereabouts, capture, and death. When Lord Nithsdale escaped from the Tower of London by his wife taking his place, the people who risked money on his life, hoping to make a profit from his impending execution, complained noisily. No sooner had they heard that the lord was really free, the same people were laying wagers on his recapture.

During periods of political unrest, Prime Minister Sir Robert Walpole's life was insured for many thousands of pounds, and when his person seemed in particular danger, speculators enlarged the odds in proportion. As soon as word got out that any great man was seriously ill, insurance would be taken out by anybody betting against his chances of recovering. Such bargains were reported in public journals, and one could imagine the effect on the invalid's already precarious health when he saw in the *Whitehall Evening Post* that he "might be considered in great danger, as his life could only be insured in the Alley at ninety per cent."

The Chevalier

One of the more bizarre cases of insurance mania involved the ambivalent adventurer known as the Chevalier d'Éon. Charles Geneviève Louis Auguste d'Éon de Beaumont was an equerry to Louis XV at Versailles, royal censor, doctor of law, and ambassador to St. Petersburg, where he became a favorite of Catherine the Great despite the fact that nobody was quite sure whether the chevalier was a man or a woman.

"This was something decidedly fresh," wrote a nineteenth-century chronicler,

a positive windfall for the wide-awake and scheming insurance brokers and the question [of his sex] was forthwith mooted at Lloyd's. At first wagers and bets were made; but as there was no readily available mode of deciding whether this extraordinary individual was man or woman, they were necessarily abandoned. Then it was decided that regular insurance policies should be opened on his sex, by which it was undertaken that on payment of fifteen guineas, one hundred should be returned whenever the chevalier was proved to be a woman. At first he pretended to be indignant, and advertised that on a certain day and hour, he would satisfy all whom it concerned. The place was a city coffee house, the hour was that of high 'change, and the curiosity of the citizens was greatly excited.

The insurances on this eccentric person's sex were, under these stirring circumstances, greatly and immediately increased, policies to a very large amount were made out, and to the rendezvous thronged innumerable bankers, underwriters and brokers. The hour approached, and with it came the Chevalier, who dressed in the uniform of a French officer, and decorated with the order of St. Louis, rose to address the assembly. It is easy to imagine the breathless attention to this teeming throng, the eager interest of some, the cool cupidity of others, the ribaldry of more and the astonishment of all, as, with an audacity only to be equalled by his charlatanry, he declared that he "came to prove that he belonged to that sex whose dress he wore, and challenged any one to disprove his manhood, with sword or with cudgel."

The spirit of the citizens had passed away, or at any rate it did not serve them on this occasion; commerce had sheathed the sentimental sword of chivalry, and none grasped the gauntlet thus thrown down by the knight. Bankers, brokers, and underwriters gaped at one another as though they had lost their senses, and while the boldness of the speech pleased many, it was far from satisfactory to those who came with the hope of winning a wager, or claiming their insurance money. The knight departed in triumph.

Large sums—in one case amounting to one hundred and fifty thousand dollars—were said to be offered him to divulge his sex. In vain. And it was then thought necessary to settle the question, if possible, in the highest tribunal, and one of the first actions tried after the act to prevent gaming in insurance arose from one of the policies on the sex of the Chevalier d'Éon, in which it appeared that Mr. Jacques, a broker, had received several premiums of thirty-five guineas, for which he had granted policies undertaking to return one hundred guineas whenever the chevalier was proved to be a woman. Lord Mansfield, the chief justice, ruled that "a policy of insurance, although not even on life, when entered into without an insurable interest, was against the purport of the act in question, and contrary to English notions of morality."

You Bet, You Lose

British underwriters also vied with each other in speculating about Napoléon's life. In 1809, Sir Mark Sykes, a banker, was giving a dinner party and conversation inevitably turned to Bonaparte and the daily danger to which he was exposed. The baronet, excited partly by wine and partly by patriotism, offered on the receipt of 100 guineas, to pay anyone a guinea a day so long as the French emperor lived. One of his guests, a clergyman, accepted the offer, but finding the company object, he said that if Sir Mark would ask it as a favor, he would let him off from his bargain. The baronet staunchly refused. The next day the clergyman sent him the 100 guineas, and for the next three years the banker paid 365 guineas. Then, thinking he had suffered enough for his idle joke, he refused to pay any longer. The man of the cloth, displeased at losing his annuity, brought an action that was eventually carried up to the highest legal authorities, and there was finally decided in favor of Sir Mark. Their lordships said that they were not disposed to give the plaintiff a life interest in Bonaparte—who did not die until 1821. By then the 100-guinea bet would have yielded more than 4,000.

For Whom the Bell Tolls

Lloyd's, the most famous insurance company in the world, was first established in the late seventeenth century when Edward Lloyd opened a coffeehouse in the City of London. It quickly became an informal center for the exchange of mercantile news, especially as it affected shipping. At first Lloyd's specialized in marine insurance, before expanding to virtually every aspect of human activity, not to mention parts of the human body, such as Jimmy Durante's nose and Liberace's fingers. Lloyd's underwriters today consist of a society of independent members who transact business on their own account and take risks on behalf of private backers, who have to be wealthy enough to take almost unlimited losses. One of the many traditions at Lloyd's is the ringing of the famous Lutine bell—once for the sinking of a ship, and twice for good news. In 1941, when the British sank the German warship *Bismarck*, the bell only rang once at Lloyd's, where any ship sunk, for whatever reason, is considered bad news.

Mining Fever

William Worthington Fowler, a broker, described the speculative fever that gripped Wall Street despite the Civil War:

March, and the first days of April, 1864, were palmy days for the bubble blowers of Wall Street. Having inflated railroad stocks to a profitable altitude, they proceeded to organize companies in all manner of those useful, costly, and beautiful things, which bountiful mother earth pours out of her lap in the rough. Samples of these things could be seen in Wall Street; brokers and bankers appeared to have been suddenly smitten with a passion for mineralogy. Their offices were transformed into cabinets of minerals, containing very fine specimens of sulphuret of lead, carbonate of copper, and oxide of iron, besides blocks of quartz bespangled with virgin gold, and lumps of coal which burned like a candle. Their talk was in mining slang, and 'pockets,' 'fissure veins,' 'faults,' 'spurs,' 'lodes,' 'pyrites,' 'chimneys,' ran all through their vocabulary. They had a deal to say about 'Comstock Ledge,' producing at that time $1,000,000 per month. They appeared to have transferred their speculative affections from Rock Island, Fort Wayne, and the railways generally, to 'The Alligator Bayou Salt Company,' 'The Big Mountain Iron Company,' and 'The Angels' Rest Quicksilver company.'

The press teemed with advertisements of these various enterprises, and some of the daily journals devoted columns to the record of what had been done, was doing, or was about to be done, in this new field of speculation. There were unsuspected gulches, where the precious metals were a drug. There were mountains of silver and copper, where junks could be had as a gift. Gold ready to be torn from the loose embrace of the maternal quartz. In fine, far off in the wilderness, as well as close to the fringes of civilization, there were hidden treasures without number, materials for wealth without stint, ungarnered, unminted, unmoulded, almost unwatched . . .

The leader of the bulls who fanned the fever of 1864 was a classic speculator by the name of Anthony W. Morse.

But by the middle of April 1864 the bears came out of hibernation.

Signs and portents of coming disaster multiplied, as that weary week drew to its close. Wise financial prophets like Jay Cooke had been heard to predict an approaching evil. The Secretary of the Treasury had been selling millions of gold, and locking the proceeds in greenbacks, in the subtreasury. Money was palpably tightening. Wild rumors were afloat, of how Morse had gone down on his knees to certain bank cashiers, and begged for a million dollars on Fort Wayne, as collateral, but without avail. At the Evening Exchange on Friday, the 15th April, he mounted the rostrum beside the president, while one of his lieutenants stood beside him. In a husky voice, and with a feeble smile upon his haggard face, he offered to sell ten or twenty thousand shares of Fort Wayne. A shiver went through the hushed crowd, and low, ominous whispers were heard: "The bull leader isn't quite himself tonight." "What's the matter with Morse? Is he in liquor?" But all these signs of disaster failed to open the eyes of the deluded multitude, who still clung to their treacherous favorites.

Over that Easter weekend the market collapsed:

The 18th of April fell on Monday. The interval of Holy-day had only strengthened the downward tendency. When he entered the regular board that morning, Morse found nearly every broker eager to sell at heavy concessions, before the call of stocks opened, and the feeling in the street was still worse. He turned and left the room. At half-past eleven o'clock, a broker rose in his seat, and announced the failure of Morse & Co. An appalling stillness, like that which precedes a tornado, followed the words, then the storm burst. The board-room seemed suddenly transformed into a Cyclopean workshop, where a hundred great trip-hammers were being plied. Pillar after pillar toppled over, till the dome fell. The palace of enchantment, builded by a strong and cunning magician of so many golden hopes, passed away like a cloud-pageant . . .

Above all the chorus of execrations was heard the word "Morse." Human nature now showed its basest side. No epithet was too vile with which to couple the name of the prostrate financier. He had fallen like Lucifer in one day, from the zenith of his fame. The men who but yesterday extolled him to the skies, now vied with each other in cursing him. His failure was irreparable. He owed millions to his brother brokers and to depositors who had trusted him. The lion of the hour had become a dead jackass. The king of the market was a lurking fugitive. Men calling themselves gentlemen, met him in the street, and showered abuse upon him. Shoulder-hitters, who had lost some of their ill-gotten gains by his fall, sought him out, and struck him like a dog . . .

Morse departed from the arena, a stripped, penniless, heart-stricken man. He had now only the shadow of a great name. He was pointed out in the streets as the man who had once set the market in a blaze, but capitalists shrunk from him as if he had the leprosy. His attenuated face now and then flitted past the streaming throng on Broadway. One day, more than a year after his failure, he was seen on the street, and Fort Wayne rose five percent. . . He became a changed man. No longer blithe and gay of mien, but morose and irritable. The vast burden of his debts and losses wore upon him. He sought relief in gambling, his old excitement, but under a new form. A gentleman who had lost by Morse's failure, one evening visited, out of curiosity, a notorious gambling hell in Twenty-fourth Street. Sitting near the dealer was one whom he remembered having seen in happier days. A gaunt, pallid face, the features sharpened by the fell disease under which he was suffering, and wearing those death-like lines with which consumption marks its prey. Alas! how changed from that Morse, who but the year before had led his dashing ranks to the summits of the market. A few months more and he lay upon his death-bed in a second-class boarding house, and without means to pay for the common necessities of life. Even when he died, his landlady held his body for the trifling debt which he owed her. It was only when some friend stepped forward and paid the sum, that the funeral rites could be performed over all that remained of what was once a king of Wall Street.

Wall Street Lays an Egg

October 29, 1929, was the culmination of a week of growing panic, as described by the *Commercial and Financial Chronicle* on November 2nd:

> The current week is one that will long be remembered in the annals of the New York Stock Exchange. The huge declines of the previous week and the worldwide publicity given to the record breaking sales on the preceding Thursday, culminated on Tuesday in the most frenzied liquidation the Exchange has ever experienced. The turnover broke all previous records and at the close had reached the unprecedented total of 16,410,030 shares. Recessions were recorded in practically every active stock, and ranged from a dozen points to 45 or more. As the week advanced prices improved but the avalanche of sales was so great that the Board of Governors of the New York Stock Exchange voted on Wednesday to defer the opening of the Exchange until 12 o'clock on Thursday, and keep the Exchange closed altogether on Friday and Saturday. This would suspend further sessions until Monday, November 4, in order to save Wall St. employees from breakdown.

Bargain

During the bull market the common stock of the White Sewing Machine Company had gone up to 48; on Monday, October 28, it had closed at 11-1/8. On that black Tuesday, somebody—a clever messenger boy for the exchange, it was rumored—had the bright idea of putting in an order to buy at 1—and in the temporarily complete absence of other bids he actually got his stock for a dollar a share.

Wrathful Jehovah

Many causes have been given for the crash and Great Depression that began in October 1929: greed, speculation, and what one newspaper editor called "a Chamber of Commerce complex." Fred Schwed, Jr., a broker who saw it from close up found a specific incident to help explain it. From his book, *Where Are the Customers' Yachts*, comes this account:

In 1929 there was a luxurious club car which ran each weekday morning into the Pennsylvania Station. When the train stopped, the assorted millionaires who had been playing bridge, reading the paper and comparing their fortunes, filed out of the front end of the car. Near the door there was placed a silver bowl with a quantity of nickels in it. Those who needed a nickel in change for the subway ride downtown took one. They were not expected to put anything back in exchange; this was not money—it was one of those minor inconveniences like a quill toothpick for which nothing is charged. It was only five cents.

There have been many explanations of the sudden debacle of October, 1929. The explanation I prefer is that the eye of Jehovah, a wrathful god, happened to chance in October on that bowl. In sudden understandable annoyance, Jehovah kicked over the financial structure of the United States, and thus saw to it that the bowl of free nickels disappeared forever.

What Did the President Know?

In 1928, on the eve of the Great Depression, Herbert Hoover prophesied, "The poorhouse is vanishing among us. We in America today are nearer to the final triumph over poverty than ever before in the history of the land . . ." The following March he became president, and, indeed, the country seemed to be booming, and the stock market—usually a harbinger of future economic conditions—was continually breaking new records. Even after the crash that began in October and bottomed in 1932, Hoover kept up his optimistic forecasts. Historian Paul F. Boller, Jr., lists the following statements issued by the White House:

November 1929: "Any lack of confidence in the economic future of the basic strength of business in the United States is foolish."

January 1, 1930: "The nation will make steady progress in 1930."

March 1930: "The crisis will be over in 60 days."

May 1930: "Normal conditions should be restored in two or three months." And: "I am convinced we have now passed the worst."

June 1930: "The worst is over without a doubt."

September 1930: "We have hit the bottom and are on the upswing."

Precedent

If it is any consolation for politicians, the same clear foresight was shown by the government of England before and during the panic of 1825. The chancellor of the exchequer, nicknamed "Prosperity Robinson," boasted in Parliament that in the past two years he had increased the circulation of currency by nearly 50 percent and that his government was "dispensing the blessings of civilization from the portals of ancient monarchy." In an 1825 speech from the throne, George IV declared: "There never was a period in the history of the country when all the great interests of society were at the same time in so thriving a condition." As if on cue, the panic of 1825 broke out, when one-eighth of the country's banks were ruined, six of the London banks stopped payment, and the two years' increase vaunted by "Prosperity Robinson" was annihilated in a few weeks.

Dazzling Insights

Calvin Coolidge, Herbert Hoover's predecessor, came up with some insights of his own, such as this pronouncement in January 1931: "The country is not in good condition." And this startling glimpse into the obvious: "When a great many people are unable to find work, unemployment results."

One day when Coolidge was visiting Hoover at the White House, and after the president outlined his latest efforts to pull the country out of the slump, Hoover expressed his frustration about the apparent lack of results and the way critics treated him.

"You can't expect to see calves running in the field," his predecessor tried to comfort him, "the day after you put the bull to the cows."

"No," replied the weary president, "but I would expect to see some contented cows."

Won't You Spare a Dime?

As the Great Depression deepened, Hoover became more isolated and hated. Everybody blamed him; Will Rogers told a joke about a man who bit into a worm-eaten apple and exclaimed: "Damn Hoover!" Another story from 1932 had Hoover walking down a Washington street with Andrew Mellon, his equally unpopular secretary of the treasury. Suddenly the president stopped and realized he had left home without cash.

"Andy, lend me a nickel, will you? I want to call a friend." Mellon offered him a dime: "You can call both of them."

Suicides

The image of people jumping from high-rise office buildings is one of the legacies of the crash of 1929. Eddie Cantor, who lost a reputed $2 million, developed a skit in which he played a hotel desk clerk and asked a broker about to check in whether he wanted the room for sleeping or jumping. Edward Robb Ellis, in his chronicle of the Great Depression, mentions a cigar manufacturer who stood on the ledge of a Manhattan hotel, and when an employee tried to rescue him, crashed onto the pavement below. But suicides took many other forms, including drowning and shooting. A man in Milwaukee left a note in which he donated his body to science; his soul to Andrew Mellon, secretary of the treasury; and his sympathy to his creditors. When James J. Riordan, president of the New York County Trust Company, shot himself at home, his friend Al Smith, "raced to Riordan's home to intercept the medical examiner, pointing out that if the full story were told at once, the bank's depositors might bring it tumbling to earth. Because of the prestige and personality of the former governor, the city official agreed to delay his announcement. Then, in the words of John Kenneth Galbraith, there was a 'long wake through which the distinguished mourners kept one eye on the corpse and the other on the clock.'"

(Galbraith, in his book *The Great Crash*, points out that contrary to legend and newspaper reports, especially from Europe, the number of suicides in the United States was below the statistical average in October and November of 1929; embezzlement, however, went up.)

Mortal Coils

Following the panic of 1874 the *San Francisco Chronicle* began to publish, under the sign of a skull and crossbones, and in a heavy black border, the names of citizens of the town who had committed suicide on account of losses suffered in stock speculations. The paper kept this up for five years on the principle that the human impact of hard times is felt long after the economy seems to have recovered. The names of sixty-five suicides were published, which the *Chronicle* used as argument against the existence of a stock exchange in San Francisco.

Sign of the Times

Soon after the 1929 crash, a cemetery in Pennsylvania was forced to put up a sign: PERSONS ARE PROHIBITED FROM PICKING FLOWERS FROM ANY BUT THEIR OWN GRAVES.

· 4 ·

MERCHANTS

TRADE AND CARRIAGES

Cultivating

In the Roman republic, there was a degree of shame attached to being in trade that made later English and German snobbery look like glowing approbation in comparison. Cato the Elder, pointing to a Roman law that branded a usurer as committing greater evil than a common thief, considered usury a form of homicide. He urged his fellow citizens to avoid making loans as dishonest investments. Cicero, in his *De Officiis*, ranked the professions according to their social acceptability. He urged gentlemen to avoid having to do anything with the gathering of taxes or the lending of money, because it would excite the ill will of men. He went on to ban from his ideal republic hired labor paid not for their skill but for mere work; small retailers, because "they make no profit except by a certain amount of falsehood"; and mechanics, because "a workshop can have nothing respectable about it." He also disapproved of all the trades that minister to the palate: fishmongers, butchers, cooks, poulterers, and fishermen. Cicero quoted with approval the comedy writer Terence, that "commerce on a small scale is vulgar, but on a large scale and importing from all quarters, and making large sales without fraud is not so very discreditable." Apart from this grudging gesture toward big business, what did Cicero think an acceptable way of making a living? He was a gentleman farmer, and he thought that nothing could be more productive, more pleasant, and more worthy of a cultivated man than agriculture.

That's Why They're Building a Chunnel

King Athelstane, the grandson of Alfred the Great, issued a statute that provided that any merchant who ventured on his own account on three voyages beyond the English Channel should be entitled to become a thane, with all the privileges of being regarded a gentleman.

Snubbing the Snobs

In later English society "being in trade" was a term of contempt well into our own century, even though many a merchant had been raised to the nobility. (Charles II, for instance, had conferred a baronetcy on the son of John Shaw, a vintner who lent him large sums of money during his years of exile in France.) So many brewers, in fact, had bought, through public service or charitable works, into the peerage, that one wit dubbed this new aristocracy the "Beerage." According to Gordon Selfridge, of department store fame, that term was coined during a riotous celebration of "Kitchen Lancers" at a county ball, when Miss Bass (later Baroness Burton) was tossed from the fray into a circle of spectators. One of the young men commented, rather too loudly, "Not quite Vere de Vere," referring to the ancient de Vere family of the earls of Oxford.

Miss Bass, whose father owned Bass's Brewery Company and was made Lord Burton, put down the provincial snob with her retort: "No, because it's Beer de Beer!"

Forgive Our Trespasses

Henry James, the American novelist who became a thoroughly British gentleman, set up house near the country estate of a retired jam manufacturer. The man had married an earl's daughter and was ashamed of the trade whereby he had acquired his large fortune. One day the ex-manufacturer of preserves wrote Henry James a letter expressing outrage at the way James's servants were trespassing on his grounds. The novelist wrote back with unusual brevity:

Dear Sir: I am very sorry to hear that my servants have been poaching on your preserves.
P.S. You will excuse my mentioning your preserves, won't you?

Motto

James Gillespie, tobacco and snuff manufacturer, used some of his large fortune to found a hospital, named after him in Edinburgh. Once he bought a new, elegant carriage and wanted to paint something personal on it. (This was before personalized license plates.) He could not think of anything, but fortunately ran into his witty friend, Henry Erskine. The future lord chancellor improvised:

Wha wad hae thocht it,
That noses had bocht it.

(Translated from Scots: Who would have thought it / That Moses had bought it.)

Commoner

Another Scot, Adam Black, the well-known nineteenth-century publisher and stationer, refused a knighthood, which he was offered for his services to literature.

"Na, na," he said in his broad Scotch accent, "it would never do to have the laddies comin' into the shop and sayin' 'Sir Adam, I'll take a pennyworth of pens!'"

Waiter

Mr. Kennet, lord mayor of London in the year 1780, began life as a waiter, and he was never allowed to forget it. When he was summoned to be questioned in the House of Commons, one of the members observed: "If you ring the bell, Kennet will come, of course."

One evening at the Alderman's Club, he was at the whist table, and Alderman Pugh, a dealer in soap and an extremely good-natured man, was at his elbow, smoking his pipe.

"Ring the bell, soap-suds," said Mr. Kennet, who had the personality of an untipped waiter.

"Ring it yourself" replied the alderman, "you have been twice as much used to it as I have."

White and Defenseless

Recently, when a made-for-TV movie on ABC called *The Children of Times Square* was attacked as being unsympathetic to minorities, Stephen White, NBC's senior vice president in charge of movies, came to the industry's defense: "We don't get letters from white businessmen, but they're really the ones who should protest. A majority of them are shown to be villainous . . . because no one will object."

Face

Most Westerners realize how seriously the Japanese take the loss of face: occasionally, it can still lead to suicide. Less known is that not only people but even firms have a "face" in Japan. The *noren*, as it is sometimes called, has a long history. Originally, it was simply the short, split curtains that were hung across the doorways of shops and restaurants. Made of heavy, blue cloth, the *noren* usually displayed the name or crest of the owner. Rather like British pub signs, in time the *noren* became a symbol or "face" for the business itself, standing for its reputation, which must be guarded. Occasionally, when a favorite employee, usually the one who married into the owner's family, went out to set up a new business, he would be allowed to use the *noren* of his previous workplace, showing a continuing relationship. This would be somewhat similar to modern franchising, where the use of a certain trademark guarantees a predictable standard of quality.

Until quite recently, when Japan began to emerge as a global trading power, many of the most established Japanese firms believed it was below their dignity to advertise for business. They maintained branches not so much to do business as to protect their "face." When they did advertise, it was not their products, but simply to announce the name of the firm and its address, its *noren*, in fact. Often one other fact was included: the amount of capital wielded by the company. This was a way of establishing rank. Frank Wertheimer, a Canadian distributor in Japan in the 1950s, recalled the dilemma of the manager of a hotel where some prominent businessmen had met. He spent hours making up a list of the firms according to their capitalization, because this was the only proper way of determining the order in which the executives' cars would be brought to the hotel entrance at the end of the conference.

Vanity

Heinrich Heine, the great German poet who lived during the first half of the nineteenth century, traveled when a young man from Hamburg to Mannheim, where he stayed at the Golden Lion hostel. While having supper in the dining room, he noticed at a nearby table an older gentleman who would occasionally look up and sigh heavily as he ate. After a time, Heine went over to him and asked the cause of his grief. Without much prompting, the man told this story:

> "My name is Müller, and I am a very rich merchant in Nuremberg. I have two hundred thousand income, an adorable wife, and charming children.

My health is excellent, and I am the most unfortunate of men."

"Why is that?"

"Ah! How to make you so terrible a confession," and the man sighed again. "I have committed a crime. I am a thief."

"Given your wealth, what hinders you from making restitution?"

"Believe me, young man, there does not pass a month that I do not give in charities, in pious works, the double, the triple, the quadruple of what I have purloined, but the claw of the vulture does not leave me a moment of repose."

"And how could a man like you be tempted to steal?" asked the poet.

"Vertigo. I had the honor of dining with the Duke of Nassau at his chateau in Biebrich. The prince, who has a very particular fondness for me, placed me on his right, and we talked during dinner of one thing and another. 'Monsieur Müller,' said the duke to me, 'how is Madame Müller?' 'Your Highness is too good,' 'And the little Müllers?' 'Very well, but Your Highness does me too much honor.' Amidst all this flattering familiarity, suddenly I saw shining before my eyes a little gilt spoon. What passed in my brain I know not, but the moment the duke turned his head I stretched my hand slyly along the cloth, took the spoon and put it in my pocket. This, sir, is what I did at the house of the Duke of Nassau."

After this recitation, Herr Müller, who had finished his third bottle, tumbled off to sleep, and in spite of so much remorse, snored like a bass viol. The next day Heine made some inquiries. He found out that the man was truly Mr. Müller, a merchant of Nuremberg, with an income of two hundred thousand, and a large family. But he had never dined with the duke of Nassau. He had invented the fable of the stolen spoon to persuade people that he was the duke's friend, willing to gratify his vanity by making himself out as a thief.

FAR AND WIDE

Silky Secrets

The Chinese manufacture of silk goes back thousands of years. An ode celebrated the process in the twelfth century B.C.:

In the eighth month they begin their spinning:
They make dark fabrics and yellow.
Our red manufacture is very brilliant.
It is for the lower robes of our young princes.

At the silk center of Shantung, the Chinese raised altars to Lui-tsu, the presiding genius of the silkworm. The altars were surrounded with groves of mulberry trees favored by the silkworm, and each year the empress of China made sacrifices at the shrine. She also used a golden implement to collect mulberry leaves for her own silkworms. Silk and the secrets of its manufacture were held so precious that for many centuries it was forbidden to take even the finished product out of the country.

Around A.D. 120 a Chinese princess married a king of Khotan. The idea of having to live among barbarians where she would have no silk so appalled her that she concealed silkworm eggs and some mulberry seeds in her headdress and thus passed through the Great Wall and the Chinese frontier with her contraband undetected. The princess began to cultivate the silkworms in her new home, but when Chinese ambassadors to her court realized what she had done, they informed her husband that his wife was harboring venomous snakes, and the king ordered the house with its precious contents, burned to the ground.

Vice Versa

American trade with China goes back to 1784, when the first U.S. vessel sailed to China from New York. Five years later, there were fifteen American merchant ships at Canton, more than from any country other than Great Britain. In those days, the balance of trade was entirely in China's favor, with the United States importing much more than it could consume and exporting the surplus Chinese goods to other countries. The trade with Canton amounted to $2 to 3 million in specie, but payment was mostly in sealskins and furs.

Fun and Profit

Gossipmongering is a popular pastime everywhere; in China it was professionalized. This from a nineteenth-century account:

> A number of elderly ladies, generally widows, make it their business to collect gossip, *on dits*, chit-chat, and stories of all sorts with which they repair to the houses of the rich, announcing their arrival by beating a small drum, which they carry for that purpose, and offer their services to amuse the ladies of the family. When it is recollected that shopping, public assemblies, and even morning calls are all but forbidden to the beauty and fashion of China by their country's notions of both propriety and feet, some idea may be formed of the welcome generally given to these reporting dames. They are paid according to the time employed, at the rate of about fifty cents an hour, and are besides in the frequent receipt of

presents—their occupation affording many opportunities of making themselves generally useful in matters of courtship, rivalry and etiquette. On these accounts they generally retire from business in easy circumstances, but are said never to do so unless obliged by actual infirmity—so congenial is the business to their female tastes.

And He Was Right

In the sixteenth century Portugese and English ships roamed the oceans of the world, vying with each other to be the first to open trade with newly discovered lands in exotic places. When the Portugese tried to establish a commercial treaty with Borneo, their efforts were frustrated by the English through an unplanned and unforeseeable circumstance. The king of Borneo received the emissaries from the Portugese vessel with special favor, and they displayed before him the presents that they had brought. For some reason there happened to be a tapestry representing the marriage of Henry VIII and Catherine of Aragon. When the king of Borneo saw the bluff figure of Henry, as large as life, he bid the strangers to pack up their presents and leave his dominions immediately. He knew, he said, why they brought him those figures: that ugly man was to come out in the night, cut off his head, and take possession of his country. There was no persuading him out of his imagination, and the Portugese were forced to abandon a commercial venture that had commenced so auspiciously.

Holy Smoke

Queen Mary Tudor ("Bloody Mary") ordered her Attorney-General Seymour to draw up the charter for a college in the new colony of Virginia, which was to be given £2,000. He opposed the grant, saying that the nation was engaged in an expensive war, that the money was needed for better purposes, and that he did not see the least occasion for a college in Virginia. The colonists responded to him that their intention was to educate and qualify young men to be ministers of the gospel, much wanted there, and begged that the attorney general might consider that the people of Virginia had souls to be saved just like those in England.

"*Souls!*" exclaimed the ever sensitive Seymour. "Damn your *souls!* Make *tobacco!*"

Behind Every Successful Man

The roots of the Mitsui Corporation, the global trading company, date back to the seventeenth century. Sokubei Mitsui was a samurai who had to renounce his class. A merchant stood almost at the lowest rung of Japanese society, below farmers and craftsmen. Only the Eta, people who handled corpses, were more despised than tradesmen. Mitsui's honorable family had become impoverished in endless civil wars serving his shogun. He now called together his household and proclaimed his intention to become a commoner: "The Mitsuis are a proud and old family, descended from the Fukiwaras whose ancestor stood on the right side of the Heavenly Grandchild when he was commanded by the Sun Goddess to go to the land of the Luxurious Reed and establish an everlasting rule . . ." Unfortunately, he now saw no choice but to give up his sword. Mitsui proposed to make money by brewing *sake* and making *shoyu*, a sauce made of fermented wheat and soya bean.

Although Sokubei made the momentous decision to enter trade in the town of Matsuzaka, he knew nothing about selling and quickly floundered. It was his wife, Shuho, who came to the rescue. She was born into a rich family of merchants, the Nagai, and was married to Sokubei at the age of 13. Shuho's thrift was legendary. According to her biography, *The Life and Deeds of Shuho Taishi*, she picked up bits of string as she walked through the streets, twined them together, and made them into a vast collection of string balls. She found a bowl with the bottom broken, and converted it into a rain pipe. Now she helped her husband by converting a part of his sake establishment into a pawnshop, a popular business in town. To compete with the more established pawnbrokers, she began the Mitsui tradition of slashing prices on interest rates. She was also a patient listener to her customers' tales of hard luck, and she encouraged them to come back by treating them to free drinks of sake and an occasional meal. Sokubei Mitsui died in 1633; Shuho survived him by more than forty years. She trained her four sons in business, especially the youngest, Hachirobei, whose talent stood out. Shuho picked Ju-san, a girl who was also from a merchant family, to be his son's wife, and then trained her daughter-in-law to take her own place. She succeeded to such an extent that Ju-san remains a role model for young Japanese schoolgirls to this day. It was her six sons who founded the six branches of the House of Mitsui, which eventually became the great international trading and banking enterprise of today.

Sing Louder

By 1861 Singer was selling more sewing machines abroad than in the United States. The vast manufacturing plant in Glasgow became so important to Clydebank that a Singer machine was incorporated into the burgh's coat of arms. Part of Singer's adaptation to so many countries in the world was manifested in having natives head up sales organizations. Indeed, in many countries, Singer is 100 percent nationalized. And when Singer salesmen found people who somehow lacked foot coordination to operate the standard treadle machine, the company came up with hand machines. When African tribesmen wanted noisier machines, on the principle that "good iron makes good noise," the Singer man obliged by loosening up the machines so that they made greater clatter.

Good Address

Mahatma Gandhi learned to sew on a Singer in jail, "It is one of the few useful things ever invented," said the holy man who later drove out the British from India with his hand-spun textile.

In Calcutta, the United States Consulate shared a building with the Singer Sewing Company, which was both a landmark and a household name. Once a letter was delivered to his "Exalted Holiness of the Consul General of the United States of America by the backside of the Singer Sewing Machine Company, Calcutta."

Surrender

Two representatives of the Singer Sewing Machine Company, one a Japanese and the other American, happened to meet at the surrender of the Korean port of Inchon in 1945. George Jones had traveled the Orient for Singer and now served in army intelligence. As a small boat of Koreans approached the American vessel that had just arrived to accept the surrender, Mr. Tani, who had been the Singer agent in Seoul, was delighted to see an old friend: "Why, it's our Mr. Jones!" he shouted.

CHARACTERS

Passion

Edmund Kean, the great star of the British stage in the early nineteenth century, was visiting Ayr in Scotland. Entering a shop, he found that the conversation was about his performance of Othello. A butcher asked very gravely whether Mr. Kean spoke all he said out of his head or if he learned it from a book. Being told how the thing was, the shopkeeper objected against paying to hear a man repeat what every person who could read might do as well for himself. This objection was met by someone observing that the actor "did not only recite the play, but he delineated the various passions which belonged to the character."

"Passion!" exclaimed the butcher with a sneer of contempt, "gang to the fishmarket if ye want to see folk in a passion! That's the place for passion!"

Every Town Should Have One

On the north side of Old Niddry's Wynd, later Niddry Street, in Edinburgh, there once stood a shop kept by an eccentric personage, who exhibited a sign bearing the singular inscription:

ORRA THINGS BOUGHT AND SOLD

which meant that he dealt in odd articles, such as a single shoe buckle, one of a pair of skates, a teapot wanting a lid, or perhaps a lid minus the teapot; in short, any unpaired article that is not to be got in the shops where only new things were sold. This trafficker in curiosities also kept, besides this stationary establishment, a moveable shop, in the shape of a tidewaiter's counting room, which usually stood at the head of the wynd, containing his own person and an assortment of "orra" things piled up around him, and having a half door, over which he communed with his customers. It is odd, but the creature made money—for he also was perhaps the greatest matrimonial matchmaker in Europe.

A Cheap Life

Robert Burns was standing one day on the waterfront at Greenock when a wealthy merchant from the town had the misfortune of falling into the harbor. The man could not swim, and he would have drowned had not a passing sailor immediately plunged in and rescued him, risking his own life in a dangerous situation. The merchant, when he recovered from his fright, put his hand into his pocket and rewarded the sailor with a shilling. There was quite a crowd collecting, and there were some contemptuous jeers about the insignificance of the sum. But Burns, with a scornful smile, asked them to restrain their clamor.

"The gentleman," said the poet, "is of course the best judge of the value of his own life."

No Handicap

Sandy Martin was a Scottish tailor who lived 300 years ago on the island of Harris, the home of the famous type of tweed. He lost his sight as a boy because of small pox, "yet so wonderfully did he possess the sense of touch," claimed a writer in 1703,

> that the loss of vision seemed to cause him but little inconvenience. Of all the tailors in the island, none were in greater repute than Sandy. Although stone-blind, he placed his customer before him, measured him quite scientifically, cut his cloth with rigid economy, sewed it firmly, smoothed it neatly, and, in short, finished his job to the entire satisfaction of his employer. But what was more surprising still, suppose that the cloth which he was to work upon was tartan, let it be however so fine and uncommon, he had the faculty of tracing out the stripes, squares and angles of the fabric, by mere delicacy of touch. It is well known that tailors who have the sight of both eyes, experience at times no ordinary difficulty in cutting and finishing a Highland tartan coat, so as to make the different squares in the cloth to coalesce diagonally at the back, and to meet angularly with mathematical correctness. But blind Martin never failed and was never known to have committed a mistake.
>
> Not satisfied with the trade of tailor, he had a second string to his bow, and acted as shoemaker also. He cut, shaped, sewed and finished a pair of shoes as firmly and neatly as most men; and his jobs, when finished, showed no indications that the performer never saw what he so exquisitely handled. In one word, he failed but seldom in any work which he took in hand. There was not a man in Harris who could more expeditiously repair a torn herring net than poor blind Sandy. However tattered the net might be, and however scattered the broken meshes, Sandy soon discovered the existence and extent of the damage, and quickly repaired it. The poor man unquestionably furnished a striking proof of the extent to which one sense may be improved by the deprivation of another; for undoubtedly the want of the sense of sight in this individual was the cause of the perfection to which he carried that of touch.

Yankee Shrewdness

The colonists of New Haven used shoestrings instead of buckles. They were cut from rawhide and called colloquially "whang." In the nineteenth century, "Shoestring Pratt" of Randolph, Massachusetts, devised a way of cutting scrap leather concentrically, pulling them straight and rolling them in their own fat. When they were round, he cut them into standard lengths. He went about in his wagon to shoemakers' factories, where he picked up waste leather and sold them back the product he made out of it.

Stratagem

Shawls became popular in the late eighteenth century both in Europe and in the newly independent United States. Jim "Jubilee" Fisk made his first fortune peddling Paisley shawls. He had formed a partnership with a traveling jeweler from Otis, Massachusetts, with the colorful name of Volney Haskell, and together they worked out a successful stratagem. One of the partners would visit a New England town and give a Paisley shawl to a well-known beauty, suggesting that she show it off in church the following Sunday. When she obliged, of course every other fashion-conscious lady wanted to have a shawl of her own. Then the very next day the other partner would show up with a whole wagonload of Paisley shawls, and he was always mobbed by the women, whose appetite had been thus whetted.

Yankee Peddlers

One of the stock characters of the American road during the nineteenth century, the word *Yankee* became a term of contempt, expressing fear, though it could also be used with pride, especially if applied by a Yankee to himself. "To Yankee" someone meant to cheat, and "Yankee peddler" was rarely used without a connotation of fraud or at least of taking unfair advantage. Before the Civil War, when more than 16,000 peddlers were licensed to roam the roads, the *Hartford Courant*, in the heart of Yankee country, defended the species:

> We may laugh at the Yankees as we will, but they are the most thriving people in the world, and "let those laugh that win". . . Take your stick, and walk out on the highway: you will not have fairly warmed yourself with the exercise before a gaily painted equipage, snug and light, drawn by a sturdy pair of Vermont horses, will come in sight. The driver is a healthy, ruddy, happy-looking fellow, comfortably wrapped up, and with a shaggy buffalo skin gathered around his feet. You see at a glance that the master's eye has had its well-known effect on the cattle. When he alights to bait, you will easily get into conversation with him. His eye is even more inquisitive than his tongue, which is saying much; but beyond this he is not disrespectful. He has a book in his pocket, and has been taught to lay aside his cap in a Christian house. He does not drink, and he does not blaspheme, and he carries no bowie-knife. . . . In a few months he will return to the banks of "the river," with money enough to stock his tiny farm. During his thousand miles of travel he will be sneered at, taxed for his license, hustled at court houses, browbeaten at inns, blasphemed at barbecues, but never cheated, never beaten, never goaded into an assault, and never seduced from his main point.

Tit for Tat

The great showman P. T. Barnum got the better of a peddler during his
early days as a country-store clerk: "On one occasion a peddler called at
our store with a large wagon filled with common green glass bottles of
various sizes, holding from a half pint to a gallon. My employees were
both absent, and I bantered him to trade his whole load of bottles in exchange for goods. Thinking me a greenhorn, he accepted my proposition,
and I managed to pay him off in unsalable goods at exorbitant prices."

Mink

Once a pack peddler in upstate New York tricked William Cook, a man
with a great reputation for honesty. Just about the time the peddler was
due for another visit, Cook's cat died. He skinned it, and when the
peddler appeared, he asked him:

"Do you buy mink-skins?"

"I'll give you ten dollars for one," the peddler offered and did not take
a closer look at the fur, knowing that Cook was a man of his word. The next
day the peddler returned to complain:

"Say, that pelt you sold me wa'nt mink. It was more like a cat."

"Well, I didn't say it was mink," Will had his answer ready. "I just
asked whether you buy mink-skins. Anybody around here will tell you
that my old cat that died was called Mink. I guess we are even now."

Deadbeat

George Hardinge, an English bookseller and politician of a century ago,
ran up a large bill for books with Triphook, a fellow bibliopolist who had
written him several times trying to collect the money, without response.
Finally, Triphook wrote expressing his fears that his client might be dead,
and concluded with the sentence: "Should the melancholy circumstance
be true, I hope the executors will pay the bill." He received the following
reply:

Dear Mr. Triphook:
What is fear'd by you
(The melancholy circumstance) is true—
True I am dead; and more afflicting still,
My legal ashes will not pay your bill;

For, oh! to name it I am broken-hearted,
This transient life insolvent I departed,
And so for you there's not a single farthing.
For my executors and self—George Hardinge.
P.S.—You'll pay the postage which these lines will cost;
The dead their franking privilege have lost.

Pricing

One fine morning when Benjamin Franklin was busy preparing his newspaper for the press, a customer stepped into the store and spent an hour or so browsing over the books. Finally, taking one in his hand, he asked the shop assistant for the price.

"One dollar," the boy answered.

"A dollar!" the customer exclaimed, "Can't you take less than that?"

"No, indeed, one dollar is the price."

The man went on browsing almost for another hour, when he asked the boy:

"Is Mr. Franklin at home?"

"He is working at the printing press."

"I want to see him," said the customer. The boy immediately went to the back and informed his boss that a gentleman was in the store waiting to see him. Franklin soon came and the browser asked him:

"Mr. Franklin, what is the lowest you can take for that book?"

"One dollar and a quarter," was the ready answer.

"One dollar and a quarter! Why, your young man asked me only for a dollar."

"True," said Franklin, "and I could better have afforded to have taken the dollar then, than to have been taken away from the business I was engaged in."

The customer seemed surprised and repeated his question:

"Come, Mr. Franklin, tell me truly what is the lowest you can take for it?"

"One dollar and a half."

"One dollar and a half! Why, you offered it yourself for a dollar and a quarter just now."

"Yes, said Franklin," and I had better have taken that price then, than a dollar and a half now."

Not wishing to inflate the price any further, the browser put down the dollar and a half and went about his business—if he had any—and Franklin returned to the printing office.

Franklin Out of Print

Benjamin Franklin, whose earliest trade was that of printer, composed
this epitaph for his tombstone, long before his death:

THE BODY
OF
BENJAMIN FRANKLIN
PRINTER,
(LIKE THE COVER OF AN OLD BOOK,
ITS CONTENTS TORN OUT,
AND STRIPT OF ITS LETTERING AND GILDING)
YET THE WORK ITSELF SHALL NOT BE LOST,
FOR IT WILL (AS HE BELIEVED) APPEAR ONCE
MORE IN A NEW
AND MORE BEAUTIFUL EDITION
CORRECTED AND AMENDED
BY THE AUTHOR

Wound Down

The following *professional* epitaph is copied from a tombstone in Lidford
Churchyard, Devon, England.

Here lies in horizontal position
The "outside case" of
George Routleigh, Watch Maker,
Whose abilities in that line were an honor
To his Profession.
Integrity was the "Main-spring,"
And Prudence the "Regulator" of all the
Actions of his Life.
Humane, generous, and liberal,
His "Hand" never stopped
Till he had relieved distress.
So sincerely "regulated" were all his move-
ments,
That he never "went wrong,"
Except when "set agoing"
By People
Who did not know
"His Key".

Even then he was easily
"Set right" again
He had the Art of disposing his "Time"
So well,
That his "hours" glided away
In one continual round
Of Pleasure and Delight,
Till an unlucky Moment put a period to
His Existence.
He departed this Life,
November 14th, 1802,
Aged 57:
"Wound up"
In hopes of being "taken in Hand"
By his Maker,
And of being
Thoroughly "cleaned," — "repaired," — and "set
agoing"
In the World to come

CUSTOMERS

Real Coffee

Many drink chicory today as a caffeine-free substitute for coffee. But in
the last century, when coffee was very expensive, some German inns tried
to save money with such substitution.

Bismarck, the "Iron Chancellor," was also known for his shrewdness.
Arriving one evening at a small inn after a hard day's journey, he
summoned the innkeeper and asked sternly:

"Have you any chicory?"

"Yes, sir."

"Bring all you have to me!" The innkeeper came back after a few
minutes with an armful of chicory.

"Is this all the chicory you have in the house?" asked Bismarck.

"Yes, this is all."

"Well, then," said the statesman, "leave the chicory here and make
me a cup of coffee."

Lesson

Dr. John Brown, a famous Scots commentator on the Scriptures, was so poor that he went into a store in Dunse to buy a halfpenny worth of cheese. The shopkeeper said he was unable to accommodate him with so small a portion.

"Then what's the least you can sell?" inquired the customer.

"A pennyworth," replied the dealer. He instantly weighed out that amount and speedily placed the cheese on the counter in anticipation of payment.

"Now," said the scholar, borrowing the tradesman's knife, "I will instruct you how to sell a halfpenny worth of cheese in future—" and he cut the small piece of cheese in two. Then he picked up one half, paid down his copper, and departed from the store.

Suspect

At the turn of the century, the Baroness Burdett-Coutts was one of the wealthiest women in the world. She was once shopping in a Paris department store, and, as she passed from one department to another, the accompanying clerk would say to the next clerk: "Two-ten." The Baroness wanted to find out what the phrase meant.

"It is just a greeting clerks are in the habit of exchanging," was the unsatisfactory explanation given. That evening, when the store's porter delivered her purchases to the hotel, she asked him if he would like to earn five francs. With that inducement, he told the millionairess that the phrase was a code word used to identify suspected shoplifters: Two-ten meant that each clerk was to use two eyes to watch the customer's ten fingers.

Berries

Charles Mathews, one of the great comic actors of the nineteenth century, was usually late in paying tradesmen. His tailor, named Berry, was quite accommodating, but when his son succeeded to the business, he sent a bill somewhat ahead of its time. The actor went into a virtuous rage and wrote the following note:

You must be a goose—Berry, to send me your bill—Berry, before it is due—Berry.

Your father, the elder—Berry, would have had more sense.

You may look very black—Berry, and feel very blue—Berry, for you and your bill—Berry.

Judgment Day

At the bottom of the Great Depression, the Hudson's Bay Company received a letter from a Canadian farmer, which was read out during the annual meeting in 1932:

> I got your letter about what I owe. Now be pachant. I ain't forgot you. Please wait. When I have the money I will pay you. If this was the Judgement Day and you was no more prepared to meet your maker than I am to meet your account you sure would go to Hell. Trusting you will do this, etc. etc.

The Loved One

An undertaker in early nineteenth-century England presented a gentleman with the bill for £67 for the burial of his wife.

"That's a vast sum," said the widower, "for laying a silent female horizontally! You must have made some mistake."

"Not in the least!" answered the coffin monger. "A handsome hearse—three coaches and six-well-dressed mutes—handsome pall—nobody, your honour, could do it for less."

The gentleman replied: "It is a large sum, but as I am satisfied that the poor woman would have given twice as much to bury me, I must not be behind her in an act of kindness; there is a check for the amount."

Pay Now, Drink Later

Frank Brower, one of the favorite black minstrels of nineteenth-century America, walked into the barroom of the Metropolitan one day, dusty and unkempt from a long journey, and asked for a glass of brandy. The saloon-keeper handed out the brandy, and then, suspicious of the man's appearance, said:

"Just pay for that before you drink it, will you?" Brower, who was about as well known in New York as any man about town, looked up astonished, and stammered:

"W-w-what?"

"Just pay for the brandy before you drink it," the bartender repeated.

The minstrel leaned across the counter: "Why," he asked confidentially, "is it so im-m-mediately f-f-fatal in its effect?"

Service Call

Sir John Bennett, a famous clockmaker on London's Cheapside, had a framed letter hanging on the wall of his private office. It read:

My dear Sir:

Since my hall clock was sent to your establishment to be cleaned it has gone (as indeed it always has) perfectly, but has struck with great reluctance, and after enduring internal agonies of a most distressing nature it has now ceased striking altogether. Though a happy release for the clock, this is not convenient for the household. If you can send down any confidential person with whom the clock can confer, I think it may have something on its works that it would be glad to make a clean breast of.

Faithfully yours,

Charles Dickens,
Higham by Rochester, Kent,
Monday night, Sep. 14, 1863.

Miller Time

When Abraham Lincoln was a young man he took a sack of grain to be ground at the mill. The owner had the reputation for being the slowest and laziest miller in Illinois. After watching him for a while, Lincoln said, "You know, I think I could eat that grain as fast as you are grinding it."

"But how long could you keep it up?" the miller replied ungraciously.

"Until I starve to death," the future president retorted.

Sending It Back

Georges Feydeau, French writer of farces, ordered lobster at Maxim's, one of those restaurants where one's dinner is seen floating about in a tank. When the dish was served, the playwright noticed that the lobster had only one claw. The waiter was summoned and offered the explanation that lobsters were very combative and because of the space problem inherent in tanks, accidents frequently happened.

"I want you to take this one back," Feydeau told the waiter, "and bring me the victor."

Room Service

Comedian Joe Frisco lived high when he had money and refused to save. (Once his agent advised him that he probably could have saved $100,000 against the next depression, to which the comic replied with his famous stutter: "With m-m-my luck there might not be a d-d-depression, and I'd be s-s-s-stuck with a hundred thousand d-d-dollars.") By the 1950s he was broke and living in a seedy residential hotel of the type that still dot the decaying center of Hollywood. One night when Frisco tried to sneak in an old friend who needed a bed for the night, he received a phone call from the manager reminding him that it would cost an extra dollar to have a guest stay in the room.

"In that c-c-case," sighed the comedian, "send up another B-b-b-bible."

The Customer Is Often Wrong

There are many anecdotes connected with inappropriate questions asked in bookstores. Once a woman with an accent came into Brentano's Fifth Avenue store in New York and asked a sales clerk to direct her to "Sex." He guided her to a small section that contained the books of Havelock Ellis and similar works. It turned out that she wanted Saks, across the street.

Another women stopped a Brentano employee and asked him, "Do you have *Fun in Bed?*" The man, who happened to be the store detective and unfamiliar with the title of the book by Frank Scully, replied modestly: "I manage."

GREAT STORES

Premiere

When John Wanamaker opened his store in 1861, he took account of business: "At the close of the first day the cash drawer revealed a total intake of $24.67. Of this sum," he noted, "$24 was spent for advertising and 67 cents saved for making change next morning."

Give the Lady What She Wants

Marshall Field was walking through his Chicago store one day when he came upon a shop assistant arguing with a customer.

"What are you doing here?" Field demanded in a quiet but firm voice.

"I'm settling a complaint," the clerk explained.

"No, you're not. Give the lady what she wants." And so Field coined the phrase that became both his company motto and the title of a book about its history.

An Innovator

In 1673, Hachirobei Mitsui opened a shop in Kyoto with a large sign that was to become famous in the history of Japanese retailing: CASH ONLY AND ONE PRICE ONLY. Until then customers mostly bought on account, which carried interest, much like our credit cards do today. By insisting on cash payment, Mitsui could slash prices below those of his competitors. Those prices were determined according to time-honored custom, by endless haggling. Mitsui became the first merchant to insist on fixed prices, a custom that spread throughout Japan. As Mitsui stores branched out, employing hundreds of men and women, the company began to establish—three centuries ago—some of the practices that Western industry did not discover until our own age: managers received a profit-sharing plan, and the company provided dormitories, baths, rest periods, and health services for their employees.

Returns

John Wanamaker pioneered a "money-back guarantee" policy in 1865. Marshall Field also offered a return policy after a customer had tried a purchase at home. Once a lady bought a cape for a specific occasion, which she returned the day after the ball, claiming that she had never worn it. Because it was a very expensive cape, the matter was brought to Field's attention. After the lady left with her refund, Field found her handkerchief tucked into the cape's pocket. Convinced that the customer is always right, the merchant said: "If she said she didn't wear it, she didn't wear it. But I guess we'd better send the handkerchief back to her."

On another day, Field was looking at the $800 price tag on a tablecloth imported from Italy. "You'll never sell it," he told A. L. Bell, the head of his linen department. A week passed, and Bell was summoned by the boss.

"Your judgment was better than mine," said Field. I was at a friend's house last night and dined on the tablecloth I said you'd never sell." It was now Bell's turn to confess.

"I'm sorry, Mr. Field. That lady took the tablecloth on approval yesterday and returned it today."

Rich All Around

It has been said that Rich's is a store that married Atlanta. Spread over two city blocks, the main store has a floor space of twenty-nine acres. It is so enormous that when a woman once asked a bus driver whether he went by Rich's, he replied, "Madam, I go by Rich's, under Rich's, through Rich's and around Rich's."

Five and Dime

Frank Winfield Woolworth hated farming so much that he offered to work in a store for free instead. The dry-goods store (so called because it did not sell liquor) in Watertown, New York, had a table of five-cent items, which sold well enough for young Woolworth to venture out on his own. With help and a $300 credit from his employers, he opened the first "Great Five-Cent Store" in Utica, New York in 1879. Despite early failures, the nickels and dimes kept adding up, and by the time Woolworth died in 1919, there were 1,081 of his stores worldwide, and a hundred of his associates and employees had become millionaires.

Founders

Sears, Roebuck and Company is the world's largest retailer, its headquarters is among the world's tallest skyscrapers, and one-third of the American population shops in its stores. Sears's success has been attributed to "bargains, brains or Ballyhoo."

Back in 1886, Richard Warren Sears was working for the Minneapolis and St. Louis Railroad, which allowed its agents to supplement their income by buying and selling goods at discounted freight rates. One of the jewelers in Redwood Falls, Minnesota, refused to accept a large, unsolicited shipment of watches. The 23-year-old Sears made a deal to buy them for $12. But instead of selling them at the suggested retail price of $25, Sears undersold the competition with a $14 price tag. He also used his connections along the railroad to help him sell. In six months he made $5,000, enough to start the R. W. Sears Watch Company, which he moved to Chicago.

When some watches were returned for repairs, Sears advertised for a watchmaker and a repairman who had his own tools. The successful applicant was Alvah Curtis Roebuck, who had been running a watch-repair operation in a delicatessen in Hammond, Indiana.

"Thus began a famous alliance," wrote Tom Mahoney and Leonard Sloane in *The Great Merchants*. "Roebuck was a tall, unusually thin man, whose black suit and high collar caused some to think of him as a Methodist minister. He was gentle and unaggressive. Sears was a handsome, mustached, restless young man of ingratiating personality, boundless optimism and incredible energy. Of him an admiring banker once said, "He could sell a breath of air!"

Items from Our Catalog

The foundation of the Sears retail empire was the catalog, which reached into millions of American homes, especially farms. An enormous amount of labor and care went into the design and writing of the catalogs to make sure that the recipients would not be offended by either the wrong stereotypes or unreachable ideals. Wrote one observer in 1940:

> The farmer is never represented as a rube with straw behind his ears; he never wears the battered straw sun hat and goatee of the vaudeville stage; he is never an Uncle Hiram with tobacco juice staining his white beard. No model, man or woman, is shown smoking a cigarette. And while the pages of women's clothes are thickly sprinkled with photographs of girls who have slender figures, there are numbers of others whose plump, matronly figures are like those of the cow-milking, chore-performing, child-bearing farm women with whom the catalog so largely deals.

Before it built up its nationwide retail chain, the most tangible asset of Sears, Roebuck was its list of catalog customers, numbering in the millions. The company took every precaution to guard this treasure and yet still had nightmares about its loss by fire or through some other calamity. To find out what would happen if the lists were destroyed, Sears ran some test advertisements in certain areas of the country, stating that they had lost their records and urging their customers to contact the company. On checking these names against the master list, the company found not only that all their old customers responded, but that they acquired quite a number of new ones. After that, Sears, Roebuck executives slept a little easier in Chicago.

The Power of Words

F. W. Woolworth, the founder of the retail store chain, had been dreaming for years about building a lasting monument to his empire. New York contractor Samuel Horowitz discussed several plans for a corporate skyscraper, but Woolworth could not make up his mind. Now that he was looking at actual designs, suddenly he got cold feet and could only see problems: what if it was the wrong image for the company, or if he could not find tenants, or if business suddenly turned sour. After one of these endless meetings, Horowitz, who had the reputation of being a super salesman, took his hat and told the chief executive: "I am going to tell you something, Mr. Woolworth. You are going to build the largest building in the world and I am going to build it for you. Good morning." And Horowitz walked out, having little to go on except his conviction that he would see his client again.

A few months later, when the project was well underway, Woolworth visited the site and told Samuel Horowitz: "Do you remember, Sam, the morning you told me I was going to build the largest building in the world and that you were going to build it for me?" Horowitz nodded.

"Well," said Woolworth, "I never was able to get that out of my mind."

Unromantic

Edward Filene, head of Boston's famous department store in the 1920s, was a complicated, restless man who turned from a shy youth with eczema into a tactless dictator. Business totally consumed him. In his thirties, while he was traveling on a streetcar with his fiancée, he ran into a business acquaintance. By the end of the ride, he had concluded a deal but lost his future bride, who had left Filene without his even noticing it.

Tribute

FDR was in the White House and times were tough when John Roosevelt began a business career working at Filene's famous bargain basement. The president's son was making $18.50 a week for keeping the bins filled. The self-effacing young man went about his humble tasks modestly, but he attracted so much attention that finally he had to be given a job in the stockrooms, where Bostonians could not gape at him.

Advice

Alfred Bloomingdale was quite stage struck in his younger days, and he backed a number of Broadway shows, a large number of which turned out to be flops. Finally, fed up with his role as an angel, Bloomingdale decided to try his wings as a producer: he felt that if he allowed his commercial instincts full play, he would make money in the theater as he had done in retailing.

He started searching for a play, found one, and nursed it along. He hired a director, who hired actors and others necessary to a production. The big night came when the play opened for its out-of-town tryout in Philadelphia. After the final curtain, it was clear to most people that the play was not going to be a hit. In fact, it was no better than the other flops that the department storeowner had simply backed. As Bloomingdale stood around in the lobby afterward, dejected, surrounded by his numerous friends from the New York theater, one of them gave him a bit of advice: "Alfred, close the play and keep the store open at night."

Comeuppance

There is a scene in *Annie Hall* in which Diane Keaton wonders whether she could withstand torture, to which Woody Allen replies: "You? The Gestapo would take away your Bloomingdale's charge card and you'd tell them everything."

However, Bloomingdale's was not always the haunt of the smart set. When it was started in 1872 by the Bloomingdale brothers, its location was in one of New York's least fashionable areas. Even after World War II, according to Mark Stevens' entertaining profile on the store, a young executive was firmly put in his place at a Fifth Avenue party. Nattily dressed Lawrence Lachman was asked by a banker's wife what business he was in.

"I've just been appointed treasurer at Bloomingdale's," Lachman beamed.

"Oh, I know that place," she replied. "That's where my maid shops."

Don't Leave Home Without It

Stanley Marcus recounts in his charming book, *Minding the Store*, that one of his customers landed in jail following a drunken brawl during a Texas-Oklahoma football game. The next morning the Oklahoma judge set bail for $250, but the man was far from his home in Dallas and knew no one in town.

The judge asked whether he knew anyone in Dallas who could help him. The man pulled out his Neiman-Marcus credit card and received the judge's permission to try to reach someone at the store. He reached a vice president, who arranged for the bail to be charged on his account, and the customer was set free.

On an even happier note, Jack Massey of Nashville was trying to get married in Dallas, when the justice of the peace asked for some local identification. The bride produced a Neiman-Marcus credit card.

"Well, if your credit is good with them, it's good with me," said the justice and went ahead with the ceremony.

Christmas Catalog

The Christmas catalog is one of the merchandising tools that made Neiman-Marcus world famous. According to Stanley Marcus, the more outrageous items were generated by the media rather than by the store. In the late 1950s Ed Murrow and Walter Cronkite would call the week before Christmas, as political news began to wind down, to get a story or two about unusual purchases by the crass and famous. Wishing to protect the privacy of rich clients and still benefit from the media attention, the store decided to include in its Christmas catalogue a variety of famous stunts: his and her Beechcraft; followed by his and her personal submersible; his and her op-art-printed silk scarves signed by Vasarely; his and her shahtoosh robes made from the world's rarest fiber, which is plucked from the neck of the ibex goat in the Himalayas. There was also the year of the his and her camel, and once the store offered to deliver a Black Angus steer on the hoof. One order to Sacramento was delivered at noon on Christmas Day; the other ran into trouble with customs half way round the world, "so we had to board and feed the animal in the quarantine station in South Africa a whole year before we could make delivery the following Christmas," writes Mr. Stanley Marcus in his engaging autobiography.

Although it is the expensive and unusual gifts that capture media attention (such as "the privacy capsule"—$800,000 and up), the more moderate are the ones that sell. One year Mr. Marcus came up with the idea of selling a version of Noah's Ark. But to balance this rather pessimistic concept, the catalogue also offered oak seedlings, presumably for the time when the waters had abated. According to Mr. Marcus:

> We offered the ark, to be made to order, complete with a staff consisting of a French chef, a Swedish masseur, a German hair stylist, an English valet, a French maid, an Italian couturier, an English curator/librarian, a Park Avenue physician, a Texas A & M University veterinarian, and a working crew of four. Included also, in pairs by species, were ninety-two mammals, ten reptiles, twenty-six birds, fourteen freshwater fish, and thirty-eight insects, priced in toto at $588,247, FOB Mount Ararat. The seedlings were priced at $10. Curiously, we received fifteen hundred orders for the seedlings and not a single for the ark. Which all goes to prove that there are more optimists in the world than pessimists!

Hot Air

At another time, Stanley Marcus wanted to be sure of reaching some important people on the store's mailing list. He realized that even beautiful catalogs get lost under the avalanche of junk mail and at the same time he wanted to bring attention to the store's gift-wrapping service. So he sent to a select list of 323 people four beautifully wrapped packages—one inside the other—with the final box containing the actual Christmas catalogue. One of the recipients was impresario Billy Rose, who had a newspaper column at the time, which is where he vented his complaint. He was pleasantly surprised on receiving the "gift," and asked his secretary to put all calls on hold. Then he began unwrapping the boxes one after another until he got to the catalog. The feeling of anticlimax was enough to send him to "Macy's basement, buy a pair of socks, and say, 'That's for Neiman Marcus.' Next Christmas, if I'm still on your list," Rose concluded, "send me a postcard, or if you want to spread yourself, a wall calendar. As I see it, it's better not to play Santa Claus at all than to put on false whiskers and come down the chimney with nothing but hot air in your bag."

Something Special

The Daily Telegraph in London once reported a story "which most satirically illustrates the intimidating potency of the Neiman-Marcus name." During the Christmas rush a hard-pressed employee accidentally gift-wrapped her lunch instead of a customer's luxurious gift. By the time she discovered her mistake the parcels had been taken to the mail. "But no one ever came forward," the newspaper commented, "to complain that he, or she, had received a stale ham sandwich and a moldy orange for Christmas. Store officials are convinced that the recipient of the extraordinary gift decided that, coming from Neiman-Marcus, it had to be something wonderfully special."

A Writer's Son

Founded in 1818, Brooks Brothers in New York is America's oldest men's clothing store. It has served stars and celebrities for many generations. Lincoln was assassinated in clothes from Brooks Brothers, and when Lindbergh arrived in Paris without luggage (thereby inaugurating a tradition), he was lent a Brooks Brother suit by U.S Ambassador Myron T. Herrick. Once Broadway writer and director Abe Burrows took his small son to the store for his first suit. All that remained was to purchase new shirts that would go with the elegant clothes.

"I want the kind with writin'," young Burrows insisted.

"You mean with your monogram?" asked the helpful clerk.

"I mean with writin'—like the Dodgers and Giants."

Thoughtless Thieves

In 1964 the lower Manhattan branch of Brook Brothers was robbed, and
the thieves got away with clothes worth $200,000. One clerk remarked:
"If they had come during our sale two weeks ago, we could have saved 20
percent."

· 5 ·

SELLING

THE PROFESSION

A Man for All Seasons

Perhaps the first person to discover that a successful salesman must first become a professional was William Maxwell, sales head of Thomas A. Edison, Inc. His definition of what that meant was: "A professional salesman is one who knows what to do and what to say and how to do and how to say it under every conceivable situation."

Made, Not Born

In the seventeenth century it was fashionable to argue whether a poet was born or made. The side that believed in native genius neatly summed up its point of view in the Latin tag: *Nascitur poeta non fit*. Today the same argument rages on the question of good salesmen and -women. Vincent Riggio, president of the American Tobacco Company in the 1950s, was considered one of the outstanding salesmen of his generation. He said: "Salesmen are made, rarely are they born; and generally when the so-called 'born salesman' gets into rough going, he fails."

Frank Bettger was a star insurance salesman in the period after World War II. He had made more than enough money by the age of 40 to retire. He could sell what would amount to a multimillion dollar policy today in about fifteen minutes. Admirers called him a born salesman. But at age 29, having tried selling for a year, Bettger had concluded that he was a hopeless failure. He told himself that he was simply not the type. Only later did he find out that nobody is cut out, that men must cut themselves out. And that, he claimed, was when he began to become a success.

Ideal

After World War II American businesses realized that they would have to return to salesmanship instead of simply filling government orders. During a convention of sales managers in Los Angeles, Harry G. Moock, then a Vice President at Chrysler Corporation, gave this description of the ideal salesman: "He has the curiosity of a cat, the tenacity of a bulldog, the friendship of a little child, the diplomacy of a wayward husband, the patience of a self-sacrificing wife, the enthusiasm of a Sinatra fan, the assurance of a Harvard man, the good humor of a comedian, the simplicity of a jackass, and the tireless energy of a bill-collector."

Professors Are Always Right

Elmer Wheeler, a supersalesman who was voted "America's Public Speaker Number One" by a poll of 500 business clubs, had flunked a public-speaking course at college. His professor told him that he would have to seek a profession where he would not come into contact with the public. At his peak, Wheeler addressed more than a million people a year.

School

William Fern, British authority on salesmanship in the period between the two world wars, observed a class for salesmen while touring America in the 1930s:

> I was a visitor to a course of high-pressure methods given to real estate gentlemen. There was no doubt in every man's mind what he was expected to do—a noted sales counsellor talked on selling methods, the treasurer told the 200 men the money that had been earned, the doctor on the property came up and told the men the healthy advantages of the estate, a well-known chairman of a real estate board had at his finger tips all the stories of fortunes made in real estate.
>
> The leading salesman of the week told them how he had done it; three men told the sales stories from the three sales magazines of the week; and the whole atmosphere reminded me of a Welsh revival I once witnessed.
>
> A grand drive was organised for the Sunday. One thousand five hundred prospects was the quota aimed at, and a special train ordered to take them

to the property and back. A network of amplifiers had been arranged all over the property for the Sunday, so that as a prospect put his name on the dotted line the event would be broadcast in stentorian tones all over the property in order to give the salesman encouragement and his prospects enthusiasm enough to have their names announced, too, over the broadcast, if they were as wise and as sensible.

Say Cheese

A small, aggressive commodities brokerage firm trains its brokers in professional voice production, the same training that singers and actors get. In the pit, where everybody screams all day, losing one's voice is the equivalent of an account executive's computer going down. Smiling is also an essential skill for a salesperson. The sales director of one of America's largest corporations hired Jay B. Iden, a director on the New York stage, to teach his salesmen to smile. Most of them thought that they knew how to smile, but Mr. Iden convinced them that in many cases their smiles were merely smirks. He taught them that smirking involved only the lips, whereas the entire face, and especially the eyes, are needed to accomplish a sincere, friendly, and attractive smile. After Iden's smile clinic the salesmen increased their sales 15 percent within three months.

Preconception

In 1962, Gerald Falick was flipping hamburgers from 5 P.M. to 3 A.M. at Royal Castle, hoping that he could use his college diploma one day to get a managerial position. After five months of working at the minimum wage, Falick was willing to try something he had deliberately avoided when he graduated from the University of Florida—selling life insurance. In the next dozen years he sold $50 million worth of insurance: "I thought that was what you did after you had failed at everything else," Falick told the *Miami Herald*. He had always wanted to be successful, though not necessarily just making money. He wanted to help people, he said, and by selling life insurance he felt he could combine the two.

Brushes with Mediocrity

Alfred Carl Fuller, whose name is synonymous with door-to-door selling, had the first door he ever knocked on slammed in his face. He left his home in Nova Scotia at 18 with $75 in his pocket. He was fired from his first three jobs (one as a conductor of a Boston streetcar, because he took it upon himself to drive the trolley when the driver failed to show up. Fuller derailed the car at the very first switch).

Alfred began knocking on doors for his brother Dwight, who had a brush company. At the end of his first day, he had sold 7 dollars' worth. He was 30 when he started making a new kind of brush in his sister's basement, a sweeper with covered ends that wouldn't damage woodwork. The company's sales went from $8,500 in 1906 to over $1 million eleven years later. He began building his powerful sales organization in 1908, by placing two small ads, one in a newspaper and one in a national magazine. Within a few weeks, 260 dealers had paid $17 and "had accepted a company catalog and Fuller's advice to be neat and polite." In the years that followed, the "Fuller Brush Man" became an American institution.

Fuller was known as "Dad" both to his friends and to his hundreds of employees. He retained a self-deprecating modesty to the end of his long life. "The company," he wrote about his brainchild, "is the product of mediocrity. Almost everyone who grew up with it in the early days was, like myself, a failure who took his job with me in desperation, often in despair."

TECHNIQUES

And a Little Child Shall Lead Them

Fred Kaiser, who was an executive for the Detroit-Michigan Stove Company in the 1950s, said that he learned an important lesson about selling from his daughter, who always insisted on buying her favorite gum drops from a particular shop. It was owned by a man named Nick, whom all the children in the neighborhood loved. They continued to patronize his store even after a more convenient shopping center opened nearby. Fred was curious and asked his little girl why she preferred to buy at Nick's shop instead of the supermarket.

"Nick always gives me more candy," she replied. "The girl in the other store always takes some away."

Upon further investigation, Fred Kaiser found that the clerks in the big store always ladled more than a pound into a bag on the scale and then took some candy out to balance the scales. Nick apparently had the opposite habit of starting with less than a pound, so that he would have to add gum drops until the scales were balanced. Although the end result was the same, the children were convinced that they got a better deal from Nick.

The Specialist

George Sutton, supersalesman in the wholesale business, told a story about how a sales manager increased the productivity of his personnel by a simple stratagem. One day he called in his salesmen and informed them that they would not be salesmen any more; they were henceforth "distribution specialists." He sent them off to take courses in psychology, merchandising, and distribution. This was just after the war, the age of Willy Loman, when most salesmen never dreamed of going to college or business school.

After the former salesmen had passed some rather stiff exams, they no longer called on prospects as one of a half-dozen competing salesmen, but as specialists who could advise clients on their various problems. When Dahl's, a supermarket in Des Moines, Iowa, placed an order for two sizes of an item, the specialist told the buyer:

"I cannot accept such an order." The buyer, used to hearing constant hard sell, could not believe his ears.

"You can't accept it?"

"No, because you can't afford the smaller size as a shelf-warmer," replied the pro: "I know from experience that you won't sell enough to warrant such an order."

The specialist may have made a smaller sale in the short term. But in the long run he had won the confidence of the buyer, who placed many repeat orders.

Elementary, My Dear Watson

Frank Bettger, insurance salesman, could deduce from a few clues what was going on around him. He was having lunch one day, at Philadelphia's exclusive Union League Club, when he noticed three men at a nearby table. He knew them: a father and son who were prominent industrialists in the community, and their lawyer. He went over to greet them and later that afternoon phoned the father to make an appointment. Within a few days Bettger sold both father and son a very large insurance policy on their business.

"Just tell me, Frank," asked the older businessman as he signed the papers, "how did you know that we happened to be discussing the reorganization of the company and that we were in the market for insurance? You have never called on me before—nobody else has, for that matter."

"I could not know, of course, what exactly you were discussing the other day," replied the salesman, "but when I see two partners having lunch with their lawyer, what is more obvious than that something is under way?"

Salesmanship

Supersalesman and best-selling author Frank Bettger quoted a story by William Power, public relations executive in the 1940s for Chevrolet Motors, who was looking to buy a house in Detroit. The realtor listened while the customer talked, and after a while it came out that William Power had all his life wanted to own a place with a tree. The real estate salesman drove him a few miles out of town to a wooded suburb and showed him the backyard of a house with eighteen trees. The house was overpriced, but each time Power tried to bring him down, the realtor simply asked him to look at the trees and then started counting them.

"Finally he sold me eighteen trees," marveled the satisfied customer, "and threw in the house!"

Closing

Shortly after two o'clock, the master mechanic stormed into the lobby, glowering fiercely.

"Let's sit down here," said Carlson, the salesman. "Do you have any leaky valves?"

"I can't buy valves," shouted the master mechanic. "The chief engineer buys them." Carlson's hearing "failed" him.

"Where do you have the most trouble with leaky valves?"

"On our caramel steam kettles," the master mechanic reluctantly admitted. "But I can't buy any valves."

By this time Carlson was demonstrating how his valve's superhard seat and disc were unblemished even after he had smashed a steel paper clip between them.

"What size valves do you use on those caramel steam kettles?" he queried.

"Three-quarter inch," answered the master mechanic. "But it's like I told you — I can't buy any."

At this point Carlson went "stone deaf" and issued this command to the baffled master mechanic:

"You write out a requisition for one 3/4 inch hardhearted valve and go in and get an order from your purchasing agent. Then you'll see how to get rid of leaky valves. Go ahead."

The master mechanic went in and got the order for that single trial valve. Carlson had done in a few minutes what the distributor and his salesmen had been unable to accomplish in twenty-five years. His ears just automatically tuned out the word no.

Enough Already

Bert Schlain, one of the gurus of salesmanship in the decade following World War II, used to warn salesmen who go on talking even after the sale had been cinched: "Samson slew ten thousand Philistines with the jawbone of an ass, and every day thousands of orders are killed in the same way."

Exit Line

There was a legendary salesman in prewar Hungary who quickly developed a reputation that he could sell anyone practically anything. Near the beginning of his career, he called on a wealthy Budapest lawyer, Dr. Alfred Ardo, a prospect he would regularly visit every couple of months. Knowing that the vacation season was just about to begin, he began offering a line of suitcases, hiking boots, and binoculars.

"I don't want any," the lawyer protested. "I don't need anything right now."

The salesman smiled and sat down. He started describing bookcases, books, men's apparel, swimsuits, and a used car in excellent condition, at a very special price. The lawyer leapt enraged from behind his desk:

"Leave me alone," Dr. Ardo yelled, "I'm extremely busy and I don't need any of these damned things!" And since he found himself up on his feet, he opened the door to show the salesman the way out. The latter was completely unfazed. He made as if to leave, and at the door he turned to the lawyer: "I know exactly what you do need, Dr. Ardo, and it's really a rather neat, little thing that will cost you practically nothing." And the salesman reached into his pocket and brought out a small brass plate with the inscription:

NO PEDDLERS OR SOLICITORS!

The lawyer laughed and bought it. The salesman later became an enormously successful stock promoter.

ATTITUDES

Another Day, Another Thought

Frank H. Davis, another great salesman in the 1940s and 1950s, told himself every night when he went to bed: "Today you lost your job. Tomorrow you start from scratch." When asked why he felt he had to do that, Davis replied: "The one thing I always feared was complacency. A man on a strange job, on a new job, gives it his best."

Frank Davis was also fond of comparing the situation of the salesman to that of the schoolteacher who was upset when a junior member of the staff got promoted over her head. She stormed into the principal's office:

"I want you to remember," she hissed, "that I have had twenty-five years of experience."

"No, my dear," the principal replied patiently, "you have merely had one year of experience 25 times."

Existential Debate

Arthur Priebe, one of the great insurance salesmen, counseled his colleagues suffering from the common affliction of "doorknob phobia," to hold a debate with themselves:

"Where am I?"

"In the hall."

"Where do I want to be?"

"In that man's office."

"What will happen if I go inside?"

"The worst that could happen is I'd be thrown back into the hall."

"Well, that's where I am now, so what have I got to lose?"

The Answer Is Blowin' in the Wind

Harry Jamieson, a Northwest hardware salesman in the 1940s, was asked how many calls he made on a prospect before giving up:

"It depends which one of us dies first," replied Jamieson, who once made 125 calls on a prospective client in a single year before the man finally placed an order. Another buyer, after Jamieson's fortieth call, finally gave in: "I cannot help buying from you," he said as he surrendered. "Your persistence has paralyzed my resistance."

Press On

Calvin Coolidge, not a man to waste words, said this about persistence: "Nothing in the world can take the place of determination. Talent will not; nothing is more common than unsuccessful men with talent; unrewarded genius is almost a proverb. Education will not; the world is full of educated derelicts. Persistence and determination alone are omnipotent. The slogan 'Press On' has solved and always will solve the problems of the human race."

Where Ignorance Is Bliss

In the early days of motor cars, people did not drive during the winter, because of the unreliability of the machines and the lack of roads. Automobiles were put up on jacks, and dealers shut down their businesses. Norval Hawkins, who was the first Ford sales manager, recalled one small dealer in South Dakota who kept sending orders through the winter months. He was a "big, awkward, gangling, farmerlike youngster who confessed that he just didn't know that he wasn't supposed to sell cars in the winter time!"

Hawkins was impressed enough to go after his sales network, and after a few years built January into the peak month for selling cars.

Mr. Fixit

Walter Chrysler was already an accomplished locomotive mechanic when in 1905 he purchased an expensive automobile, borrowing most of the money for it. He drove it to a garage and proceeded to dismantle the whole automobile between forty and fifty times. When he felt he could reassemble the machine blindfolded, Walter Chrysler was satisfied that he could build a better car at a lower cost. Even as a fabulously wealthy industrialist, he never lost his zest for mechanical work. Stranded motorists were startled as Chrysler would pull up, bolt from his own car, and fix their motor in a jiffy. Then he would hand them one of his business cards and express the hope of seeing them become his customers in the future.

Warning

Here is another story from those early days when one had to be practically a mechanic to buy a used car. Paul Hoffman, who after World War II became the administrator of the European Recovery Program, began in the automobile business in Chicago when he was 18 and the motor car was even younger. One day, a veterinarian dropped by the lot and asked young Hoffman for a demonstration of a used 1905 Jackson model. The eager young salesman offered to drive him home and found to his horror that the doctor lived on a farm, some forty miles away. Hoffman knew that it was pure recklessness to drive the car beyond city limits, no matter that the Jackson Automobile Company advertized its product with the slogan: "No hill too steep; no sand too deep."

By some miracle, with a great deal of banging and pounding, the used Jackson made it to the veterinarian's home. The veterinarian was so impressed that, as soon as he entered his kitchen, he took out a pen to sign the purchase papers. Then he stopped and looked at Hoffman.

"One question, son. If you were me, would you buy this car?"

The young salesman swallowed hard. He needed badly to make the commission. As he briefly struggled within himself, his eyes fell upon an embroidered notice in the doctor's kitchen with the warning: "Jesus hears every word you say."

There was no sale that day.

Gospel True

There is a long tradition in America, reaching back to the Puritans, of taking inspiration for every kind of human activity and profession from the one book universally read, the Bible. But it was in the twentieth century that Jesus was directly recruited by the chamber of commerce and Madison Avenue as the Great Salesman or Model Executive, as described in Bruce Barton's bestsellers, *The Man Nobody Knows* and *The Book Nobody Knows*. Here is an eyewitness description of one of these preachers of commerce, the legendary Don Ingall of Quality Products, who traveled around spreading the gospel of salesmanship in the 1930s:

> Don Ingall stood facing us. He was silent for a little while. His alert eyes roved around the room, as if he were trying to determine in his own mind the type of men he was about to address.
>
> "Fellows," he said in an informal manner, "I have come here for the purpose of helping you to become better salesmen. I know of no surer way to help you than to recommend that you all study the greatest book on salesmanship that has ever been written, or will be written." He paused, then smiled in reply to the incredulous looks on our faces.
>
> "This book will tell you about the greatest salesman who ever lived or ever will live," he continued. "I want you to become better acquainted with him. I want you to study his methods, learn how he handled difficult

situations. The book is packed with excellent illustrations, but tonight I am going to discuss only one of them."

Don Ingall fumbled in his pocket, then drew forth a small, well-worn Bible. He thumbed through it and found the place he wanted.

"I am going to read the story of a sales experience that happened to the Great Salesman. We are going to study how He handled a situation, and see how His method can be applied to your own selling practices. The story is found in the eighth chapter of John. 'Jesus went unto the mount of Olives. And early in the morning he came again into the temple, and all the people came unto him; and he sat down and taught them.'"

Don looked up and smiled. "Here are a few points of interest to begin with. I'll just list them. You can enlarge the thought to suit yourselves. First, Jesus came into the temple. He began the day right by seeking the guidance of God. Now this does not mean that we have to go to church every morning, but we can at least pause a few moments and ask for divine blessing and spiritual help for the trials of the day. Second, the time was early in the morning. Jesus did not lie in bed until noon. The salesman who goes out to his customers early in the morning does so with a mind that is fresh, not fagged with the worry, detail and irritation of the day. Third, the people came to Him. Your customers may be up early. Be the first salesman to see them. Fourth, Jesus sat down. Informality is one of the secrets of good selling. Be natural. Do not put on a false front. It doesn't fool anybody but yourself . . ."

To Sell or Not to Sell

One of the more curious books in my library is one by William Burruss, published in Chicago during World War II. Its title is *Shakespeare the Salesman.* Mr. Burruss applied scenes, situations, or speeches he might find in *Hamlet* or *Julius Caesar* to the world of selling. Here, for example, is his meditation on Mark Antony's famous speech:

> Shakespeare realized what Mark Antony is up against. He isn't approaching a prospect who is friendly and interested. He is approaching a rather hostile audience, and his first job is to get the attention of the audience.
>
> They didn't kill a ruler every day in Rome, so this was an unusual event. There had been tremendous emotional excitement. Brutus had made a sales presentation, and the audience was sold on not only the fact that Brutus was a very honorable man, but that Brutus was right in what he did and in what he advocated . . . . Into this howling emotional mob came Mark Antony bearing the dead body of Caesar. In this act he excited the curiosity of the crowd. But that act alone would not calm the excited mob.
>
> He had to face the fact that he must use the four laws of a sale, the first of which is to get attention. You remember how he struggled to get attention:

Friends, Romans, countrymen, lend me your ears,

he shouted. But, he didn't get their attention. I've always felt sorry for Mark. I went over to Italy several years ago and looked at the place where Mark made that speech. I can visualize the crowd milling around, talking, excited and antagonistic.

My mind went back to an experience I had when I went on a trade trip for the Chamber of Commerce at Kansas City, Missouri. It was a good many years ago, and we had a marvelous band. Every time we would stop at some small town, the band would play a selection to see if we couldn't get some of the crowd to come to the platform. The crowd would gather around the rear end of the train. The band would stop, and then I would hop up on the platform and make a speech. Then the band would have to play another selection to see if we couldn't get some of the crowd to come back.

Mark Antony didn't have any band. If he had had a band, it would have been a great help.

The Old Question

Bennett Cerf, founder of Random House, was invited to tour the plant of a large paper mill that supplied many of the New York publishers with paper. The sales manager hosted the representatives of a dozen invited publishers. The food was excellent, the wine flowed freely, and when the sales manager rose to make his pitch, he was applauded warmly by both the customers and his large sales force.

"Fellows," he said with a catch in his voice, "just fifteen years ago today our mill received its very first paper order from a book publisher."

A salesman in the rear of the room piped up: "And when are you going to fill it?"

Convergent Humor

Delays plague the computer industry, where products are regularly announced six months to a year before they are ready. One purpose behind this is to generate orders. Another is to intimidate the competition.

Often the product encounters unexpected problems in development and needs several months to be "debugged"; sometimes there is a shortage of parts. During one of the periodic shortages of microprocessor chips, Convergent Technologies could not get its new computer, called NGen, to its customers. Intel was backlogged with orders, and there were simply no chips. The problem was that the company's sales organization had already sold and promised large quantities by a certain delivery date. One day, the top salespeople in his organization trooped into boss Allan

Michels's office and presented him with an enormous Marine combat boot that had a large bullet hole in it. It was an artist's rendering of what it means to shoot oneself in the foot.

Michels, an entrepreneur with a sense of humor, kept it proudly mounted in the office. To dramatize the plight of his company, Michels then drove to see the president of Intel. Once in the other executive's office, he went down on his knees and handed him a doll of the Cookie Monster, with these words taped on it: "Give me chips!"

LIFE OF A SALESMAN

It's the Truth

Comedian George Gobel defined *salesman* as "a fellow with a smile on his face, a shine on his shoes, and a lousy territory."

On the Road

In the eighteenth century most of America was a vast, dangerous, and lonesome place for traveling salesmen. Gideon Lee, who was to become the greatest leather merchant in New York, took his merchandise to Georgia, but his vessel was shipwrecked at Cape Fear, and he barely saved himself just with the clothes on his back. Accompanied by a faithful friend named Smith, who nursed him while he had been sick at St. Mary's, Lee had no other means of getting to the North than on foot. The journey was a tedious and dismal one: several days through the pine barrens of North Carolina, without finding a house in a day's travel. Smith was a brother Yankee and bore the hardships with courage and humor.

"One day," Gideon Lee used to relate, "we were trudging along, nothing to be seen but the pitch-pine forests before and behind and on both sides of us; shoes worn out, and our feet bleeding, myself before, and Smith following after; neither of us had exchanged a word for some time, when Smith suddenly spoke out in his nasal twang:

"Mr. Lee!"

"Well, Smith, well what about it?"

"I wish I could hear it thunder?"

"Hear it thunder? Why do you wish so?"

"Because they say that thunder is God's voice, and if I could only hear it thunder I should know I was on God's earth; as it is now, I don't know where I am."

Hus'ling

One of the most popular books a 100 years ago was the autobiography of a typical American salesman, J. P. Johnston's *Twenty Years of Hus'ling*, which gives a frenetic portrait of a man willing to go anywhere and do anything. Johnston started in Ohio, raising and selling sheep and trading in cattle and chicken. He then went into the restaurant business, and next the watch trade. He manufactured soap for three weeks, joined a circus, went broke and was jailed, learned telegraphy, founded a jewelry and spectacles business, then retired from the same. Halfway through the book he shows his willingness to try yet something else:

One day I met James Forster, an old acquaintance, who was engaged in the insurance business. He asked me if I didn't think I would make a good insurance agent.

I told him I had never tried it, but I knew I would.

He asked how I knew so much, if I had never tried it.

"Because I am no good at anything else," I answered.

He asked how I would like it. I assured him I was ready to try it, and that I owned a nice horse and buggy to travel over the country with.

He then took me to his office and after giving me a few instructions, gave me the necessary papers and sent me out.

The very first day I took three applications. The company insured on the installment plan, by issuing a policy for five years, the first payment of forty cents a hundred per year, was to be paid when the application was taken, and the balance made payable in equal annual installments. The agent's commission was the first installment, or twenty percent of the gross amount.

I was not long in learning that the rate charged by this company was just about double that of any other in existence, but the people readily fell in with the idea of paying their insurance by installments.

I gave it a week's trial and was immensely successful, and turned my applications over to Mr. Forster, but was careful to sign my name to them in full, as sub-agent.

He made an equal division of commission with me, which I was not satisfied with. I then quit, when Mr. Forster called in about a week to see why I didn't keep "hus'ling" as I had been doing so nicely.

"Well," said I, "Mr. Forster, it's against my principles to steal and give someone else half. I can't afford to go out and rob my neighbors and acquaintances, and give you any part of it." He had no more to say.

Martyrs

The following is a classic tale of the sophisticated peddler by Eli Perkins, the great nineteenth-century humorist:

A Philadelphia book agent [or traveling salesman] importuned James Watson, a rich and close New York man, living out at Elizabeth, until he bought a book—the *Early Christian Martyrs*. Mr. Watson didn't want the book, but he bought it to get rid of the agent; then, taking it under his arm, he started for the train which takes him to his New York office.

Mr. Watson hadn't been gone long before Mrs. Watson came home from a neighbor's. The book agent saw her, and went in and persuaded the wife to buy another copy of the same book. When Mr. Watson came back from New York that night Mrs. Watson showed him the book.

"I don't want to see it," said Watson, frowning terribly.

"Why, husband?" asked his wife.

"Because that rascally book agent sold me the same book this morning. Now we've got two copies of the *Early Christian Martyrs* and—"

"But, husband, we can—"

"No, we can't either!" Mr. Watson interrupted. "The man is off on the train before this. Confound it! I could kill the fellow—"

"Why, there he goes to the depot now," said Mrs. Watson, pointing out the window at the retreating form of the book salesman making for the train.

"But it's too late to catch him, and I'm not dressed."

Just then Mr. Stevens, a neighbor, drove by, when Watson pounded on the glass in a frantic manner, almost frightening the horse.

"Here, Stevens," he shouted, "you're hitched up; won't you run your horse down to the train and hold that book agent until I come? Run! Catch 'im now!"

"All right," said Mr. Stevens, whipping up his horse and tearing down the road. Mr. Stevens reached the train just as the conductor shouted "all aboard!"

"Book agent," he yelled, as the salesman stepped onto the train. "Book agent, hold on! Mr. Watson wants to see you."

"Watson? Watson wants to see me?" repeated the seemingly puzzled book agent. "Oh, I know what he wants! He wants to buy one of my books; but I can't miss the train to sell it to him."

"If that's all he wants," said Mr. Stevens, driving up to the car window, "I can pay for it and take it back to him. How much is it?"

"Two dollars for the *Early Christian Martyrs*," said the book agent, as he reached for the money and passed the book out through the window.

Just then Mr. Watson arrived puffing and blowing, in his shirt sleeves. As he saw the train pull out he was too full of utterance.

"Well, I got it for you," said Stevens; "just got it."

"Got what?"

"The book—*Early Christian Martyrs*, and—"

"By—the—great guns!" moaned Watson, as he placed his hand to his brow and fell exhausted onto a seat.

No Remedy

Mrs. Calvin Coolidge found it hard to say no to the kind of book agent as fictionalized by Eli Perkins. Long before her husband became president, Mrs. Coolidge was talked into buying an expensive medical book on home remedies by a fast-talking door-to-door salesman. She was afraid to tell her husband how much she had spent, but left it lying about the house. One day she picked up the book and happened to glance at the flyleaf. There in her husband's handwriting were the following words: "Don't see any recipes for curing suckers."

Out of Africa

Myron Cohen was a silk salesman who became one of the best-known stand-up comics in the 1950s. He said: "Material has always played an important role in my life." Here are two typical Myron Cohen stories about New York garment-district salesmen who are out of their element.

A salesman, whose hobby was entomology, had finally saved up enough money to go to Africa in search of some rare specimens. Cutting his way through the equatorial jungle he came to a small village, where he was astonished to run into his old friend Benjamin Gross, whose absence had been noted in the garment center.

"Benny, what on earth are you doing here?" he exclaimed.

"I'm the local witch doctor," said Ben, "but what are you doing here?"

"I'm looking for a certain insect for my collection." Ben reached for a nearby tree and brought down a bug on the palm of his hand.

"Is it this one?"

"No, that's not it." Benny went to another tree and brought another insect.

"Is it this?"

"No, Ben, I'm sorry."

The witch doctor tore off a branch that was crawling with different insects.

"No," the entomologist shook his head sadly. "All these are a dime a dozen back home. What I came for is much more rare, Ben."

"Well, I guess I don't have it," the witch doctor shrugged, "but thanks for letting me show you my line."

Two salesmen went wild game hunting in Africa. Walking single file through the jungle, they came to a clearing. Suddenly Jack whispered to Milton in front of him:

Don't t-t-turn around t-t-too quickly, but is that a lion behind me?"

"You're asking me?" Milt shot back, "Am I a fur salesman?"

· 6 ·

ADVERTISING

SIGNS AND NAMES

Barbers

If you have ever wondered about the meaning of the red, blue, and white sign outside barbershops, it goes back many centuries, when barbers not only shaved, but also pulled teeth and bled their customers in various surgical procedures. According to one antiquarian source the sign is "the historic memorial of the time when barbers practised phlebotomy, and patients undergoing the operation had to grasp a pole in order to accelerate the discharge of blood. As the pole was thus liable to be stained, it was painted red, and when not in use, the owner suspended it outside the door with the white linen swathing bands twisted around it. In later times, when surgery was dissociated from the tonsorial art, the pole was painted red and white, or black and white, or even with red, white and blue lines winding about it, emblematic of its former use, and the soap basin was appended thereto."

John Gay's fable of the goat without a beard thus describes a barber's shop:

His pole with pewter Basons hung,
Black rotten Teeth in order strung,
Rang'd Cups that in the Window stood,
Lin'd with red Rags to look like blood,
Did well his threefold Trade explain,
Who shav'd, drew Teeth, and breath'd a Vein."

The Jolly Barber

Jonathan Swift had a living in the county of Meath, and he was daily shaved by the village barber, who became a great favorite with him. While lathering Dean Swift one morning, the barber said he had a great favor to request of the reverend. His neighbors had advised him to take the little public house at the corner of the churchyard, which he had done, in the hope that by combining the profession of publican with his own, he might gain a better support for his family.

"Indeed," the Dean agreed, "and what can I do to promote this happy union?"

"Some of our customers have heard much of your reverence's poetry, so that if you would but condescend to give me a smart little touch in that way, to clap under my sign, it might be the making of me and mine forever."

"But what do you intend for your sign?" asked Swift.

"The Jolly Barber, if it please your reverence, with a razor in one hand and a full pot in the other."

"Well, in that case there will be no great difficulty in supplying you with a suitable inscription." Without hesitation Swift took up his pen and instantly scratched out a couplet which came to be affixed to the sign, and remained there for many years:

> Rove not from pole to pole, but step in here,
> Where nought excels the shaving—but the beer.

Partners

Occasionally partners have more in common than business interests: their names seem to complement each other. The following curious and apt names of partnerships were collected from old English signs and business directories: Carpenter & Wood; Spinage & Lamb; Sage & Gosling; Rumfit & Cutwell, and Greengoose & Measure, both tailors; Single & Double; Foot and Stocking, hosiers. One is not quite sure whether to believe that Adam & Eve were two surgeons who practised in Paradise Row, London, though Byers & Sellers did have a shop in Holborn.

"Sometimes the occupation of persons harmonizes admirably with their surnames," a nineteenth-century antiquarian continues:

> Gin & Ginman are innkeepers; so is Alehouse; Seaman is the landlord of the Ship Hotel, and A. King holds the "Crown and Sceptre" resort in City Road. Portwine and Negus are licensed victuallers, one in Westminster and

the other in Bishopsgate Street. Mixwell's country inn is a well-known resort. Pegwell is a shoemaker, so are Fitall and Treadaway, likewise Pinch; Tugwell is a noted dentist; Bird an egg merchant; Hemp a sheriff's officer; Captain Isaac Paddle commands a steamboat; Mr. Punt is a favorite member of the Surrey wherry [rowing] club; Laidman was formerly a pugilist; and Smooker or Smoker a lime burner; Skin & Bone were the names of two millers in Manchester; Fogg and Mist china dealers in Warwick street: the firm afterward became Fogg & Son, on which it was naturally enough remarked that the "son had driven away the mist." Mr. I. Came, a wealthy shoemaker in Liverpool, who left his immense property to public charities, opened his first shop on the opposite side of the street to where he had started as a servant, and inscribed a sign: "I CAME from over the way."

Finally, Going & Gonne was the name of a well-known banking house in Ireland, and on their failure in business some one wrote:

> Going & Gonne are now both one
> For Gonne is going and Going's gone.

Alas, Poor Shakespeare

In the second half of the eighteenth century there was a great increase in the general use of signs throughout London, "not only for taverns and ale-houses, but also for tradesmen, which furnished no small employment for the inferior rank of painters, and sometimes even for the superior professors. Mr. Catton painted several good signs," wrote James Elmes in 1825,

> but among the most celebrated practitioners in this branch, was a person of the name of Lamt, who possessed a considerable degree of ability. His pencil was bold and masterly, and well adapted to the subjects on which it was generally employed. Mr. Wale, who was one of the founders of the Royal Academy, and appointed the first Professor of Perspective in that institution, also painted some signs, the principal of which was a whole length of Shakespeare above five feet high, which was executed for, and displayed before the door of a public-house, at the north-west corner of Little Russell Street, Drury Lane. It was enclosed in a sumptuous carved gilt frame, and suspended by rich iron work. But this splendid object of attraction did not hang long, before it was taken down, in consequence of the act of Parliament which was passed, for paving, and removing the signs and other obstructions in the streets of London. Such was the total change of fashion, and the consequent disuse of signs, that this representation of the immortal Shakespeare was sold for a trifle to a broker, at whose door it stood for several years, until it was totally destroyed by the weather and other accidents.

Relatives

Financier Otto Kahn one day drove past a modest storefront in New York that sported a sign: "Abraham Kahn, Cousin of Otto Kahn." The tycoon called his lawyer, who threatened the store owner with a suit unless the sign was taken off. Not long afterward, Mr. Kahn asked his chauffeur to drive by the store again. As the limousine slowed down, the financier saw that the old sign was gone. In its place was a freshly painted one: "Abraham Kahn. Formerly cousin of Otto Kahn."

Pure Miracle

Procter & Gamble introduced a white soap in 1870 and called it in a forthright manner: White Soap. A few years later, workers accidentally let some air get into the vat while mixing the soap and were amazed to see that the bars now floated. This miracle prompted Harley T. Procter to rename the product Ivory Soap, based on a passage from the forty-fifth Psalm:

"Out of ivory palaces they have made thee glad."

What is in a Name?

In 1939 Ernest Henderson and his partners began to think about building a chain of hotels. What to call it? They owned the Stonehaven in Springfield and Lee House in Washington, and had just purchased their third one in Boston, called the Sheraton, which had a huge neon sign advertising its name in the night sky. Henderson and his partners thought it would be too expensive to replace the sign, so they decided to call the whole chain the "Sheraton." Henderson later came to be himself nicknamed "Mr. Sheraton" out of the same chain of events.

As Henderson tells it in his highly readable memoirs, his company pursued a strategy of buying up the most distinguished hotels in a community, with the result that it had to fight many a local battle with newspapers and society leaders who disliked the changing of their favorite landmark's name. The controversy of changing Boston's Copley Plaza to the Sheraton Plaza went on for years. The most dramatic headline came out in Worcester, a town situated somewhat west of Boston. Here the Bancroft Hotel had been named after a son of Worcester who had founded the Naval Academy at Annapolis. After it had been acquired by Sheraton, one local paper, anticipating the change of name, ran the headline: "Barbarians from the East Desecrate Memory of Worcester's Greatest Citizen."

And Ricardo Played Him on TV

The popular brand Maxwell House coffee was named after a hotel in Nashville, Tennessee. The coffee was so excellent at the Maxwell House that after drinking it, Teddy Roosevelt came up with the immortal words: "It's good to the last drop."

Good Reasons

When H. J. Heinz registered his trademark in 1896, he already sold more than fifty-seven varieties of his condiments. He simply liked the deliberately unround number of fifty-seven.

George Eastman's favorite letter happened to be *K*, so he invented a name that begins and ends with it. Then *Kodak* didn't mean anything. It does now.

Run a Mile

At about the time the people at R. J. Reynolds Tobacco Company were looking for a brand name for their new Turkish tobacco, the circus came to Winston-Salem, North Carolina. With it came an aged dromedary, named "Old Joe," who became the inspiration for Camel cigarettes. The tobacco people did not know the difference between the animals. The word *dromedary* means "runner" in Greek. If you want a camel, however, you could walk a mile.

And a Parrot Shall Lead Them

Ashton-Tate and its leading data-base software dBase II (and dBase III) are all but household names to the corporate world. Both names are the creation of an advertising man, Hal Pawluk, who advised entrepreneur George Tate to change the name of a software program he had acquired, from Vulcan to dBase II. Pawluk felt that the term sounded technical, descriptive, and an advance from dBase I, which in fact had never existed. The renamed product proved an instant success, helped by some other unconventional advertising ideas. The first notorious ads in January 1981 carried a picture with the headline: "dBase II vs. THE BILGE PUMPS", which did not please the manufacturer of the depicted bilge pump. At the COMDEX industry fair in Las Vegas, George Tate had a blimp with the name dBase II circling *inside* the convention center. The blimp was tethered to his booth.

Ashton-Tate is also a concoction. Pawluk came up with the name, even though there was no Ashton at the time: he simply liked the sound of the name. And there is no longer a Tate, since the entrepreneur had been felled by a sudden heart attack. But the company did acquire a large South American blue parrot called Ashton. The mascot has her room at corporate headquarters in Torrance, California, and a staff member is assigned to keeping her happy. Ashton is also a spokesperson: she likes to startle visitors with the names of Ashton-Tate products she memorizes from tapes. She can reel off "dBase," "Framework," and at last sighting was busily trying to master "Rapidfile" in time for the new product's release.

Billboard

E. Joseph Cossman, evangelist of the mail-order business, used billboards outside his offices to intrigue passersby or to impress special customers. In his book, *How I Made $1,000,000 in Mail Order*, Cossman describes flying from Los Angeles to New York to see a man called Dave Geller on business. After waiting fruitlessly for a couple of hours while Geller was in conference, Cossman had enough and flew back home. After a few days, Geller called to say that he would be flying out to the West Coast specifically to apologize. As he arrived at the parking lot, an enormous billboard greeted him:

"Thanks, Dave Geller, for coming all the way from New York to spend ten minutes with us." The two men became close friends and business associates.

After that, Joe Cossman expanded the use of the billboard to reflect his own philosophy and moods; he gives several pages of one-liners at the back of his book. Examples:

"If you must cry over spilled milk, condense it."
"The most inflammable kind of wood is the chip on the shoulder."
"A halo has to slip only a few inches to become a noose."
"Having fun is like insurance. The older you get, the more it costs."

One morning Cossman put up a joke:
"If you tilted the country sideways, all the loose ends would fall into Los Angeles."

Los Angeles was not amused. The office received thirty phone calls, two special delivery letters, and a telegram, and three people appeared in person to protest. After that, Cossman kept to more philosophical and general topics.

Dodgers' Fan

The late Ralph Carson, a pioneering advertising man in Los Angeles (whom I was priviledged to know in his last years, when we were both teaching at the University of Southern California), was an avid baseball fan and may be the man most responsible for getting the Dodgers to the West Coast. When he heard that Walter O'Malley was willing to consider a move from Brooklyn, Carson used his talents and resources in advertising in a one-man campaign to persuade the team. He personally paid for large ads in cities where the Dodgers were rained out, quoting the weather report and temperatures that day in Los Angeles.

In 1957, Ralph Carson tried to put up a billboard three blocks from Ebbets Field with the message: "GOOD LUCK TEAM—NEXT YEAR IN LOS ANGELES." Not surprisingly, the Outdoor Advertising Association of Brooklyn rejected his proposal. Next year the Dodgers moved anyway.

USE AND ABUSE

Singing in the Rain

Hachirobei Mitsui was a forerunner of modern advertisers. In seventeenth-century Japan, umbrellas made of oil paper and decorated with delicate painting were popular with Japanese housewives. Mitsui had large quantities made with his symbol and a message promoting the store, and on rainy days he gave the umbrellas away with a minimum purchase. Word quickly spread throughout Yedo, and Japanese ladies soon arranged to be caught in the rain near his store, thus spreading thousands of colorful advertising messages throughout the town.

The inventive pioneer did not stop there. He introduced billboard advertising by putting up large wood-block prints on vacant buildings. Some of these ads were executed by famous artists of the day and later became collectors' items. Noting the new popularity of theater, Mitsui also patronized playwrights, commissioning them to write plays in which characters talked about his store in favorable terms.

Advertising

P. T. Barnum attributed much of his success to his techniques of advertising. In his memoirs he advised:

You may advertise a spurious article, and induce many people to call and buy it once, but they will denounce you as an imposter and swindler, and your business will gradually die out, and leave you poor. This is right. Few people can safely depend upon chance custom. You all need to have your customers return and purchase again. A man said to me, "I have tried advertising, and did not succeed; yet I have a good article."

I replied, "My friend, there may be exceptions to a general rule. But how do you advertise?"

"I put it in a weekly newspaper three times, and paid a dollar and a half for it."

I replied, "Sir, advertising is like learning—a little is a dangerous thing."

And How It Works

Barnum liked to quote a nameless French writer about the power of advertising: "The reader of a newspaper does not see the first insertion of an ordinary advertisement; the second insertion he sees but does not read; the third insertion he reads; the fourth insertion, he looks at the price; the fifth insertion, he speaks of it to his wife; the sixth insertion, he is ready to purchase; and the seventh insertion, he purchases."

Scruples

John Wanamaker, who practically invented the modern department store, was also the first to run full-page advertisements. His motto: "The customer is always right"—which is still a byword in American business as much in the breach as in its observance—was matched by equally high standards of advertising. One of Wanamaker's advertising men was so scrupulous that he could only write copy when he was convinced of its absolute truth. One day, the men's clothing department wanted to advertise a sale of neckties reduced from a dollar to only 25 cents. The ad man inspected the ties personally and asked the buyer:

"Are they any good?"

"No, they're not," came the honest reply.

The ad man scratched his head and went to work. After wrestling with his conscience, he came up with the following copy: "THEY ARE NOT AS GOOD AS THEY LOOK, BUT THEY ARE GOOD ENOUGH AT 25 CENTS."

The demand was so great that Wanamaker's had to buy several more weeks' supply of cheap ties.

In Other Words

Elmer Wheeler, the salesman who contributed the immortal line "Don't sell the steak, sell the sizzle!" to the language, was constantly looking for sentences that would sell a product. His tests account for the phenomenon that hardly anything costs a round figure, because Wheeler found there are many people who would buy a product for $2.98, but would not pay $3 for it. "But if the price is $2.60," he asserted, "people will think that you have raised it from $2.50." An appliance could be sold more easily for two dimes a day than for $79.50, as the Hoover company found out. Sales, however, can be increased not simply by rewording the price. The vacuum cleaner manufacturer changed a warning signal which said DANGER to the more practical TIME TO EMPTY, and saw a big jump in sales.

To the Pure in Heart

At the beginning of the century there were battles fought over the question of pasteurizing milk. Nathan Straus compared the arguments of legislators opposed to pasteurization to that of the Maine milkman:

"A lady summering in Maine told her milkman severely: 'See here, this milk of yours is half water and half chalk. What do you mean by advertising it as pure?'

'Madam,' said the milk manufacturer with withering scorn, 'to the pure all things are pure.'"

Plus ça Change

The early subscriber to Alexander Graham Bell's telephone system had a number of problems to overcome. There was no switchboard, so one could only call another set that one also leased. In order to reassure existing and future customers, the fledgling company was forced to advertise in words that might be appropriate for some phone companies today: "Conversation can be easily carried on after slight practice and with the occasional repetition of a word or sentence. After a few trials, the ear becomes accustomed to the peculiar sound."

Medical Advice

When Hires root beer made its appearance at the Philadelphia Exhibition of 1876, the advertisements claimed it was "soothing to the nerves, vitalizing to the blood, refreshing to the brain." The soft drink was supposed to give children strength and help "even a cynic to see the brighter side of life." Coca-Cola, too, was first sold more like medicine. The company recommended its product as relieving "physical and mental exhaustion," which was later diluted to "the pause that refreshes." 7-Up originally was touted as a hangover remedy in the post-Prohibition era with the slogan: "Takes the *ouch* out of *grouch.*"

The company didn't seem to care what the customer might do with the *gr* that was left.

Trademark

The Coca-Cola Company tried early to register Cola as its own exclusive trademark. The application failed on not one but two separate grounds: if the drink did contain Kola nuts, then it would be a descriptive term, which means that anybody else had the right to use it (as Pepsi-Cola and others eventually did). On the other hand, if it did not have Kola nuts, then it would be a deceptive term and nobody could use it. The company seemed to do quite nicely without a trademark for cola, and decided to promote the even more ambiguous *coke* instead.

Pass the Perrier

With all the pure water being sold in stores or delivered at home these days, it is amusing to come across this advertising slogan from the 1840s for Hostetter's Stomach Bitters, which contained 44 percent alcohol and was recommended for conditions ranging from dysentery and shakes to nervousness and gloom: "Harmless as Water from the Mountain Springs."

A Closer

Albert D. Lasker, often regarded as the father of modern American advertising, possessed tremendous powers of persuasion and salesmanship. The worst thing he could say about anybody—and he did say it about a businessman who got a government appointment—was: "he is not a *closer,*" that is, he could not secure a sale. One of the earliest incidents that John Gunther relates in his fascinating biography, *Taken at the Flood,* took place in 1899, when young Lasker had heard through the grapevine that the Rheinstrom Brothers, liquor manufacturers in Cincinnati, were about to start a substantial advertising campaign. Lasker had also heard that the account was more or less promised to Charles Austin Bates in New York. As Gunther says: "For Lasker to compete against Bates was like an unknown boy tenor competing with Caruso."

The young man got on a train from Chicago to Cincinnati and went straight from the station at 7 A.M. to the liquor firm, where he saw the owner opening the mail. (Apparently, in those days, even in very large firms, the boss always opened the mail to prevent any embezzlement or spying.) Abe Rheinstrom was anything but encouraging: "What do you want?" Lasker handed him his card and introduced himself.

"I had heard, sir, that you are going to advertise, and my firm sent me down to solicit—"

"How dare your firm send a young boy like you down—disturbing me in my most important work of the day, early in the morning! Get out!"

Lasker had to leave the office, feeling foolish, having insisted to his employers at Lord & Thomas that he be the one sent. His next stratagem was to intercept Mr. Rheinstrom at home, where Lasker deduced he was likely to go for lunch and a little nap. He called the client at his home and spoke so fast that he could not be interrupted:

"I'm - the - young - man - you - kicked - out - of - your - office - this - morning. - I - came - down - from - Lord - & - Thomas. - If - I - go - home - without - seeing - you - I'm - liable - to - lose - my - position. - What - difference - does - it - make - to - you - just - to - give - a - few - minutes? - Maybe - it's - the - turning - point - in - the - career - of - a - young - man. - It - may - be - the - making - or - breaking - of - me. - Can't - I - come - to - see - you - for - a - few - minutes?"

Rheinstrom agreed. Three hours later, Lord & Thomas had the account.

What Is Advertising

As Albert Lasker mastered other aspects of the business and techniques of advertising, he was troubled by the fact that he could not sum up exactly what "effective advertising" was. He asked his mentors, he studied slogans, he let the word out in conversations what he was seeking to know. One day in 1904, one of the office boys at Lord & Thomas handed him a note in the middle of a meeting. It read simply: "I am in the saloon downstairs, and I can tell you what advertising is. I know that you don't know. It will mean much to you. If you wish to know what advertising is, send the word 'Yes' down by the messenger. — John E. Kennedy."

The man seemed crazy, and, against the advice of his partners, Lasker went down to see him for a minute, which stretched into hours, until after midnight. There were two concepts that Kennedy shared that day that were to revolutionize advertising: first Kennedy asked Lasker what he thought of the essence of advertising, and he replied, "News."

"No, news is a technique of presentation, but advertising is a very different thing. I can give it to you in three words."

"I am hungry. What are those three words?"

Kennedy said: *"Salesmanship in print."*

The second concept was Kennedy's belief that one had to tell the reason *why* people should buy something. Out of that, copywriting was born.

Writing

Aldous Huxley wrote: "It is much easier to write ten passably effective sonnets, good enough to take in the not too inquiring critic, than one effective advertisement that will take in a few thousand of the uncritical buying public."

Claude Hopkins, who became Albert Lasker's top copywriter and closest friend, could barely write a grammatical sentence. One of his secrets was never to write for the masses: "Ads are not written to interest, please, or amuse. You are not writing for the *hoi polloi*. You are writing on a serious subject—the subject of money spending. And you address a restricted minority."

Nose

David Ogilvy had early sales experience before going into advertising. He recalls selling rather expensive kitchen stoves at a trade fair in London. Since each sales pitch would take more than half an hour, he had to select prospects carefully: "I learned to smell them; they smoked Turkish cigarettes, a mark of aristocracy, like an Old Etonian tie," he wrote in *Confessions of an Advertising Man.* Later, this sense became more refined if metaphorical: "Once I came away from a New York luncheon of the Scottish Council with the presentiment that four of the men I had just met for the first time would one day become my clients. And so it turned out."

Psychology

David Ogilvy used to tell a story about Max Hart. The men's clothing tycoon summoned his advertising manager to complain about his latest campaign: "Nobody reads that much copy," he asserted.

The ad manager begged to differ. "I'll bet you ten dollars, Mr. Hart, that I can write a whole newspaper page of solid type and you will read every word of it." Hart eagerly accepted the bet.

"I won't have to write even a paragraph to prove my point," the ad man continued. "I'll just give you the heading:

THIS PAGE IS ALL ABOUT MAX HART."

Misleading

Campbell Soup used to advertize that it produced twenty-one different kinds of soup, and listed them. But the list actually contained twenty-two brands. In some years as many as 700 people would write to the company about this discrepancy. Executives of the company were delighted with their deliberate mistake, because it caused the ads to be talked about and gave them feedback about how carefully their advertising was read.

Anticipation

Ben Duffy, head of the Batten, Barton, Durstine and Osborn (BBDO) advertising agency in the 1950s, landed his largest accounts by putting himself into the client's position. In preparing to meet with Vincent Riggio, president of the American Tobacco Company, Duffy wrote down the questions he would ask if he himself were the prospective client, and then jotted down his answers.

When the time for the interview came, Duffy presented his answers and waited. Riggio reached for a drawer and pulled out a list of questions he had prepared. When he glanced through them he realized that they had all been answered. The two then went to lunch to celebrate the deal.

Expenses

Advertising companies are notoriously free spenders in good times, and being the chief financial officer at a Madison Avenue agency must be among the least gratifying of jobs. Yet Robert Feland at Batten, Barton, Durstine and Osborn became a legend within the industry during the 1950s, his literate memos treasured and retold like epigrams. Fred Manchee, in *The Huckster's Revenge*, quotes a few: "I do not mind being cursed for trying to hold down payroll and other controllable expenses. That could be a source of pride. I do greatly dread being cursed for not trying hard enough, for yielding when I should have been firm, for being agreeable when expenses could have been held down by being disagreeable. For that I would feel shame forever."

About employees asking for personal loans, Feland ruled: "We tell them frankly that we will assist the unfortunate, but we cannot undertake to help fools."

A regional officer failed to heed his belt-tightening drive, so Robley Feland wrote him:

> When James the Sixth of Scotland became James the First of England, he moved from Edinburgh Castle to London. Immediately after crossing the line from Scotland into England he encountered two vagrants by the wayside. He knighted one and had the other hanged, just to show that he was really King of England.
>
> This is a much more thorough job than you have been doing to date. You have knighted a lot of people, but you have as yet hung no vagrants!

The Eye of the Beholder

When the British author G. K. Chesterton was visiting New York he was taken on a night tour of the glittering lights of Times Square and Broadway. As he gazed at the cascade of neon flashing the names of various products at passersby, Chesterton remarked: "How beautiful it would be for someone who could not read."

Smart Kids

In 1971 Ralph Nader attacked the advertising claims made by the Ted Bates Agency for Profile bread and Wonder bread, both manufactured by the food giant Continental Baking, a subsidiary of ITT. Commercials claimed that Profile bread had fewer calories per slice than other bread, while Wonder bread advertised that it helped "build strong bodies in twelve ways." Television commercials depicted kids who were visibly growing by leaps and bounds thanks to this beneficial product.

In March 1971, the Federal Trade Commission agreed with Nader that Wonder bread had exactly the same nutrients as other bread, and that Profile bread had fewer calories only because it was more thinly sliced. The company appealed and won, at least in the case of Wonder bread. The judge ruled in favor of the company on the grounds that children did not believe TV commercials anyway.

The Primrose Path

Placing commercial products in movies is big business: one agency has over thirty clients signed up at a hefty $50,000 each a year. Though such deals have been around for decades, the product-placement business got a major boost in 1982, when Reese's Pieces candy was featured prominently in Steven Spielberg's *E.T.* Universal Studios first approached M&Ms, but were turned down. Subsequently, Reese's Pieces were used without the company's knowledge. Presumably, they did not sue Universal when sales of their candy suddenly jumped 65 percent after the film was released. However, it gave critics something to worry about. Peter Rainier, movie critic for the *Los Angeles Herald-Examiner* called it a "pernicious trend. . . you get the feeling that if the *Wizard of Oz* were made today, the yellow brick road would be brought to you courtesy of Carpeteria."

Rich Gore, a merchandising consultant, persuaded MasterCard not to pay to have its product seen in *Death Wish III*. He gave this rationale to the credit card company: "It stars Charles Bronson and is a shoo-in hit. But it takes place in the ghetto and shows lots of people getting blown away. I don't think that would do MasterCard any good."

Concern

Once when Batten, Barton, Durstine and Osborn (BBDO) was doing a campaign to boost the circulation for the *New Yorker*, Tax Cumings found himself in an elevator with Harold Ross, the legendary editor of the magazine. To make conversation, and out of genuine pride at the way the campaign had worked, Cumings asked, "Do you realize, Mr. Ross, that the *New Yorker* now has 250,000 readers?"

"Indeed," the editor asked. "And how are they all?"

MERCHANDISING

Shrewd as a Hatter

P. T. Barnum tells the story of the first Jenny Lind concert in New York, when tickets were so much in demand that an auction was held. A small businessman bought the first ticket but not just to listen to the famous Swedish Nightingale:

Genin, the hatter, bought the first Jenny Lind ticket at auction for two hundred and twenty-five dollars, because he knew it would be a good advertisement for him. "Who is the bidder?" said the auctioneer, as he knocked down the ticket at Castle Garden. "Genin, the hatter," was the response. Here were thousands of people from the Fifth Avenue, and from distant cities in the highest stations in life. "Who is Genin, the hatter?" they exclaimed. They had never heard of him before. The next morning the newspapers and telegraph had circulated the facts from Maine to Texas, and from five to ten millions of people had read that the tickets sold at auction for Jenny Lind's first concert amounted to about twenty thousand dollars, and that a single ticket was sold at two hundred and twenty-five dollars to "Genin, the hatter." Men throughout the country involuntarily took off their hats to see if they had a "Genin" hat on their heads. At a town in Iowa it was found that in the crowd around the Post Office, there was one man who had a "Genin" hat, and he showed it in triumph, although it was worn out and not worth two cents. "Why," one man exclaimed, "you have a real 'Genin' hat; what a lucky fellow you are." Another man said, "Hang on to that hat, it will be a valuable heir-loom in your family." Still another man in the crowd, who seemed to envy the possessor of this good fortune, said, "come, give us all a chance; put it up at auction!" He did so, and it was sold as a keepsake for nine dollars and fifty cents! What was the consequence to Mr. Genin? He sold ten thousand extra hats per annum, the first six years. Nine-tenths of the purchasers bought from him, probably, out of curiosity, and many of them, finding that he gave them an equivalent for their money, became his regular customers. This novel advertisement first struck their attention, and then as he made a good article, they came again.

Why Spend?

William Wrigley, Jr., founded the company that bears his name in 1891, with a total of $32. Although continually strapped for cash in the early days, he pioneered one of the tenets of modern advertising: create a need first and then fill it. He spent more than $100,000—a fortune in those days—on his first two ad campaigns with very little to show for them. His response was to more than double his advertising budget, which finally stopped the tide of red ink just short of bankruptcy. By the 1920s Wrigley was spending $4 million a year promoting his one product.

When Philip K. Wrigley took over from his father, he maintained the same formula. Once asked during a transcontinental plane trip why he continued to advertise when he already had one of the most successful products in the world, the chewing-gum tycoon replied: "For the same reason the pilot of this plane keeps the engine running when we're already twenty-nine thousand feet up."

Ground Floor

Back in 1905, John P. Burkhard, publisher of a new magazine called *Field and Stream*, was trying to drum up some advertising business. He had heard about an ex-bicycle maker in Detroit by the name of Henry Ford, who had gone into automobiles. Burkhard contacted Ford and sold him on an advertising contract worth $1,200. But his new customer was short of cash and offered the publisher a choice between a new Ford coupe or $1,200 worth of stock in the equally new Ford Motor Company. Without a second thought Burkhard chose the automobile, and having no use for it, he turned it over to his printer for credit. Had he taken the stock, he would have become a millionaire in a few years.

Rates

M. I. Pitkin, promotion manager for *Cosmopolitan's* in the 1940s, used to tell about a circus advance man named Flanagan who dropped in at the office of a smalltown newspaper and inquired about the cost of a full-page ad.

"One hundred bucks."

"And a half-page?"

"One hundred bucks."

"And a quarter-page."

"One hundred bucks."

"Your rates aren't very elastic," Flanagan fumed. "How on earth do you calculate them?"

"That's easy," the editor hastened to soothe him. "Your show is due here on July 12th. I've got the only paper in town. And on the 13th I've got a bill due for exactly one hundred bucks."

Publicity

Late in the last century, W. J. Arkell bought a venerable magazine called *Judge*, which badly needed to improve its balance sheet. In the next few years the problem grew steadily worse, and finally there was no money to spend on advertising. At this point, the owner came up with a desperate idea to create publicity for the ailing publication:

I knew many members of Congress, and induced one, a close personal friend, to introduce a bill in the House of Representatives in which I offered two million dollars for the privilege of printing an advertisement of *Judge* on the backs of postage stamps. This bill of course created a sensation at the

Capitol, and hundreds of newspapers throughout the United States attacked it. Some of the editorials held the measure up to ridicule, while others opposed it seriously as a dangerous precedent. It looked for a time as though, in spite of this opposition, the bill might pass, as they were very hungry for money in Washington at the time. But of course I did not want the bill to go through, for I did not have the money to put up on a contract. So by arrangement another of my friends in the House, when the bill came up for consideration, made a riproaring attack upon it. In his speech he said it was all right, perhaps, for *Judge* to advertise on the backs of postage stamps, but it was a dangerous precedent, as the newspapers had declared, for when the *Judge* contract ran out, some person might come along with a pile ointment, and he would want to advertise that on the backs of postage stamps. His speech killed the bill. This delighted me. In addition to the free advertising I got from the proposal, and in the newspapers, I received thousands of letters from persons the country over, some favorable, and many others quite unfavorable. But I concluded that even the writers of these letters, if they were not familiar with *Judge*, would at least buy a copy to find out what the magazine was like.

Spokesman

Long before Lee Iacocca, founder Walter Chrysler was the spokesman for Chrysler automobiles. He was the first to use his own face and words in every advertisement for his product. Chrysler also was among the first to use a public relations man and ghost-writer to obtain a vast amount of free newspaper space by expressing himself on every conceivable subject. When he found out that farmers formed the largest group of Chrysler customers, he became an expert on farming, commissioning innumerable columns of advice to farmers, all of which were printed for free.

Getting It Right

During the 1912 presidential campaign, three million copies were about to be printed of Theodore Roosevelt's convention speech. The small booklet was also adorned with photographs of Roosevelt and Governor Hiram Johnson of California, his running mate, but the publisher noticed just in time that nobody had bothered to get permission to reproduce the photographs. In such a case, the copyright law provided for a penalty of $1 for each copy printed. The presses were halted until the chairman of the campaign committee came up with an idea of how to get around this $3 million land mine. He dispatched a telegram to the Chicago photographic agency that owned the copyright:

HUGE PUBLICITY OPPORTUNITY TO RUN YOUR PHOTO-
GRAPHS WITH THREE MILLION COPIES OF ROOSEVELT
SPEECH. HOW MUCH?

Within an hour came the reply:

APPRECIATE OPPORTUNITY BUT CAN ONLY PAY $250.

My Kind of Town

In the heyday of the Chicago newspaper wars, immortalized on stage and
screen in *The Front Page*, the *Tribune* came up with a stunt that increased
circulation by an astounding 250,000 in three days and practically im-
mobilized the Windy City. In 1921 the *Chicago News* began the circulation war by distributing what amounted to free lottery tickets. When this
noticeably increased the number of newspapers its rival sold, the *Tribune*
decided to adopt the sincerest form of flattery and launched what became
known as the "Cheer Checks" campaign.

The logistics of printing and distributing more than 25 million "Cheer
Checks" for drawings of lucky numbers were minutely planned. On the
morning after Thanksgiving, the announcement of the scheme was made
in a double-page spread. Printers were called from their homes, and the
ticket presses worked overtime. A supply of 25 tons of special paper,
bearing the *Tribune's* watermark (to avoid counterfeiting) had arrived that
day from a Wisconsin mill. By Saturday evening five million coupons had
been distributed. There was a constant throng of people outside the
Tribune building, wanting more coupons. To ensure wider distribution,
the *Tribune* mailed out 1.5 million envelopes, and handed out 40,000
posters as well as 2.5 million flyers explaining the scheme. The daily
draw of prizes was listed in the paper, and the surge of demand for extra
copies stretched the organization to the utmost.

Curiously, from an advertising point of view, every piece of promotion
for the campaign made plain the *Tribune's* dislike for the stunt. The other
newspaper had inaugurated a highly demoralizing lottery—the announcements explained—that it attempted to disguise as charity, so the
Tribune felt obliged to stop the practice by doing everything better and on
a larger scale, without a pretense of charity. It was constantly emphasized
that the *Tribune* would be only too glad to stop if the affair were frowned on
by the authorities.

According to a contemporary (and biased) account, put out by the
Tribune,

This elimination of the false mantle of charity had one unexpected effect.
Multitudes of people who would not participate as recipients of charity were

keen to collect Cheer Checks and willing to win prizes when it was plainly a business proposition. Banks put *Tribune* Cheer Checks in the pass books of depositors. Bakers wrapped them with hundreds of thousands of loaves of bread. The largest corporations in Chicago asked for the privilege of distributing them to their employees. Department heads in the Post Office wrote for bundles to be given to their forces. A Sunday school superintendent got some for his classes. Thousands of merchants stood in line in all kinds of weather to get allotments. The attempt to distribute them house to house had to be abandoned because the men doing the work would sell them or keep them in the hope of winning.

Finally the government stepped in to stop the craze by reminding the newspapers that lotteries were illegal in Illinois. "No one was more anxious to accede," the *Tribune* writer remarked piously, "than the newspaper that started the stunt."

Buy Low, Sell High

Stanley Arnold, who became known for his million-dollar ideas, started in retailing. His father opened Cleveland's first supermarket in 1937, which gradually expanded to a chain of fifteen Pick-N-Pay stores, one of which young Stanley managed. During a record blizzard that swept Cleveland, Stanley Arnold had the first of his "million-dollar" marketing ideas. As he sat in one of the fifteen empty stores in the numbed city, plans for an unprecedented retailing event began to take shape in his brain. He asked all able-bodied employees to report to work the following day. When they did, Arnold asked them to make large snowballs in the parking lots. That day 7,900 snowballs were packed into grapefruit crates, 80 to a box, which were then taken to a deep freeze facility, where Arnold had arranged for the snowballs to be kept at twenty degrees below zero for an indefinite period.

Everybody was convinced that the boss's brain had been frostbitten, while he was busy finding out from the Weather Bureau when the year's worst heat wave, based on statistical averages, was most likely to occur. He was told the middle of July. Armed with that piece of information, Arnold took the train to New York and went to see Charles Mortimer, then President of General Foods. Arnold proposed a joint promotional sale of General Food's Birdseye Frozen products. The sale to be held during the hottest week of July, was to be called "A Blizzard of Values," and young Stanley wanted General Foods to provide an array of prizes. There was nothing unusual in such cooperation between manufacturer and retailer. What raised the eyebrows of several vice presidents was the giveaway that

the mild-mannered Stanley proposed as his contribution to lure Cleve-
landers into the stores—snowballs.

Summer came, and for once the long-term forecast was accurate. In the
100-degree heat, special contingents of Cleveland's finest had to hold
back hysterical women in the parking lot to keep them from mobbing the
already crowded stores. During five days of Pick-N-Pay's "Blizzard of
Values" some 40,000 General Foods samples were given away, along with
7,900 grapefruit-sized snowballs. As Stanley Arnold concludes in his
thoroughly engaging book (*Tale of the Blue Horse and Other Million
Dollar Adventures*), "thousands of customers had a good time, and the
food industry began to take notice of the great potential of *excitement* as an
ingredient in selling."

The People Business

Later in his career, in the 1950s, Stanley Arnold was working at Young &
Rubicam, where he was asked to come up with a marketing campaign for
Remington Rand. The company was among the most conservative in
America, and its chairman, appropriately enough, was General Douglas
MacArthur. Intimidated at first by a company that was so much *a part of
America*, Arnold also found in that phrase the first inspiration for a
campaign. After two weeks of thinking about what it meant, he paid a
personal visit to the New York offices of Merrill, Lynch, Pierce, Fenner
and Beane, and placed with them the ultimate odd-lot order: "I want to
purchase," he told the broker, "one share of every single stock listed on
the New York Stock Exchange."

The clerk was a little astonished: "Mr. Arnold, we believe in diversifi-
cation, but this is incredible."

"I'm glad to hear it," said Stanley Arnold, who had worked hard
precisely to elicit such a response.

After a vice president tried to talk him out of it, the order finally was
placed. It came to more than $42,000 for one share in each of 1,098 com-
panies listed on the Big Board at the time. Arnold now took his diversified
portfolio into a meeting of Remington Rand's board of directors, where he
argued passionately for a sweepstakes campaign with the top prize called
"A Share in America." The conservative old gentlemen shifted around in
their seats and discussed the idea for a while.

"But Mr. Arnold, we are not in the securities business," said one.

"We are in the shaver business," rejoined another.

"I agree that you are not in the securities business," said the million-dollar idea man, "but I think you also ought to realize that you are not in the shaver business either. You are in the people business."

The company bought the idea.

You'll Never Get to Heaven with a Grand Piano

Around the turn of the century there was a coupon craze, as retailers sought to retain customer loyalty by offering prizes. Nat C. Goodwin, a famous vaudeville comedian, was offered some coupons in a store after he laid in a large amount of necessities.

"I don't want 'em;" Goodwin answered.

"You had better take them, sir," the clerk persisted. "We redeem them with very handsome prizes. If you can save up a thousand coupons, we give you a grand piano."

"Say, look here," said the actor, "if I ever drank enough of your whisky or smoked enough of your cigars to get a thousand of those coupons, I wouldn't need a piano. I'd want a harp."

Going Out of One's Way

The various bonus mileage programs that airlines devised in the 1980s to foster customer loyalty has had some strange fallout. Many companies have denied their employees private benefits from such programs, after discovering that they were sometimes flying the most roundabout routes in order to get more mileage. A rather extreme example of going out of one's way to qualify for bonus coupons came when TWA flight 847 was hijacked in June 1985, and was flown four times between Algeria and Beirut. Larry Hilliard, regional director of corporate communications for TWA, revealed that Deborah Toga, wife of one of the hostages, had enquired whether these trips qualified under the airline's Frequent Flyer program. They did.

· 7 ·

CORPORATE CULTURE

BIG BUSINESS

Think

Thomas Watson built the ailing Computing-Tabulating-Recording Company into the global colossus we know as International Business Machines (IBM). More than that, he is the man most responsible for making this the age of the computer, a machine that began by counting faster than humans and that is now rapidly overtaking us in other areas. Watson is remembered for plastering his stationery, all the offices at IBM, and his home with the slogan: THINK. The monthly house organ, in fact, was called "THINK." But this was not the only exhortation he used. Rather, it was the last of five keywords: "Read—Listen—Discuss—Observe—Think." And especially in the early days of the company's existence, he put all kinds of other motivational slogans and truisms on the walls, such as:

"There is no such thing as standing still."
"We must never feel satisfied."
"Time lost is time gone forever."
"Teaching is valueless unless somebody learns what is taught."
"We forgive thoughtful mistakes."

According to legend, Watson devised his THINK slogan when he was managing sales at National Cash Register, where he developed his unique talents under the stern taskmaster John Patterson. At a meeting of advertising heads, which was going nowhere, Watson jumped to his feet: "The trouble with every one of us," he shouted, "is that we don't think enough. We don't get paid for working with our feet—we get paid for working with our heads. Any man on the selling force could make two dollars where he now makes one if he would think along the right lines. 'I didn't think,' has cost the world millions of dollars."

Not everybody went along with Chairman Watson's thinking. One day, when people came to work at IBM headquarters, they found this addition scrawled under each THINK slogan by an anonymous wit: OR THWIM.

Mr. Sloan

Few people have been as influential in shaping the modern American corporation as Alfred P. Sloan, Jr., who ruled General Motors for thirty-five years. Although a man of deep sympathy, he was also very aloof. He never called anybody by his first name, which Peter Drucker attributes to the formal upbringing of the later Victorian generation. Whenever he found there was a new elevator man in the GM building in Detroit or New York, he would introduce himself: "I am Mr. Sloan. What is your name?" If the man answered, "I am Jack, sir," Sloan would become livid: "I asked for your name, sir."

And he would never forget that name.

The Idea Factory

3M is the Minnesota corporation that grew from being a maker of mediocre sandpaper into an international conglomerate that makes everybody's list of excellent companies. The main reason, according to Thomas Peters and Robert Waterman (authors of the bestselling *In Search of Excellence*) is its championing of ideas and deep belief that ultimately they will succeed. The invention of Scotch Tape in 1930 is enshrined in legend:

> The salesmen who visited the auto plants noticed that workers painting new two-toned cars were having trouble keeping the colors from running together. Richard G. Drew, a young 3M lab technician, came up with the answer: masking tape, the company's first tape. In 1930, six years after Du Pont introduced cellophane, Drew figured out how to put adhesive on it, and Scotch Tape was born, initially for industrial packaging. It didn't really begin to roll until another imaginative 3M hero, John Borden, a sales manager, created a dispenser with a built-in blade.

Jumbo

At a time when American manufacturing is said to be in decline and in full flight from foreign competition, U.S. civilian and military aircraft is still the number-one choice all over the world. The Boeing 747 is widely considered the best and safest airplane ever built. The first one, completed in September 1968, took four years and $1.5 billion to build, and the effort almost sank the company, throwing the Seattle area into a depression. The project sounds a bit like the construction of the pyramids: 7,000 mechanics worked to put together four and a half million parts inside the largest building ever made. The final assembly plant at Everett, Washington, encloses 200 million cubic feet, covering an area of 43 acres. During the eighteen months it takes to assemble the giant airplane, Boeing provides customers with a free office at the assembly plant where they can supervise personally every stage of construction.

Let Me Count the Ways

Roger von Oech gives creativity workshops in Silicon Valley to some of the most creative companies in America. One of his exercises gets people to describe their company in a graphic metaphor or simile. Giving some of his favorite examples from the workshops (in his book *A Whack on the Side of the Head*), von Oech does not reveal the companies' names, but then again, the corporate culture that spawned these images may be archetypal anyway.

"Our company is like Peter Pan," wrote one participant, "it's childlike, and wishes to retain the good parts of being a small company even as it grows larger. Our president is like Tinkerbell—the spirit and imaginative force of the company. Our chief financial officer is like Wendy—he's practical, has both feet on the ground, but he's also pulled along in the magic. Our chief competitor is like Captain Hook, but we'll overcome him with imagination rather than guns and knives."

Another, perhaps recalling the famous "belly" speech by Menenius in Shakespeare's *Coriolanus* wrote: "Our company is like a giant human body. Administration is the guts. Sales and marketing are the mouth. Corporate management is the mind making decisions. Research and development is the reproductive system. And the secretaries and the technicians are the skeleton that supports the body."

That some of the managers were less than comfortable with their company is revealed in the following metaphors:

"Working here is like a nightmare. You'd like to get out of it, but you need the sleep."

Or: "Our company is like a galley ship without a drummer. We've got some people rowing at full beat, some at one-half beat, some at one-quarter beat, and some dead beats. Also, the captain is steering by the wake."

And the most ambiguous statement of all: "Working here is like urinating in a dark suit. It's warm and it feels good but it doesn't show."

Battles

In the chairman's office at the London headquarters of Shell Transport and Trading, from time immemorial, there was hung a Dutch old master: Jacob Bellevois's depiction of the Battle of Medway in 1667. It shows, with historical accuracy, all the British ships being sunk, on fire or in retreat. This seemed an unbalanced view of Anglo-Dutch relations, so the current chairman commissioned a new English master, John Groves, to paint the battle of Terschelling, where the British fleet sank a large Dutch flottila. The painting will hang in the headquarters of Royal Dutch Shell in The Hague, perhaps to remind the leaders of this binational conglomerate of the virtues of competition.

Covert Action

"Never tell anyone what you are going to do till you've done it," said Cornelius Vanderbilt to a friend who asked him for the secret of success in business. In 1850, the Pacific Mail Steamship Company had a virtual monopoly of the immensely lucrative cargo trade between San Francisco and Panama. Vanderbilt naturally wanted to have a piece of this action. One day, the Commodore was observed in his office standing before a man of the Western Hemisphere and placing his finger successively on three points. The first of these was San Juan de Nicaragua on the Atlantic shore; the second was the lake of Nicaragua; the third was the port of San Juan del Sur, on the Pacific. Here was a route that, if possible, would save nearly one thousand miles of travel and put money in the purse of whoever secured it.

Vanderbilt silently investigated the practicability of the route and made all his arrangements with a view to its establishment. A few days later, his new steamer *Prometheus* lay at the dock, fired up and furnished with coal and all other provisions for a cruise. Vanderbilt went on board, and asking a friend to give his good-bye to Mrs. V., ordered the lines cast off and the prow turned southward. In due time he made his appearance in Nicaragua, where he lived for six weeks on toast and tea, took care of his health, and then returned to New York, where he organized what became known as the Nicaragua Accessory Transit Company.

Obsession

When it comes to business, IBM has raised secrecy to a high art. In fact, the National Security Council and the CIA should hire Big Blue to help plug their leaks. When IBM went to Microsoft to develop its operating system for the personal computer (DOS), it required extraordinary security measures from the tiny and generally laid-back company in Washington State. The room where the project was being developed had to be windowless, unventilated, and locked at all times. IBM sent its own file locks, and when Bill Gates, the owner of Microsoft, had trouble installing them, IBM sent its own expert installer. In fact, the industrial giant was obsessively sending people to check up on Microsoft.

Close collaboration behind locked doors, however, does not necessarily breed intimacy. Gates told *PC World* magazine how, after a year of Herculean labor on the operating system for the IBM PC, he found it "an anticlimax when I got a form letter from IBM a week after we'd finished the thing, which said, 'Dear Vendor: You've done a fine job.'" (Big Blue is not insensitive to its own blunders, and, according to Gates, it apologized "an appropriate number of times.")

Top Secret

It is noteworthy how the habit of secrecy, developed for good business reasons, can become so much ingrained in the corporate culture (or government, for that matter) that it affects the private lives of its executives and employees. *Time* magazine's 1983 profile of IBM revealed that Chairman John Opel would divulge only that he drove a six-year-old car, but not what make it was. When the same question was put to Don Estridge, the man in charge of the unit that created the IBM personal computer, his instant reaction was reportedly, "Oh, no, I don't want to get into that. You don't need to know that."

Public Relations

In 1940, Peter Drucker was editor for *Fortune* magazine, which had just published a somewhat critical article about IBM in its tenth anniversary issue. Drucker describes in his autobiography the conversation he had with Thomas Watson, who called to speak with the writer of the article.

"I'm afraid, Mr. Watson," I said, "that the writer is not available. You will have to discuss the story with me; I am the editor in charge of it."

"I don't want to discuss the story," said Mr. Watson, "I want to speak to the writer personally."

"Give me your message," I said, "and I'll see that he gets it."

"Tell that young man," said Watson, "that I want him to join IBM as our director of public relations; he can name his own salary." I thought this might be one of his 'persuasion' attempts of which I had heard.

"You realize, Mr. Watson," I said, "that the story will come out in the magazine whether the writer stays on the staff or not."

"Of course," said Watson, "and if the story does not appear, I withdraw my offer."

"Mr. Watson," I said, "have you read the story?"

"Of course," he said, quite irritated, "I always read what's written about me and my company."

"And you still want the writer as your director of public relations?"

"Of course," said Watson, "at least he takes me seriously!"

Estranged Relations

Peter Drucker was working on the newly launched *Fortune* magazine in the early 1930's when Alfred Sloan hired Paul Garrett as the first public relations officer at General Motors.

"What's your main job?" Drucker asked him.

"To keep *Fortune* away from GM," was Garrett's reply.

Elephants Dancing

The personal computer revolution caught IBM off guard. The world's largest computer manufacturer was suddenly facing competition not from Burroughs or the Japanese, but from kids working out of their parents' garage. The giant corporation responded with an intrapreneurial approach by establishing a small, nonbureaucratic IBU, or Independent Business Unit, within IBM. Frank T. Cary, former chairman of Big Blue, commented that the unit was an answer to the question: "How do you make an elephant dance?"

And another elephant story: a Congressional subcommittee under Emanuel Celler in 1969 investigated the dangers conglomerates posed to competition. International Telephone and Telegraph (ITT) was one of six companies singled out. Under Harold Geneen, ITT had become one of the largest conglomerates in the world, with more than a thousand companies under one corporate roof. Geneen argued that under the ITT system there were just as many companies competing. In fact, they gave each other mutual support and input, which helped them to be more competitive.

Chairman Celler listened to this clever argument for a while and then said, "You remind me of what somebody said before this committee some years ago: 'Every man for himself,' said the elephant as he danced among the chickens."

EMPLOYEES

Try It Sometime

Irvin S. Cobb, the American humorist, was down and out in New York, trying to get a job with a newspaper. He was almost 30 years old and had a wife and a sick child to support. He got turned down by every newspaper he visited. In fact, most often he could not get to see anyone in a position to hire him. So Cobb wrote a letter to each one of them, which ended with this paragraph:

> This is positively your last chance. I have grown weary of studying the wallpaper design in your ante-room. A modest appreciation of my own worth forbids my doing business with your head office boy any longer. Unless you grab me right away, I will go elsewhere and leave your paper flat on its back right here in the middle of a hard summer, and your whole life hereafter will be one vast, surging regret. The line forms on the right; applications considered in the order they're received. Triflers and professional flirts save stamps. Write, wire, or call at the above address.

The next day Irvin Cobb was offered four jobs.

Syndication

Emmet J. McCormack, one of the founding partners of Moore-McCormack Lines, began his business career as a 14-year-old Brooklyn urchin looking for work in New York. He visited four shipping companies and asked each whether it needed the services of an office boy. Each came back with the same reply: there was simply not enough work to justify hiring him full time. So young McCormack sat down and figured out a solution to both his and their problem: he offered each company his services as one-quarter of an office boy. They hired him by putting up $1 a week each. The shipping tycoon always remembered his first business achievement: getting hired as a "syndicated office boy."

How to Get Fired—Maybe

As most managers know, it is more and more difficult to fire employees, even for "just cause." Many firms are paralyzed by fear of lawsuits into retaining incompetent or troublesome staff. However, in some countries, the problem is worse than in others. Thomas Horton, a New York management consultant, wrote in the *Wall Street Journal* about the manager of a West German chemical company who was asked if it was at all possible to get fired at his firm.

"I suppose," the man replied, "if you were to spit the director-general straight in the eye, he might fire you; or he might just say that it was raining."

The Good Old Days

In 1958 an office manager at the Boston *Herald* was cleaning out some old files and came across these rules of conduct for employees, originally issued in 1872:

1. Office employees each day will fill lamps, clean chimneys and trim wicks. Wash windows once a week.
2. Each clerk will bring in a bucket of water and a scuttle of coal for the day's business.
3. Make your pens carefully. You may whittle nibs to your individual taste.
4. Men employees will be given an evening off each week for courting purposes, or two evenings a week if they go regularly to church.
5. After thirteen hours of labor in the office, the employee should spend the remaining time reading the Bible and other good books.
6. Every employee should lay aside from each pay day a goodly sum of his earnings for his benefit during his declining years so that he will not become a burden to society.
7. Any employee who smokes Spanish cigars, uses liquor in any form, or frequents pool and public halls or gets shaved in a barber shop, will give good reason to suspect his worth, intentions, integrity and honesty.
8. The employee who has performed his labor faithfully and without fault for five years, will be given an increase of five cents per day in his pay, providing profits from business permit it.

Thank You for Not Smoking

British publishing tycoon Robert Maxwell hates cigarettes and has outlawed them in certain areas of his offices. One day, as he was walking through such an area, the boss saw a man obliviously smoking away. Maxwell immediately pounced on him, reminding the man that the penalty for breaking his rule was immediate termination.

"How much do you earn?" he asked the unfortunate wretch.

"Seventy-five pounds a week," replied the smoker. Maxwell reached into his pocket and took £300 from his wallet.

"Here's a month's pay; you're fired."

The man took the money and left, without revealing, however, one essential fact: he was not an employee, but a delivery man waiting for a receipt, when he found himself suddenly enriched for his smoking habit.

Employee Fires Boss

Colorful New York journalist Jimmy Breslin stole a march on his employers at the American Broadcasting Company, (ABC) when he announced in a brief ad on the front page of the *New York Times*: "ABC Television Network: Your Services, such as they are, will no longer be required as of 12/20/86.—Jimmy Breslin."

In fact, ABC had already decided to cancel its late night show "Jimmy Breslin's People," but had not gotten around to letting him know. The feisty journalist had not endeared himself to his boss. When complaining about the scheduling of his show in New York, he suggested in a column that Bill Fyffe, the manager of WABC-TV "do the honorable thing and jump in front of a bus."

Dick Cavett, whose show was canceled at the same time by ABC, took a more traditional approach toward the hand that might yet feed him. Being told by his agent that his "time slot was going out of business," Cavett remarked, "Now I know how Gimbels' clerks felt."

Lunch Break

J. C. Penney started as a lowly clerk in a general store. On the first day, an older employee suggested that they take their lunch together. Penney agreed, ate quickly, and, as soon as he finished, he headed back to the store.

"Don't be a sucker, take your time," said the more seasoned employee, but the future department store magnate ignored the advice. Within two months Penney was made manager of the store. Other promotions followed in quick succession, and soon he started his own chain, which eventually expanded to 1,500 stores across the United States. The attitude of not cheating his employer by taking a longer lunch break stood him in good stead as an independent businessman. Whereas his competitors were often thinking of how to take the most money from the public, J. C. Penney lay awake at night figuring out better ways of serving his customers, and this proved to be a major ingredient in his success.

How to Remain Indispensable

William Randolph Hearst offered one of his top columnists, Arthur Brisbane, a six-month sabbatical, all expenses paid, as an appreciation for services rendered. He was surprised to hear Arthur Brisbane refuse this gift and asked him why.

"First of all, I'm afraid," the journalist reasoned, "that if I quit for six months, the circulation of your newspapers may go down. And secondly, I'm afraid that it may not."

Productivity

British writer Arnold Bennett often heard his publisher boast about his secretary's remarkable efficiency. Bennett was working on a book about how people could become more productive, and, on a visit to the publisher's office, he asked the secretary for the secret of her efficiency.

"It is not my secret," she replied, "it's his. Every time I do any job, no matter how insignificant, he praises me so extravagantly that I feel I must live up to it."

Thrift

In the early days of the *New Yorker,* the offices were so small and sparsely furnished that Dorothy Parker preferred to spend her days at a nearby coffee shop. One day, the editor found her sitting there.

"Why aren't you upstairs, working?" demanded Harold Ross.

"Someone was using the pencil," Mrs. Parker explained.

Promotion

When William S. Knudsen, later president of General Motors, was still a workman, his foreman sent for him.

"Bill, could you lick any man in your department?"

"Sure!"

"Could you lick any two?"

"Sure!"

"Could you lick any three!"

"Could be."

"Could you lick any four?"

"Maybe . . ." Bill hesitated.

"Could you lick any five?"

"No."

The boss paused, and Bill waited to hear what this was all about.

"Well," he continued, since you realize that you can't lick them all, I'm going to put you in charge of them."

Marrying the Boss's Daughter

In 1822 M. Labouchère was a humble clerk working at the banking house of Hope & Company in Amsterdam, when he was sent by his employers to negotiate a loan from Mr. Baring, the London banker. He displayed in the affair so much ability that he won the esteem and confidence of the great financier.

"Sir," said Labouchère one day to Baring, "your daughter is a charming creature; I wish I could persuade you to give me her hand."

"Young man, you are joking; for you must know that Miss Baring could never become the wife of a simple clerk."

"But, what if I were in partnership with Mr. Hope?"

"Oh, that is quite a different thing; that would entirely make up for all other deficiencies."

Labouchère returned to Amsterdam and said to his patron: "You must take me into partnership."

"My young friend, how can you think of such a thing? You know that it is impossible. You have no personal fortune—"

"I know," Labouchère interrupted politely, "but what if I became the son-in-law of Mr. Baring?"

"In that case, of course, the affair would soon be settled, and so you have my word."

Fortified with these two promises, M. Labouchère returned to England and two months later married Miss Baring.

Confusing

Employees at a Taiwanese high-tech firm, Tatung, (makers of the Einstein computer) which established a new factory in Telford, Shropshire, are not permitted to laugh. According to a report in the British *Financial Times,* Mr. C. S. Lin, the company secretary, said that he did not wish to discuss the ban on laughter, but made it clear that "the provisions are already part of the conditions of employment." Well, Einstein would have smiled.

On the other hand, according to a 1985 AP dispatch, U.S. District Judge David O. Belew, Jr., ruled that American Airlines had the right to fire Robert W. Cox for not smiling enough. Cox, suing the airline, contended that he had met all requirements for the job except for the smile. But the judge said that the airline's policy of requiring a "friendly facial expression" was essential in the competitive airline industry. So American Airlines is still doing what it does best, without Mr. Cox's services—who perhaps should apply for a job with Tatung.

Modern Times

After Bell & Howell introduced an automated mail delivery cart, there was some concern about adverse reaction to working with a robot. After an informal survey, Michael Skrzyck, salesman at the company, summed up the findings: "It's not dehumanizing. We find workers give it a personal name and sex and send it get-well cards when it's being serviced."

GETTING PAID

Expensive Lecture

P.T. Barnum recollected an argument he had with one of his employees:

One of the ushers in my Museum once told me he intended to whip a man who was in the lecture room as soon as he came out.

"What for?" I inquired.

"Because he said I was no gentleman," replied the usher.

"Never mind," I replied, "he pays for that, and you will not convince him you are a gentleman by whipping him. I cannot afford to lose a customer. If you whip him, he will never visit the Museum again, and he will induce friends to go with him to other places of amusement instead of this, and thus, you see, I should be a serious loser."

"But he insulted me," muttered the usher.

"Exactly," I replied, "and if he owned the Museum, and you had paid him for the privilege of visiting it, and he had then insulted you, there might be some reason in your resenting it, but in this instance he is the man who pays, while we receive, and you must, therefore, put up with his bad manners."

The usher went along with Barnum's sermon and promptly asked him for a raise, if he was expected to be abused in order to promote his employer's interest.

The Wrong Argument

Henry Rosenfeld, who worked in New York's garment district, used to tell a story about a faithful cutter who, having labored in the same place for twenty-five years, finally asked for a raise.

"Sam, business is bad right now. I can't afford it," the boss said.

"But I'm doing the work of three people," Sam replied truthfully.

The boss exploded: "Three men's work! Tell me their names, and I'll fire them!"

The Right Way

Mark Woods, president of the American Broadcasting Company in the 1940s, was working in his office when an employee managed to slip by his secretary.

"I just had to see you, Mr. Woods," he said with a desperate look in his eyes. "I've asked my immediate supervisor for a raise, and he said I couldn't have one. But I really ought to get more money."

"Why?" asked the bewildered chief executive.

"Well, for one thing, there are three companies that want me."

"What three companies?"

"The light company, the gas company and the phone company," said the man.

Woods gave him a raise—for his sense of humor.

Fees

W. A. Richardson employed Abraham Lincoln to execute a lease on a house in Quincy, Illinois. The lease arrived in the mail, without a mention of payment. Richardson sent back $25, which he thought a fair price for the legal services rendered. After a few days he received a reply:

February 21, 1856: I have just received yours of the 16th inst., with a check on Flagg and Savage for twenty-five dollars. You must think I am a high-priced man. You are too liberal with your money. Fifteen dollars is enough for the job. I send you a receipt for fifteen dollars and return you a ten-dollar bill. Yours truly, A. Lincoln.

Abraham Lincoln was once cross-examining a famous surgeon who had given expert testimony for the other side. The doctor had made some highly exaggerated statements, and now Lincoln got on his feet and asked him very slowly, carefully weighing each word: "Doctor, how much money are you to receive for testifying in this case?"

The witness hesitated and asked the judge whether he should answer. The judge ruled the question proper. The witness then named a fee so large that there were audible gasps in court. Lincoln stretched himself to his full height, and his voice rose to a high pitch with indignation: "Gentlemen of the jury, big fee, big swear!"

Then he sat down. And won the case.

Hide the Bushel Too

Stanley Diller was an economics professor, enjoying high prestige and low salary until he decided to go into private industry at the age of 40. He started the bond research department at Goldman, Sachs, and later he moved over to Bear, Stearns and Company, where his earnings and bonuses skyrocketed to more than half a million dollars. Aware of the suspicions with which professors are sometimes regarded in the real world, Diller has taken off the Ph.D. from his business card and asks his colleagues never to call him "doctor."

"It could cut my salary at least by 75 percent," he says only half in jest.

Expense Account

When Gene Fowler was a journalist working for the Hearst papers in the early 1920s, he covered the discovery of three missing U.S. Navy balloonists in a remote part of northern Canada. While most of the press corps were content to wait for the lost heroes to turn up in Toronto, Fowler and some enterprising colleagues rented a private railroad car, filled it with every variety of booze and edible delicacy, and set out for Moose Factory, the picturesque name for the northern outpost. When he got back from his junket to the offices of the *New York American,* the now sober reporter found himself having to itemize and justify $1,200 worth of expenses. Fowler listed all the provisions he imagined that a northern expedition could involve: parkas, snowshoes, dogsled, and a team of huskies.

The paper's finance department returned the expense account as inadequate. At this point, Fowler attached an elaborate and moving story about his rented pack of dogs, and how the head dog unfortunately died as a result of a mishap, how he compensated the owner and spent another $20 for a commemorative headstone to mark the spot where the faithful dog fell. The accounting office promptly returned this too, with the unfeeling comment that the items failed to add up by a buck or so. Whereupon the exasperated Fowler scribbled at the bottom of the list: "Flowers for the bereft bitch—$1.50."

Expensive Account

When Louis Sobol was starting on his career as a reporter he was given the assignment to cover the last few days of railroad magnate W. H. Harriman. Members of the press took up quarters in an exclusive hotel in nearby Tuxedo, New York, and waited. Finally, the millionaire died, and it was time for Sobol to turn in his story and his expense account. His managing editor studied the latter for a long time before responding, "If this is Mr. Harriman's will you're showing me, it's worth a story on its own."

CLASS STRUGGLE

Knights of Labor

The brutal methods of industrialization and the naked cynicism of capitalism inspired the forces of socialism and utopianism to organize workers in the second half of the nineteenth century. Some of the early organizers used medieval guilds and secret societies as models: the Molly McGuires were born of the violence of the Irish famine; the Noble Order of the Knights of Labor was founded by a Philadelphia garment-cutter, Uriah K. Stephens, and six of his colleagues. Stephens, a Mason, was especially attracted to secret rites, and he insisted on keeping the Knights of Labor so secret that its name could not even be mentioned to outsiders. This caused a problem with announcing meetings, some of which were held in the forest, others in rented meeting halls. Announcements in the press referred to the organization simply by five asterisks (*****). When the initiated saw the mark appear on a sign or the door of some auditorium, hordes of them would show up. The problem was that the curious would also flock there, which destroyed the point of secrecy. In the 1880s, when unemployment was general, the leadership of the Knights of Labor urged workers to smash beer and milk bottles in order to increase employment in the glass industry.

In 1885, the Knights of Labor organized its first successful strike when railroad tycoon Jay Gould announced a 10 percent cut in wages and 5,000 shopmen struck his lines. Gould backed down but retaliated a few months later by firing many union members. The Knights of Labor answered with a boycott of all rolling stock owned by Gould. Labor victory was complete and especially sweet, given the opponent. It was Jay Gould, the archetypal Wall Street capitalist, who had once boasted: "I can hire one half of the working class to kill the other half."

No Cigar

Samuel Gompers, founder of the Federation of Trades and Labor Unions in 1882 (which later became the American Federation of Labor), started work at the age of 10. Born into a poor family in mid-nineteenth-century London, he was indentured to a cigar maker at one shilling a week. His father also belonged to The Cigarmakers' Society, which had an emigration fund to enable its underemployed members to make the passage to America. The Gompers family made the journey during the Civil War. As Samuel later recorded:

> For the first year and a half after we came to New York I worked with my father at home. Father paid a deposit for materials and worked at his bench at home instead of in a shop. At that time home work was not exploited as it was later under the tenement-house system. When I determined to find work outside, I had the self-confidence that goes with mastery of a trade. In hunting for a job, I chanced to fall in with another cigar maker much older than I. Together we went from shop to shop until we found work. With a bit of nervousness but with sure, quick skill I made my first two cigars, which the boss accepted, and I became a permanent workman in the shop.
>
> My first job as a journeyman was at Mr. Stachelberg's on Pearl Street. I was then between sixteen and seventeen. There was much unrest in the shop. The men were discontented. They asked me to present to the

employer their grievances and the new conditions they wanted. When I did so, Mr. Stachelberg told me that I, a mere boy, ought to be ashamed of representing men old enough to be my father and that I ought to be at home where my mother could "dry me out behind the ear." I told him that the men were entitled to have whomever they chose. When Stachelberg found that I couldn't be intimidated, he tried to bribe me. He sought me out in conversation, offered to treat me to beer, and to do everything to alienate me from the men. However, I stuck by them men and finally succeeded in winning the case.

Don't Touch the Grass

The panic of 1893 produced vast unemployment and even starvation in many parts of the United States, and the first march by protesters on Washington. Jacob Selcher Coxey, a horse breeder and owner of a stone quarry in Massillon, Ohio, issued a proclamation that it was the duty of government to relieve social distress, and that he intended to use force, if necessary, to make it act for the poor, by organizing the unemployed into peaceable armies that would march on the Capitol and beg along the way for food. The newspapers and politicians treated the whole thing as a joke, but the idea found receptive ears throughout the country. "On to Washington!" was the general battle cry, and by the spring of 1894, armies of "Coxeyites," altogether some 20,000 strong, were on a march from a dozen different states from as far away as California and Oklahoma. Hordes of tramps marched through the cities, carrying banners and singing hymns. They begged food from farmers, occasionally stole a train or were helped to transportation by authorities anxious for the ragged hoboes to pass through their territories. As the movement grew, there was also growing hostility. A preacher in Hoboken, New Jersey, delivered a sermon, the Christian gist of which was: "All we owe a tramp is a funeral." The New York *Herald* editorialized about the way to get one in a hurry: "The best meal for a regular tramp is one of lead, and enough of that to satisfy the most craving appetite."

Many of the marchers, discouraged by growing trouble with the police and lack of food, deserted and hiked back home. Less than 1,000 arrived in Washington, where the final indignity awaited Coxey. It was the first of May, and as the "General" was about to address his ragtag army, he and his closest adjutants crossed the lawn toward the Capitol steps. They were immediately arrested, tried, and briefly jailed for violation of a statute that forbade the bringing "into notice any party or organization or movement on the Capitol grounds," and also for trampling on the grass. It was an ignominious end to the first national crusade by the poor.

And Each Actor Came upon His Ass

In the days before the Actors' Equity Association, formed in 1913, performers were exploited by managers. There were no standard contracts, so the actor rarely knew what he or she was getting into. Rehearsal periods were unpaid, and they could last between six and eighteen weeks. John Goldsworthy had a two-year contract with the Shubert brothers in New York: he spent fifty-seven weeks rehearsing for various shows that only played for a total of twenty-two weeks. Another New York actor spent twenty-two weeks rehearsing but only played four nights in three productions, all of which closed after one or two performances. He was paid only for the time played.

The formation of Actors' Equity was greeted with indifference by the public and derision by management. The *New York Review*, a newspaper generally representing the Shubert family's interests, commented on July 12:

> An actors' union or any sort of cooperative protective organization having actors exclusively for members, is doomed to failure because the foundation upon which any such sort of League must stand to be successful is absolute equality. It is quite absurd to suppose that any actor would admit that any other actor is his equal. In no other profession of art do egotism and jealousy show themselves more luridly.
>
> Every actor considers himself the nonpareil of his own line and wants a larger salary than any other competitor. Therefore to regulate pay and form of contract would be an impossibility, because on these questions no set of actors will stand together. The minute one of them found a backer and had a chance to go starring, the adopted form of contract would be consigned to limbo. Where there is jealousy, envy, vanity, and the refusal to admit that one's fellow is one's equal there can be no union or joint action.

The first series of actors' strikes against managers were staged six years later, when the union had about 2,000 members. There were large throngs on Broadway seeking refunds, while some of the prettiest actresses demonstrated for Equity in Wall Street, where the managers got backing for their entertainment. Although some well-known actor-managers, such as E. H. Sothern, resigned from Equity when the strike was called, others showed solidarity. James O'Neill, the playwright's father, wired his support from his tour, while Lionel and John Barrymore reaffirmed their refusal to "go into any production unless every principal part in it is filled by a member of the Association." The actors also got support from the fledgling motion picture industry, and from a less expected source—almost to a man the drivers of New York's taxicabs were with Equity. Many of them had stickers pasted on their windshield demanding "Equity for Actors," and, as reported in the *New York American*, Sidney Jarvis, one of the striking actors, hailed the cabdriver who had been hired to convey a couple of acrobats from the Winter Garden to the Century Roof.

"Do you know," Jarvis demanded, "that you're helping a couple of scabs there to break the actors' strike?"

"What? Get the hell out of my cab," the driver shouted, and his passengers in their spangled tights had to make their way on foot.

Bluff

In 1913, when New York performers tried to organize the Actor's Equity Association, they found a formidable opponent in George M. Cohan, the greatest star and producer on Broadway. The original Yankee Doodle Dandy threatened to shut out the union from his productions, and, to make his opposition perfectly clear, he purchased in the New York papers large ads with the following notice: "I'd sooner lose every dollar I have and make my living as an elevator operator than do business with Actor's Equity."

The union took his bluff seriously because the next day they hung out a sign: "Wanted—elevator operator. George M. Cohan preferred."

Violence

There have been few employers who have hated unions with greater passion or fought them more eloquently than General Harrison Gray Otis, publisher of the *Los Angeles Times* at the turn of the century. He was chiefly responsible for making Los Angeles—in direct contrast with the highly unionized San Francisco—an open-shop town. Otis remained a military man even in peacetime, built himself a residence called "The Bivouack," and made the *Times* building into a medieval fortress. In 1890 he broke a printer's strike against his paper and soon organized a Merchants' and Manufacturers' Association, primarily to organize employers against labor unions. While professing to be against the closed shop, the General made it virtually impossible for any manufacturer or contractor to hire union labor in Los Angeles.

Otis was disliked even by some of his business friends; he was universally hated by his enemies. One of his newspaper rivals called him a "surly old swill dispenser," while Hiram Johnson, a liberal politician, described him as "depraved, corrupt, crooked, putrescent." People frequently thought aloud: "It's a wonder somebody doesn't blow him up!"

On the first of October 1910, at one o'clock in the morning, the *Times* building was dynamited. Out of a 100 people working in the building, 20 were killed, and another 60 injured. Although the plant was entirely wrecked, and the General himself away in Mexico making a real estate deal, the paper came out the next morning with only a slight delay. It carried the headline: "UNIONIST BOMBS WRECK THE TIMES," and it was printed at a backup plant only two blocks away, where Otis had set up auxiliary equipment, expecting just such an emergency. On his return he wrote an editorial in his most unrepentant style:

> O you anarchic scum, you cowardly murderers, you leeches upon honest labor, you midnight assassins, you whose hands are dripping with the innocent blood of your victims, you against whom the wails of poor widows and the cries of fatherless children are ascending to the Great White Throne, go mingle with the crowd on the street corners, look upon the crumbled and blackened walls, look at the ruins wherein are buried the calcined remains of those whom you murdered . . .

Nonviolence

As a labor lawyer, Mahatma Gandhi involved himself in disputes between bosses and employees, during which he developed some of his unusual techniques of bargaining that proved so successful in securing India's independence from the British. Before he would begin arbitration, Gandhi insisted that workers renounce violence, including against scabs. He made them promise that they would never beg for alms: if necessary, they should take other jobs. Finally, they had to pledge that they would remain firm, no matter how long their strike lasted. During a three-week strike against millowners in Ahmedabad, the laborers were losing heart, and in order to strengthen their resolve, Gandhi came up with his most famous negotiating technique. He captured the moment in *The Story of My Experiments with Truth*, originally published in 1929:

> One morning—it was at a mill hands' meeting—while I was still groping and unable to see my way clearly, the light came to me. Unbidden and all by themselves the words came to my lips: "Unless the strikers rally," I declared to the meeting, "and continue the strike till a settlement is reached, or till they leave the mills altogether, I will not touch any food."
>
> The labourers were thunderstruck. Tears began to course down Anasuyabai's cheek. The labourers broke out, "Not you but we shall fast. It would be monstrous if you were to fast. Please forgive us for our lapse, we will now remain faithful to our pledge to the end."

"There is no need for you to fast," I replied. "It would be enough if you could remain true to your pledge. As you know we are without funds, and we do not want to continue our strike by living on public charity. You should therefore try to eke out a bare existence by some kind of labour, so that you may be able to remain unconcerned, no matter how long the strike may continue. As for my fast, it will be broken only after the strike is settled."

[Gandhi's gesture caused him other problems of conscience. His religious convictions could not allow his fasting to be taken as an aggressive act against the owners of the mill. He believed that they must arrive at their decision without coercion:]

I tried to set the mill owners at ease. "There is not the slightest necessity for you to withdraw from your position," I said to them. But they received my words coldly and even flung keen, delicate bits of sarcasm at me, as indeed they had a perfect right to do. The principal man at the back of the mill owners' unbending attitude toward the strike was Sheth Ambalal. His resolute will and transparent sincerity were wonderful and captured my heart. It was a pleasure to be pitched against him. The strain produced by my fast upon the opposition, of which he was the head, cut me, therefore, to the quick. And then Sarladevi, his wife, was attached to me with the affection of blood sister, and I could not bear to see her anguish on account of my action.

Anasuyabai and a number of other friends and labourers shared the fast with me on the first day. But after some difficulty I was able to dissuade them from continuing it further.

The net result of it was that an atmosphere of good will was created all round. The hearts of the millowners were touched, and they set about discovering some means for a settlement. Anasuyabai's house became the venue of their discussions. Sjt. Anandshankar Dhruva intervened and was in the end appointed arbitrator, and the strike was called off after I had fasted only for three days. The mill owners commemorated the event by distributing sweets among the labourers, and thus a settlement was reached after twenty-one days' strike.

At the meeting held to celebrate the settlement, both the mill owners and the Commissioner were present. The advice which the latter gave to the mill hands on this occasion was: "You should always act as Mr. Gandhi advises you."

Takeover

In the bruising battle for the takeover of Transworld Airlines (TWA), financier Carl Icahn was accused of everything from greed to heartlessness. Icahn prepared his strategy by winning concessions from the pilots' union. He praised them for their professionalism and heroism, especially during the Beirut hijacking in 1985. And just when everybody around the table began to feel a comfortable glow about their future boss, Icahn is reported to have come to the point: "The only problem is you get paid too much money."

According to Moira Johnston's book, *Takeover*, when the president of TWA, C. E. Meyer, flung in Icahn's face that he was simply out to make a buck, the financier calmly replied: "If we are psychoanalyzing each other, why don't you admit what you really care about is your job, and you're afraid I'm going to take it away from you."

The financier's persuasion did not work with all the unions. The Independent Federation of Flight Attendants felt that its largely female membership had been singled out for discrimination, and it struck the airline. At the height of the dispute, in the spring of 1986, Mr. Icahn was about to board a flight on his new airline, when the following message appeared on the crew's computer terminal: "Passenger needs assistance. Has no heart."

If You Can't Lick Them

A few years back, when the Chrysler Corporation put Lane Kirkland, president of the United Auto Workers Union, on its board of directors, it was considered an almost desperate solution to wringing further wage concessions from the workers. However, the roof did not cave in on the capitalist system, and Chrysler's comeback is one of the great success stories of the 1980s. Another recent example of such cooperation was provided by Trusthouse Forte, the British real estate giant, which bought three grand hotels in Paris. The unions, playing on the nationalist fervor that had kept the British and the French at or near each others' throats since the Norman conquest, now campaigned passionately against the foreign takeover. Chefs, bellboys, and waiters were parading outside their hotels. Rocco Forte, finding that the Hotel Plaza-Athenée was virtually run by by the unions and that management had all but relinquished its responsibilities, decided on a bold move: he offered the job of managing director to the union shop steward, who was also the chief concierge. As Walter Goldsmith and David Clutterbuck describe it in their book, *The Winning Streak*:

> The new managing director introduced a regime of remarkable employee participation, quite unlike anything found elsewhere in THF [Trusthouse Forte]. An employee consultative committee took over the handling of lateness, absenteeism and other disciplinary matters. An incentive scheme was worked out under which the employees shared with THF all profits

above 5 per cent of turnover. In return, the labor force was reduced by 20 percent. Profits rose dramatically to three and a half times the level on acquisition. The remaining employees saw their annual income double over a five-year period.

Even though the ex-shop steward had been virtually running the hotel before, the recognition of this fact worked wonders. For one thing, he did not have to fight management anymore.

Ford's Prayer

Henry Ford disliked unions and fought any attempt at organization that might challenge his paternalistic rule. "Labor union organizers are the worst pest that ever struck the earth," was one of his milder comments. His right-hand man, Harry Bennett, set up a private militia of over 3,000 to fight unionization. This force included ex-convicts, ex-policemen, and pugilists, whom he described as "a lot of tough bastards but every goddam one of them is a gentleman."

During the 1930s, before unionization of the auto industry, there were underground cells of militant workers. One of them put out a penny sheet, printed *samizdat*, called "The Ford Worker." One particular issue contained the following parody of the Lord's Prayer:

Our Father, who art in Dearborn, Henry be thine name.
Let payday come. Thy will be done in Fordson as it is in Highland Park.
Give us this day our six bucks (plus forty cents?)
And forgive us our laziness as we forgive thee for speeding us up.
Lead us not into intelligent thought or action
But deliver us from all Freedom, for thine is true slavery,
Thy power over us forever and ever. Amen.

Union Strikes for Wage Cut

The following actual news item reads like a parody of a management fantasy.

Local 32 of the International Association of Heat and Frost Insulators staged a one-day strike in Newark, New Jersey, because a contract offer included too much money: "We turned down the original offer," alleged James Grogan, business manager for the union, "because it would have just about priced us out of the market."

The walkout by the 400-member local ended when management gave in to the union's demand for substantially *less* in wages and fringe benefits. . .

And Man Bites Dog

When Jack H. Brown, president of Stater Brothers in San Bernardino, California, was suspended by the board of directors, members of the Teamsters and United Food and Commercial Workers staged noisy demonstrations to help their boss regain control of the company. The unions considered Jack Brown as one of their own, a chief executive who, starting at age 13, climbed up the ladder through every phase of a supermarket operation. When some supermarket chains were struck by the Teamsters in 1985, Brown refused to lock out the union. The power play against Brown at Stater Brothers was staged by Board Chairman Bernard Garrett, who had no background in the grocery business. Commenting on the unusual situation (*Fortune* magazine headlined the article: "Man Bites Dog"), Ron Heiman, the steward of the Teamsters remarked: "It's the first time in history we have picketed for management."

But the Union Marches On

Another dispatch from the labor front: the Oregon Court of Appeals recently awarded $950.30 in workers' compensation benefits to Peter F. McCabe, a harried union chief who suffered a stroke while having sex. His attorney argued that as chief executive officer of his union (which is not identified) the 35-year-old McCabe was exposed to a great deal of stress. Indeed, the stroke occurred immediately following a union meeting, when the victim paid a visit to a motel in Eugene, Oregon.

Hot Air

Walter Reuther, long-time president of the United Auto Workers, was flying to Washington, D.C., to lobby Congress for labor legislation. Flying over the Capitol, the DC-4 suddenly rose 500 feet, then bounced back and finally landed. Reuther asked the pilot what caused the sudden bump. "I should have known better," replied the pilot, "we have all been warned not to fly over the Capitol dome when Congress is in session, because of all the hot air and rush of political gas."

Reuther then turned to his traveling companion, who happened to be Martin Wagner of Gas, Coke and Chemical Workers Union of the CIO. "Martin, your union has jurisdiction over gas plants. It's time you organized Congress, which is the largest gas plant in America."

· 8 ·

MANAGERS AT WORK

PEOPLE

Ends and Means

Stephen Girard, who made his fortune from trading all over the world in the early days of the United States, insisted that his employees follow his precise instructions to the letter. In turn, he would take full responsibility for the consequences, even if he was proven wrong. One of his best captains sailed back to Philadelphia, having purchased his cargo of tea at an unauthorized port, and was summoned by the boss.

"Captain," Mr. Girard said sternly, "you were instructed to purchase your cargo at———"

"That's true, Mr. Girard," the captain replied, "but upon reaching the port, I found I could do so much better, that I felt justified to proceed—"

"You should have obeyed your orders, sir," was the retort.

"I was influenced by a desire to serve your interests, sir. The result ought to justify me, since it puts many thousands more in your pocket than if I had bought where I was instructed."

"Captain, I take care of my own interests," the merchant said. "You should have obeyed your orders even if you had broken me. Nothing can excuse your disobedience. You will hand in your accounts, sir, and consider yourself discharged from my service."

Girard was as good as his word, and though the captain's disobedience had vastly increased his profits, he never received him into his service again.

Expensive Lesson

In his early career as a tea merchant, John Jacob Astor allowed his pettiness over five hundred dollars to cause him a loss of seventy thousand. An insurance company had informed the captain of one of his ships that he had to have a chronometer on board. The captain came and spoke to Mr. Astor on the subject, who advised him to buy one.

"But I have no five hundred dollars to spare for such a purpose," said the captain, "and the chronometer should belong to the ship."

"Well," said the merchant, "you need not pay for it now, pay when you can." The sailor still objected, and after prolonged haggling, Astor finally authorized him to buy the chronometer and charge it to the ship's account.

It was done. The day of departure was at hand. The ship was hauled into the stream. The captain, according to custom, handed in his account. Astor, subjecting it to his usual close scrutiny, objected to the item of five hundred dollars for the chronometer. He alleged that there had been an understanding between them that the captain would finally pay for the instrument. The sailor recalled the entire conversation and firmly held to his position. Astor, too, insisted on his own recollection. The captain became so profoundly disgusted that, important as the command of the ship was to him, he resigned his commission. Astor found another captain and the ship sailed for China.

Another house, which was engaged in the China trade, knowing the worth of this "king of captains," as Astor himself used to call him, bought him a ship and dispatched him to Canton two months after the departure of Astor's vessel. The captain, put upon his mettle, employed all his skill, and had such success that he returned to New York with a full cargo of tea just seven days after the arrival of his former vessel. Astor, not expecting another ship for months, was confident of monopolizing the market and had not yet broken bulk, nor even taken off the hatchways. His former captain arrived on a Saturday. Advertisements and handbills were immediately issued, and on the Wednesday morning following, as the custom then was, the auction sale of the tea began on the wharf—two barrels of punch contributing to the atmosphere of the occasion. The cargo was sold to good advantage and the market was glutted, so that Astor lost the entire profits of the voyage. Meeting the captain some time later on Broadway, the merchant admitted: "I had better have paid for that chronometer of yours."

Perfection

John H. Patterson, despite his many innovations for the welfare of his employees, ruled National Cash Register with an iron fist. He particularly hated yes-men executives and complacent employees. One incident recounted in Isaac Marcosson's book about the company, *Whenever Men Trade*, describes how Patterson called his secretary into his office. When J. H. Barringer came in, Patterson asked him to join him at the window:

"Do you see that dog in the snow?"

"No," the secretary replied truthfully.

"Are you sure you don't see a dog there?" Patterson insisted.

"I am sure," said Barringer.

This was Patterson's way of testing whether his secretary had the independence of mind to become an executive. Barringer passed, and later was made vice president.

On the other hand, Patterson fired people at the drop of a hat. He never wanted to hear that something could not be done: this alone could provide grounds for instant dismissal. One of his foremen once reported that everything within his department was functioning smoothly, with 100 percent efficiency.

"Then you are perfectly satisfied?" asked Patterson. The man replied in the affirmative.

"All right," said the boss, "you are fired." Although he wanted perfectionists, he thought that perfection itself would only breed complacency.

A Legend in His Own Mind

Although most corporations are in constant search of excellence, they may not want to find absolute perfection. Here is a story from the early days of the Dow Chemical Company. A man, eager to be hired, approached Herbert H. Dow, in conversation with the head of his electrical department, and asked about a job he had heard about. The man went on at great length about his qualifications, and stressed more than once that he had never, under any circumstances, made a mistake. Dow finally interrupted him: "We have three thousand people working here, and on the average, they make three thousand mistakes each and every day. I couldn't insult them by hiring somebody perfect."

Hands Off

Romance in the workplace is both commonplace and inevitable; most managers have to face the problems of productivity and disrupted relationships both in the office and back at home. The executive of a major electrical appliance firm recalled (in a *Wall Street Journal* article) being phoned by the wife of one of his top managers, a handsome and aggressive man. She said she knew that her husband was having an affair with one of the secretaries at the plant, whom she wanted the executive to fire. The wife claimed that this had happened at her husband's previous workplace, where she had succeeded in getting the secretary fired. The executive knew that the wife's claims were not unfounded. On the other hand, he did not think that the relationship had affected either employee's performance and did not seem to disturb their colleagues. Rather than become involved in a domestic issue, he told the wife that if he had to fire anybody it would be her husband, who held a position of higher responsibility. She never called again.

The authors of the same *Journal* article recalled an old story told about Horace Lorimer, famed editor of the *Saturday Evening Post*. He had been running a serialized novel in the magazine, and one installment ended with a beautiful secretary having a romantic dinner with her boss. When the next episode opened with the two of them having breakfast together, many readers wrote in to express their moral outrage. In a subsequent issue, Lorimer issued an editorial disclaimer: "The *Saturday Evening Post* is not responsible for what its characters do between installments."

Welfare

In the 1880s, the early days of the National Cash Register Company (NCR), a shipment of defective registers was returned from England to the plant in Dayton, Ohio. Apart from the $50,000 tied up in the deal, the very reputation of the fledgling enterprise was at stake. John H. Patterson, the founder and owner of the company, faced the crisis head on. He moved his office to the factory floor to investigate what could have caused such a breach of quality control. The answer was not difficult to find. The factory floor was dark and dirty; the drinking water smelled foul; the workers felt unclean and were grumbling. Moving swiftly and decisively, Patterson had the place cleaned up and provided his men with individual lockers where they could keep a change of clothes. He also gave his workers free lemonade. In the longer term, he redesigned the factories so that 80 percent of the wall space was replaced with glass. In fact, several decades before the architects of the Bauhaus began propagating modern industrial design, NCR pioneered the so-called daylight factory. Morale improved, and after a time there were no defective returns.

One day in 1904 Patterson noticed a female employee trying to warm a cup of coffee on a radiator. When he realized that she would eat nothing else warm for the entire day, he instituted free hot meals first for female employees, then later for all workers. In the decades that followed, NCR installed showers and baths, dining rooms, recreational facilities, and health clinics; it instituted rest periods, movies during lunch hour, night classes, and organized vacations. It was the birth of the modern welfare corporation.

Caring

One of Patterson's pupils was Thomas Watson, who later developed at IBM extensive programs in education, health care, and recreation. Watson was not simply an executive who declared that his door was always open and then waited for people to come to him. He was continually visiting factories and spent hours talking with the workers, so that many of them considered him their friend rather than their boss. One day an employee flew in from Endicott to New York to see Watson. Doctors had just told him that a younger brother had an incurable disease and would not live long. The distressed employee thought maybe Watson could do something that was beyond the medical resources of a small community. Within hours, the patient was under the care of a famous specialist in a top hospital, thus relieving his brother's anxiety. The employee then tried to apologize for perhaps overstepping himself, but Watson interrupted him: "When I said bring your problems to me, I meant exactly that."

Duty

Alfred P. Sloan, Jr., disapproved of his executives calling each other by their first names. He held it against Mr. Wilson, president of General Motors under him, that he was on a first-name basis with his vice presidents. Peter Drucker quotes Sloan on his own management style:

> It is the duty of the Chief Executive Officer to be objective and impartial. He must be absolutely tolerant and pay no attention to how a man does his work, let alone whether he likes a man or not. The only criteria must be performance and character. And that is incompatible with friendships and social relations. A Chief Executive Officer who has "friendships" within the company, has "social relations" with colleagues or discusses anything with them except the job, cannot remain impartial—or at least, which is

equally damaging, he will not appear as such. Loneliness, distance and formality may be contrary to his temperament—they have always been contrary to mine—but they are his duty.

Summing Up

Chrysler Chairman Lee Iacocca once said: "If I had to sum up in one word what makes a good manager, I'd say decisiveness. You can use the fanciest computers to gather the numbers, but in the end you have to set a timetable and act. And I don't mean rashly. I'm sometimes described as a flamboyant leader and a hip-shooter, a fly-by-the-seat-of-the-pants operator. But if that were true, I could never have been successful in this business."

Some have claimed that Iacocca had been planning to become chairman of Chrysler from before his birth, and that his name is really just an acronym for "I Am Chairman Of Chrysler Corporation [of] America."

Metaphysics

Once a distinguished visitor to Henry Ford's auto plants met him after an exhaustive tour of the factory. The visitor was lost in wonder and admiration. "It seems almost impossible, Mr. Ford," he told the industrialist, "that a man, starting 25 years ago with practically nothing, could accomplish all this."

"You say that I started with practically nothing," Ford replied, "but that's hardly correct. Every man starts with all there is. Everything is here—the essence and substance of all there is."

METHODS

Color Coding

Robert Owen, sometimes described as the father of personnel management, sometimes as one of the many parents of socialism, faced up to the many problems of manufacturing and business relations caused by the early upheavals of the Industrial Revolution. In his textile factories in Scotland, Owen introduced several new techniques of dealing with employee problems. As he recounts in his autobiography, published in 1857, this is how he stopped pilferage:

In one department in which theft had been carried on to a ruinous extent, and in which a hundred thousand of the kind of objects pilfered passed daily through four different sets of hands, I devised a plan by which, without counting, should one be taken, the loss would be at once discovered, and in whose department it occurred. I had also a daily return presented to me every morning of the preceding day's operations, and frequent balances in every department.

But that which I found to be the most efficient check upon inferior conduct was the contrivance of a silent monitor for each one employed in the establishment. This consisted of a four-sided piece of wood, about two inches long and one broad, each side coloured—one side black, another blue, a third yellow, and a fourth white, tapered at the top, and finished with wire eyes, to hang upon a hook with either side to the front. One of these was suspended in a conspicuous place near to each of the persons employed, and the color at the front told the conduct of the individual during the preceding day, to four degrees of comparison. Bad, denoted by black, and No. 4—indifferent by blue, and No. 3—good by yellow, and No. 2,—and excellent by white and No. 1.

Then books of character were provided, for each department, in which the name of each one employed in it was inserted in the front of succeeding columns, which sufficed to mark by the number the daily conduct, day by day, for two months; and these books were changed six times a year, and were preserved; by which arrangement I had the conduct of each registered to four degrees of comparison during every day of the week, Sundays excepted, for every year they remained in my employment. The superintendent of each department had the placing daily of these silent monitors, and the master of the mill regulated those of the superintendents in each mill. If anyone thought that the superintendent did not do justice, he or she had a right to complain to me, or, in my absence, to the master of the mill, before the number denoting the character was entered in the register. But such complaints very rarely occurred. The act of setting down the number in the book of character, never to be blotted out, might be likened to the supposed recording angel marking the good and bad deeds of poor human nature. . . This simple device and silent monitor soon began to show its effects upon the character of the workers. At first a large proportion daily were black and blue, few yellow and scarcely any white. Gradually the black were changed for blue, the blues for yellow, and the yellows for white. And for many years the permanent daily conduct of a very large majority of those who were employed deserved and had No. 1 placed as their character on the books of the establishment. . . Never perhaps in the history of the human race has so simple a device created in so short a period so much order, virtue, goodness and happiness, out of so much ignorance, error and misery.

On Time

Samuel Smiles wrote in his nineteenth-century bestseller, *Self Help*:

Men of business are accustomed to quote the maxim that "Time is money"— but it is more; the proper improvement of it is self-culture, self-improvement, and growth of character. An hour wasted daily on trifles or in indolence, would, if devoted to self-improvement, make an ignorant man wise in a few years, and employed in good works, would make his life fruitful, and death a harvest of worthy deeds. Fifteen minutes a day devoted to self-improvement will be felt at the end of the year. An economical use of time is the true mode of securing leisure: it enables us to get through business and carry it forward, instead of being driven by it. On the other hand, the miscalculation of time involves us in perpetual hurry, confusion and difficulties; and life becomes a mere shuffle of expedients, usually followed by disaster. Nelson once said, "I owe all my success in life to having been always a quarter of an hour before my time." And it was wittily said by Lord Chesterfield of the old Duke of Newcastle: "His Grace loses an hour in the morning and is looking for it all the rest of the day."

Timeliness

When George Washington's secretary excused himself for the lateness of his attendance and laid the blame upon his watch, his master quietly said: "Then you must find another watch, or I another secretary."

Time-Saver

Henry Ford discovered a good way of saving time. Rather than summoning one of his managers to see him when he had a problem to discuss, Ford himself would make the visit to that executive's office. Ford said that he developed this method when he discovered how much easier it was for him to "leave the other fellow's office than I can get him to leave mine."

The Eyes Have It

Most sales or management training presentations today are given with visual aids: overhead projectors, slides, and colorful graphs and pie charts. One of the first people to realize the power of such displays was the founder of National Cash Register (NCR), John H. Patterson. In the early days of trying to sell his product he found out what most teachers know: that the eye is much mightier than the ear. Following up his observation with solid research, Patterson came up with the fact that the optic nerve is twenty-two times stronger than the one controlling hearing. So in his sales presentations he instituted black boards, charts, and the pedestal, which was simply a large easel to hold charts.

Patterson's visual sense proved useful to him when he opened NCR's first showroom in Paris. His manager Jules Vuillaume attracted a large number of prospective purchasers (P.P.'s, as Patterson used to call them) all waiting to see a demonstration of the amazing new American cash register. There was only one small problem: Patterson did not speak a word of French. But he forged ahead, using charts and drawings, as he did in training his salesmen back in Dayton, Ohio, and the language barrier collapsed.

After a while, Patterson came to rely so much on his pedestal, charts, and pyramids that he could not be articulate without them, even in English. He had pedestals installed in all NCR offices, factories, and showrooms. There was even a pedestal in his bedroom just in case he woke up with an idea in the middle of the night.

The Soul of Wit

When Peters and Waterman were conducting their interviews at 3M, they were astonished that proposals for a new product rarely exceeded five pages. When asked about it, a vice president said: "We consider a coherent sentence to be an acceptable first draft for a new-product plan."

Another Wack

In discussing managers who want to get down to brass tacks, Roger von Oech likes to quote Karl Albrecht's saying that these people "never give themselves the opportunity to consider steel tacks, copper tacks, plastic tacks, sailing tacks, income tax, syntax or contacts." Van Oech, consultant to many of the most innovative companies in Silicon Valley, is fond of a definition he once heard of the four parts that make up a computer: "There is hardware, software, firmware and liveware."

Hire Talent

Andrew Carnegie attributed his success to others whom he had the good sense to hire. He composed the following epitaph for himself: "Here lies one who knew how to get around him men who were cleverer than himself."

Robert Townsend, in his "Guerrilla Guide" at the back of his bestseller, *Up the Organization,* advises executives to hire the best people available. He says that whenever he hired anybody he'd ask himself: "How would I like to work for him—or her—some day?" He also quotes Leo Rosten: "First-rate people hire first-rate people; second-rate people hire third-rate people."

Early to Rise

P. D. Armour, owner of the Chicago meat-packing concern, hired an office clerk without telling him what time to report to work. The new employee turned up Monday morning at eight o'clock to find the boss and his entire staff already deep into their daily tasks. The next day the young man came at seven o'clock, only to receive a glowering stare from Armour. The third day the clerk arrived at 6:30 A.M. His boss looked up from his pile of papers: "Young man, just what is it that you do with your forenoons?"

Do It Now

During the first decade of this century, long before there were any efficiency experts, somebody came up with the idea of hanging up in the office signs that simply said: "DO IT NOW!" The head of a large business firm bought a great number of these supposed cures against procrastination and had them hung up in front of all his numerous employees. After a few days, he was startled by the results. The cashier had skipped out with $20,000, the head bookkeeper had eloped with the best secretary, three clerks had asked for a raise, and the junior office boy had gone out West to become a highwayman.

Dead Files

Samuel Goldwyn's secretary was trying to make room in her filing cabinets and asked her boss for permission to destroy files that had been inactive for more than ten years.

"Go ahead," said the movie mogul, "but make sure you keep copies."

How to Get Good Reports

Sam Cherr, one of the three founders of Young & Rubicam, the advertising agency, had a simple way of getting the best work out of the people he managed. All marketing plans had to be put into writing, and some of these detailed reports often ran to 200 pages. Stanley Arnold recalls bringing such a report to Cherr, who said nothing for a few days, until its author could stand it no longer and asked what he thought of it. Cherr simply asked: "Is that the best you can do?"

Well, of course, everything always can be improved, the report had been done under deadline pressure, and Stanley readily conceded that he could probably do better. He took back the plan, rewrote the 200 pages, and resubmitted it. Again, there was no reaction, until the writer dropped by to ask: "How did you like my marketing report, Mr. Cherr?" And Mr. Cherr asked again the same question: "Is that the best you can do?"

Arnold now had several days in the interval to think about the report's shortcomings, so he conceded again that he could do better. Spending the entire weekend to rewrite it, the tired executive brought back a wholly rewritten report on Monday morning. By Wednesday, he could hardly stand it and simply had to know whether Sam Cherr had liked the report. And Cherr asked the third time: "Is that the best you can do?"

And when the author finally replied, with some degree of truthfulness: "Yes, Mr. Cherr, that's the best I can do," Sam Cherr replied: "In that case, I'll read it."

Private Line

In 1981 Jack Welch became the youngest chief executive officer in the history of General Electric (GE), at the age of 45. Welch acquired his highly successful reputation as a GE group manager. He installed a private line in his office for the sole use of his purchasing agents, who would report to him the moment they negotiated a deal. Welch always interrupted whatever meeting he was having to take the call and would congratulate the agent in a loud voice for knocking another nickel or dime off the price of one of GE's products. He then followed up with a hand-written note of appreciation.

Consultants

An expert has been defined as a man (or woman) at least fifty miles from home. The classic definition of a consultant is a man (or woman) who borrows your watch and charges you for telling you the time.

"We're somewhat like eunuchs," a management consultant once confessed, "we can tell other people what to do, but we can't do it for ourselves."

As the head of one consulting firm said, looking through the brochure of a rival: "It reminds one of a lost government looking for a country."

The first consultant, according to Hal Higdon's book *The Business Healers*, is identified as Han Fei Tzu, imperial advisor and founder of the legalist school of Chinese philosophy. In the West, the much-maligned Machiavelli has been generally regarded as the first hired gun (or poisoner) in management. The invasion of American business by efficiency experts began in the late nineteenth century, and the giant Booz, Allen & Hamilton management consulting firm in Chicago was founded in 1914.

While studying at Northwestern University, Edwin G. Booz was deeply influenced by Professor Walter Dill Scott of the psychology department there, who had conducted one of the earliest marketing surveys and believed that it was more important to hire the right person for a job than to time him or her at work. When Booz later began his Business Engineering Service, he asked the State Bank of Evanston for a loan to help set up his office.

"What is it you are selling?" the banker asked. Booz explained his theory that most problems in business were people problems. The bank not only loaned him the money, but hired him to study problems at the bank. It was his first consulting job.

Shooting the Messenger

Frederick W. Taylor, one of the famous time-study experts, was fired by Bethlehem Steel, for being too critical of company practices. Edwin Booz was known for his bluntness, something that most management consultants learn to avoid. When Sewell Avery hired Booz to rescue Montgomery Ward during the Great Depression, the consultant moved into an office at the mail-order company.

One day Avery asked Booz point blank, "Ed, what's the main problem at Montgomery Ward?"

"You," Booz replied with equal directness. Apocrypha has it that this exchange terminated their relationship.

After Edwin Booz's death, his company kept up the tradition, in a more devious manner. The president of a company in Wisconsin was close to retirement and wanted to make an impartial decision about his successor. He secretly hired Booz-Allen to evaluate the five vice presidents in his company. The consultants came and discreetly completed their job, but, before the president could implement their recommendation, he died. The board of directors, unaware of the report, appointed a new president. The new president found the report in one of the old president's drawers, and saw that he was not the consultants' choice. He is reported to have buzzed his secretary: "Please, Mrs. Jones, have somebody go through the factory and the offices, and if there are any Booz-Allen men around, tell them they are fired."

Machiavelli 101

Laurence Shames, author of *What They Don't Teach You About at Harvard Business School*, remembers something they did teach there. During the 1940s, when Harvard's Business School began moving into national prominence, the course to take was something called Administrative Practices, known as "AdPrac." The catalogue described AdPrac's aims in such innocuous and worthy terms as teaching the future manager how "to obtain action by working through people . . . maintaining harmony between the individuals and groups of which [an] organization is composed . . . [and by utilizing] the capacities of the individuals concerned to the greatest advantage." The students, who knew better, dubbed the course "Machiavelli for Beginners." Future conglomerateur Harry Figgie, Jr. summed up the lesson he learned in that class as "how to saw the rungs out of someone's ladder without his even knowing it."

Mary Cunningham felt that AdPrac did not go far enough. When she became victim of well-publicized infighting at Bendix Corporation she felt unprepared, as she wrote in her book *Powerplay*: "I wasn't very savvy when I first went to work for Bendix. Oh, I was intelligent, and like most of my classmates at the [Harvard] Business School, ambitious, but I lacked any real know-how about how the corporate world operates. What I knew about the world and people I'd learned from reading Plato and Thomas Aquinas. A crash course in Machiavelli might have been more relevant."

Life Class

Realtor Frank Morrow confesses that he learned to become an entrepreneur despite attending Stanford University's Graduate School of Business. He took all the required classes in finance, accounting, and marketing, but he claims to have learned the most about business from a drawing course in the art department. Artist Nathan Olivera taught that all art is a series of discoveries from the first line. The hardest thing to do is to put down the first line, but the artist has no choice. "The same is true of business," says Morrow. "A lot of business school types analyze things to death and never get around to acting. Perhaps more them should take drawing courses."

And If You Can't Draw

A manager once asked Peter Drucker, the management guru, what skills he should master in order to become a better manager.

"Take up the violin," Drucker advised.

ULCERS

It Is More Blessed to Give

Sam Bronfman had a legendary temper. "The salvos of curses," writes his biographer Peter Newman, "were directed with the care of an artillery officer observing the detonations from his battery of guns. He could adjust the range and impact of his outbursts so that if calling someone a son of a bitch didn't produce the desired effect, he would move on to tagging him 'a son of a son of a bitch,' and escalate from there."

If name hurling did not work, Bronfman would also resort, literally, to stick and stones. His quaking executives sometimes had to duck objects that the boss would throw at them. Once, he hurled a paperweight at a vice president, which was stopped only by the window divider from crashing through to the Manhattan pavement below. A commemorative plaque was made of this incident, and Seagram executives would nervously point to it whenever Sam Bronfman began to work himself up.

These outbursts left Bronfman himself relatively undisturbed. Once, when his nephew Gerald warned that he'd get ulcers if he did not mind his temper, Sam came back with the famous reply: "Listen. I don't get ulcers. I give them."

The Forest from the Trees

Once one of Seagram's auditors recently was back from Caracas, where he was checking the expenses of a subsidiary company, when he ran into his boss at the Montreal head office.

"How's business in Venezuela?" asked Sam Bronfman.

"I don't know, Mr. Sam. I was there to look at the books."

This reply stuck with Bronfman. For years afterward he would recount the exchange as an astonishing example of the man's stupidity: "Imagine," he would tell any visitor or employee, "going all the way to Venezuela and never asking how business was!"

Drive

Andrew Carnegie inspired his subordinates with his own energy and restlessness. However astounding might be the results obtained by the Carnegie Works, the captain at the head was never satisfied. As each month's output surpassed that which had gone before, Carnegie always came back with the same cry of "More." "We broke all records for making steel last week!" a delighted superintendent once wired him, and immediately he received his answer: "Congratulations. Why not do it every week?"

Positive Reinforcement

Andrew Carnegie was showing a delegation through one of his plants when he stopped to talk to a gray-haired, stooped employee.

"Let's see, Wilson," he asked, "how many years exactly have you been working for me now?"

"Thirty-nine, sir," Wilson beamed. "And may I add that in all those thirty-nine years I made only one trifling mistake."

"Good work," grunted the steel magnate, "but from now on, please try to be more careful."

Paperwork

Thomas Edison worked as a so-called telegrapher in his early career, and this was one of his favorite stories of those pioneering days: "Some linemen were busy putting up telephone poles through a farmer's fields. The farmer presently appeared and ordered them off his land, whereupon they showed him a paper giving them the right to plant poles wherever they pleased. Not long afterward a big and vicious bull charged the linemen, while the old farmer sat on a nearby fence and yelled: 'Show him yer papers, darn ye, show him yer papers!' "

Crisis Management

Henry Kissinger, when secretary of state, is reported to have looked at his calendar and told an aide: "There cannot be a crisis next week. My schedule is already full."

Just Testing

John H. Patterson, founding chairman of National Cash Register (NCR), set up rigid standards for quality control. In the early days of the company, Patterson was showing visitors around the factory, when he came to a row of newly manufactured registers. They had all been just tested. One had been found defective, which a worker was supposed to have taken away for repair. As bad luck would have it, the boss picked the malfunctioning machine to demonstrate the principles of the cash register. After a few frustrated attempts to get it to work, Patterson turned to his guests and said: "Here is one that's defective. Let me show you what we, do here with registers that do not work properly." Patterson then picked up a hammer and, with the zeal of a Luddite, attacked the machine and smashed it to smithereens.

Bearing Gifts

Henry Ford liked to be generous with gifts. He would give cars, tractors, and real estate to his associates and employees, often telling them, "Now this is yours for life." But if he ever turned on that person, he usually took back his gift. He once told his right-hand man, Harry Bennett: "Never give anything without strings attached to it."

It was Bennett who after his boss's death wrote about a man named Ash, who worked for Henry Ford at the Rouge power plant. They went back several decades, working as fellow mechanics for Thomas Edison. Ash was completely devoted to his job and to Henry Ford. To reward him, Ford one day gave him a new car. Ash felt a tremendous sense of gratitude, and whenever he heard that Ford would be visiting the plant, he would run out to the parking lot and start polishing the gift. This act, however, had the reverse effect on the boss. Getting back one day from the plant, Ford said to Harry Bennett: "That fellow Ash hasn't done a lick of work since he got that car. You go and take it away from him."

Bennett did what he usually did in such circumstances—nothing. But after a few days Ash's car disappeared and was never found again.

Memos

Jed Harris, the famous Broadway producer of the 1930s, was greatly disliked. In fact, Laurence Olivier had such a bad experience with him that he modeled his version of Richard III on Harris, in both makeup and character. At one time when Dick Maney worked as a publicist for Harris, the latter decided that everything should be written down in a memo. Maney thought this a big waste of time, and to make his point, bombarded Harris with memos like:

TO: Mr. Harris
FROM: Mr. Maney
RE: What time is it?

or:

TO: Mr. Harris
FROM: Mr. Maney
RE: Whatever happened to Dorothy Arnold?

Meetings

Homer Livingston, president of the American Bankers Association in the 1950s, was giving a speech to a large gathering of bankers in Louisville, Kentucky, when the microphone went dead. Livingston, raising his voice, asked if the back row could hear.

"No," shouted a man. At this point, another man stood up in the front row, and shouted back: "Then I'll change places with you."

Stop the World

According to Norman Augustine, president of the Martin Marietta Corporation, some organizations have no other function but to have meetings. He notes Parkinson's Law that all meetings must always be a whole hour, regardless of the subject discussed. He thinks that probably the only way to reduce the duration of meetings would be to speed up the rotation of the Earth:

> If, for example, the Earth would rotate not in twenty-four but in eighteen hours, meetings would almost certainly be scheduled each day and a 33 percent increase in management productivity automaticaly realized, assuming the basic real workday remained unchanged. . . . If the Earth could be made to rotate twice as fast, managers would get twice as much done. If the Earth could be made to rotate twenty times as fast, everyone else would get twice as much done since all the managers would fly off.

Chairman of the Bored

As John Z. De Lorean climbed up the corporate ladder at General Motors, (GM) he had to attend more and more meetings with the top executives who worked, ate, and sometimes slept on the fourteenth floor of GM Headquarters in Detroit. Sometimes, during presentations, De Lorean was appalled to find that a considerable number of them would nod off: "Not loud, snoring sleep, mind you. Just quiet repose. They would sit in their chairs, arms folded, heads on their chest, quietly dozing. If it was a film presentation, and the lights were turned off, half the meeting could be asleep." In J. Patrick Wright's book about De Lorean, *On a Clear Day You Can See General Motors,* the maverick automaker relates what made him quit General Motors:

The most embarrassing, and probably the most ridiculous meeting I attended "upstairs" involved a presentation to the Industrial Relations Policy Group in the fall of 1972. A young guy from the labor relations staff was talking about an obscure personnel point which he proposed that we change. It was an insignificant matter by any corporate standard, having to do, as I remember, with adjusting a transferred employee's pay rate upward to correlate with the cost of living in his new locale. It simply meant that what may be a great salary in some place like Selma, Alabama, isn't worth much in New York City. If a guy gets transferred from Selma to New York, he should get more money to maintain his standard of living. So what were we doing in a big meeting of top brass listening to this presentation? I couldn't answer that question.

Looking around I counted up about $10 million worth of executive talent listening to and watching this presentation of cost-of-living graphs, color slides, industry analysis charts and company-by-company comparisons. The presentation finally ended. A couple of guys who were dozing in their seats blinked awake, and the room of executives looked toward the chairman for an indication of what we were going to do, as usually happened. The chairman in this case was Richard C. Gerstenberg, a fairly trim, hard-working finance man, who was born in Mohawk, New York, and presented a friendly, folksy, almost farm boy manner common among other GM executives. Gerstenberg's speech was often salty, but not offensive, and his delivery staccato and forceful. He snapped, "Goddamnit I don't like to be surprised."

We were all stunned because the point of the meeting was so insignificant anyway. "What is Gerstenberg so surprised about?" I thought.

"We can't make a decision on this now," he continued. "I think we ought to form a task force to look into this and come back with a report in 90 to 120 days. Then we can make a decision."

He then rattled off the names of the members of the task force he was appointing. There was an eerie silence after the chairman spoke. It lasted for what seemed like half a day. The whole room was bewildered but no one had the courage to say why.

Finally, Harold G. Warner, the snow-white-haired, kindly executive vice-president, who was soon to retire, broke the silence. "Dick, this presentation is the result of the task force that you appointed some time ago.

Most of the people you just appointed to the new task force are on the old one."

Everyone became a little nervous and somewhat embarrassed. Gerstenberg flushed in the face and then said something which I cannot remember. I guess we accepted the recommendation from the Industrial Relations Policy Group on the matter, but I remember saying to myself as the meeting ended: "What the hell am I doing here?"

John Z. De Lorean left General Motors soon afterwards to start his ill-fated sports-car manufacturing venture.

No Substitute

The CEO of a large and well-known corporation had posted the following inspiring slogans in his conference room:

"Intelligence is no substitute for information."
"Enthusiasm is no substitute for capacity."
"Willingness is no substitute for experience."

One day the slogans were taken down, after somebody had scribbled underneath: "A meeting is no substitute for progress."

Hard Man, Soft Name

When Harold Geneen left Raytheon for ITT, Raytheon's shares dropped six and a half points. But even long after he had been running ITT, he remained a mystery man outside of management and investment circles to such an extent that the press often misprinted his name as Geheen or Green. People were not even sure how to pronounce his name. There was a joke about it inside ITT: "Is the *g* hard as in God, or soft as in Jesus?"

Jack's Kingdom

Jack Tramiel, Polish-born survivor of Nazi death camps, came to New York and founded a small business repairing typewriters in the Bronx. By the early 1980's that company had developed into Commodore International which had become the largest manufacturer of home computers in the world. Then Tramiel abruptly left the company and simultaneously announced that he had bought Atari from Warner Communications, which meant he was going into direct competition with his former brainchild.

A fifth-grade dropout, Jack Tramiel would not have been a model student at the Harvard Business School. Jim Finke, who served once as president at Commodore, said that "there are no strong barons in Jack's kingdom. There is only a strong king." One of his former marketing vice presidents described Tramiel's "eyeball" style of management: "If there's a single embarrassing document on your desk, sooner or later Jack will swoop in, pick it out of the pile, and then look out!" Another ex-employee confided to *Business Week* that Tramiel "is like a magnesium flare lit in a dark room. You may be left awed—but also choking because all the oxygen was used up."

A tough competitor, who talks of business not as a sport but as war, Tramiel is unabashed and unapologetic. He told a reporter: "I'm not in business to be loved; I'm here to make money."

Circumlocution

Donald Regan, when he was running the over-the-counter department of Merrill Lynch, became the youngest partner at the brokerage firm before leaving to become chief of staff to President Reagan. Once questioned about his habit of dressing down subordinates, Regan was reported to have replied in the great tradition of Irish bull: "I don't chew people out. I remind them of their heritage, and who their parents were, and whether or not their parents were married, and a few things of that nature."

Central Planning

On becoming Kremlin boss, Gorbachev expressed the hope that better planning might produce an extra 2 percent growth in Soviet industry. As examples of poor planning, he authorized an exhibition of shoddy and defective goods produced by Soviet workers, including a whole consignment of boots with high heels attached to the toes.

· 9 ·

THE
SPIRIT OF
ENTERPRISE

CHILDHOOD

The Big Question

Gideon Lee, one of the early leather merchants in New York, recollected his childhood:

> I remember when I was a lad living with my uncle, it was my business to feed and milk the cows. And many a time, long before light in the morning, I started off in the cold and snow, without shoes, to work, and used to think it a luxury to warm my frozen feet on the spot just before occupied by the animal I had roused. It taught me to reflect, and to consider possibilities; and I remember asking myself: "Is it not possible for me to better my condition?"

The Real Horatio Alger

When Horatio Alger was attending Harvard, he first rented rooms from a certain Mrs. Curran, who one day appeared in the nude in front of the young scholar. "I shall have to move," he confided to his diary, "to where there is more respect for decency." So Horatio acquired his next Cambridge landlord: a kindly old man who was trying to run a bookstore. Mr. Floyd Thurstone was obviously more interested in helping his tenants with their studies than in his business, which was rapidly heading for bankruptcy. Young Horatio, out of sympathy for his landlord, entered an essay contest. He worked feverishly at an essay about Socrates, which was awarded the first prize of $40. He then offered the money toward the mortgage, which saved the bookstore and the Thurstone house. His act of generosity did not go unrewarded. Horatio was facing uncertain prospects after graduating from Harvard Divinity School, when Mr. Thurstone suddenly died, and in a Dickensian turn of events, left everything he owned to Horatio—a ring, a watch, and $2,000 in cash.

Alger, who had studied divinity only to please his father, now took the money and went off to Europe, where a Parisian café singer finally initiated him into the facts of life.

"I was a fool to have waited so long," wrote the future patron saint of entrepreneurs: "It is not nearly as vile as I had thought."

The First Dollar

P. T. Barnum typified not only American showmanship and a genius for advertising, but an all-round talent for business. He began young:

> My organ of "acquisitiveness" was manifest at an early age. Before I was five years of age, I began to accumulate pennies and "four-pences," and when I was six years old my capital amounted to a sum sufficient to exchange for a silver dollar, the possession of which made me feel far richer and more independent than I have ever since felt in the world.
>
> Nor did my dollar long remain alone. As I grew older I earned ten cents a day for riding the horse which led the ox team in ploughing, and on holidays and "training days," instead of spending money, I earned it. I was a small peddler of molasses candy (of home make), ginger-bread, cookies and cherry rum, and I generally found myself a dollar or two richer at the end of a holiday than I was at the beginning. I was always ready for a trade, and by the time I was twelve years old, besides other property, I was the owner of a sheep and a calf, and should soon no doubt have become a small Croesus, had not my father kindly permitted me to purchase my own clothing, which somewhat reduced my little store.

Honest Toil

President Lincoln once described to William H. Seward, his secretary of war, how the first dollar he made caused him to feel about himself:

I was about eighteen years of age. I belonged, you know, to what they call down South, the "Scrubs"; people who do not own slaves are nobody there. But we had succeeded in raising, chiefly by my labor, sufficient produce, as I thought, to justify me in taking it down the river to sell. After much persuasion, I got the consent of Mother to go, and constructed a little flatboat, large enough to take a barrel or two of things that we had gathered, with myself and little bundle, down to New Orleans.

A steamer was coming down the river. We have, you know, no wharves on the Western streams; and the custom was, if passengers were at any of the landings, for them to go out in a boat, the steamer stopping and taking them on board. I was contemplating my new flatboat, and wondering whether I could make it stronger or improve it in any particular, when two men came down to the shore in carriages with trunks, and looking at the different boats, singled out mine, and asked: "Who owns this?" I answered, somewhat modestly: "I do." "Will you," said one of them, "take us and our trunks out to the steamer?" "Certainly," said I.

I was very glad to have the chance of earning something. I suppose that each of them would give me two or three bits. The trunks were out on my flatboat, the passengers seated themselves on the trunks, and I sculled them out to the steamboat. They got on board, and I lifted up their heavy trunks and put them on deck. The steamer was about to put on steam again, when I called out that they had forgotten to pay. Each of them took from his pocket a silver half-dollar, and threw it on the floor of my boat. I could scarcely believe my eyes as I picked up the money.

You may think it was a very little thing, and in these days it seems to me a trifle; but it was a most important incident in my life. I could scarcely credit that I, a poor boy, had earned a dollar in less than a day—that by honest work I had earned a dollar. The world seemed wider and fairer before me. I was a more hopeful and confident being from that' time.

Sunday School

Andrew Carnegie was the son of poor weavers. Before he left Scotland for the New World at the age of 10, he attended Sunday school.

"What teaching can you quote from the Bible?" the minister asked young Andrew, who immediately provided the Scottish proverb:

"Take care of your pennies and the pounds will take care of themselves."

"Be you not ashamed of yourself, lad"; said the clergyman, "that saying is surely not in the Bible."

"It ought to be," replied the future industrialist.

Organizer

Although Andrew Carnegie was known as the "Steel King," he did not know very much about the manufacturing of steel. But he knew how to handle people, and it was his talent for organization and leadership that made him rich. When he was still a boy in Scotland, little Andrew found a pregnant hare. Soon he had a whole nest of furry little bunnies, but nothing to feed them. Then he had a bright idea. He asked all the boys he knew in the neighborhood to gather enough clover and dandelions for feed, and, in return, he promised to name a bunny after each one of them.

Later in life Carnegie said that his conscience troubled him for exploiting his playmates in this manner, but that he gave them the only reward at his disposal. However, the lesson stayed with him. When Carnegie wanted to sell his steel to the Pennsylvania Railroad, he built a vast new steel mill in Pittsburgh and named it the "J. Edgar Thomson Steel Works." J. Edgar Thomson happened to be president of the Pennsylvania Railroad, and he was so delighted at having the new works named after him, that he did not need any further persuasion to order all the steel he needed from Carnegie.

The Making of a Commodore

Cornelius Vanderbilt early showed the stuff he was made of. He was riding racehorses when he was 6 and began his love affair with open water by assisting his father on his boat. The older Vanderbilt was a farmer on Staten Island and started the ferry to New York in order to sell his produce there. Sometimes other business came his way, as when he was contracted to transport the cargo from a ship that ran aground near Sandy Hook. The lighters that were to carry the goods to the city could not reach the ship, and it was necessary to haul the cargo, transported in wagons, across the sands from the vessel. The 12-year-old Cornelius was placed in charge of this operation. He loaded his lighters, sent them up to New York, and then started for home with his wagons. When he reached South Amboy, the future Commodore found he had no cash to get himself, his wagons, horses, and men back to Staten Island. The ferry passage amounted to $6, and he was momentarily at a loss about how to raise the money. Finally, he went to the tavern keeper, to whom he was a total stranger, and asked for a loan of $6, offering to leave one of his horses, which he promised to redeem within two days. The taverner was so impressed by the boy's energy that he loaned him the money, and the party got back home. The pawned horse was promptly redeemed.

The Whiskey King

Jack Newton Daniel displayed his business ingenuity early. At the age of 6 he ran away from his family in Lincoln County, Tennessee, where, as the youngest of ten children, he was known as the runt, and convinced a neighboring family to adopt him. With one stroke he became the oldest child in his new household. When he was 7, Jack was offered a job as a houseboy by Dan Call, who combined his calling as a Lutheran minister with making a living as a merchant, farmer, and whiskey distiller. Young Jack was eager to learn about the mysteries of making moonshine and sour mash. And when Dan Call's congregation pressured him to choose between the pulpit and his still, he offered his 13-your-old apprentice the opportunity to buy his distillery on credit. Jack had been saving his salary of $5 a month, as well as learning the business, so in 1860 he bought the whiskey business that to this day bears his name.

Let There Be Dark

Herbert Hoover was working in his uncle's real estate office in Oregon, when the company got into financial difficulties. The partners held a meeting late into the night to see how they could get themselves out of the mess, but ended up bickering and shouting at each other. In the middle of all the name-calling the lights suddenly went out, so the partners, after they were united by complaining about the gas company, decided to postpone their problems and stumbled home. When Uncle John was about to lock up the office, he noticed his nephew appear near the gas valves outside, and he became suspicious:

"Bert! Did thee turn out the lights?"

"They were only running up the gas bill," answered the future secretary of commerce and president of the United States "and there was no use in that kind of talk."

The Whiz Kid

According to *People* magazine, Bill Gates is to software what Thomas Edison was to light bulbs—"part innovator, part entrepreneur, part salesman, and full-time genius." The future founder of Microsoft became involved with computers and business while in seventh grade at a Seattle private school. One summer he earned more than $4,000 programming the school schedules on a time-share mainframe. He and his school buddy, Paul Allen, became computer hackers who broke into and crashed the data banks of such companies as Burroughs and Control Data. A year later they decided to go straight and founded a small company called Traf-O-Data, which used a new Intel 8008 microprocessor to analyze traffic patterns in Seattle. The company grossed $20,000 that first year: Bill Gates was 15.

The following year, he went to Congress—as a page—and witnessed from close up the 1972 Nixon-McGovern campaign. The young entrepreneur bought up 5,000 Democratic campaign buttons, just after Senator McGovern dumped Senator Eagleton as his running mate. Gates paid five cents for the suddenly obsolete political weapons, which he soon resold as historical and rare memorabilia, often at $25 each. At 17, Bill took a formal leave of absence from his school. He and Allen were hired by TRW to develop software at a reported salary of $30,000. Later he dropped out of Harvard to start Microsoft, which became the top software company in the world. Recently he also became the world's youngest self-made billionaire, at thirty. He might go back to Harvard one day—although more likely as a professor.

Confidence

Steve Jobs, cofounder of Apple Computer, was 13 when he had a class project to do at Homestead High School in Los Altos, in what was to become California's Silicon Valley. He had to build a frequency counter to measure the speed of electronic impulses. The device needed parts that were beyond his budget, and young Steve started to phone around. He made a collect call to Burroughs in Detroit. He also got through directly to Bill Hewlett in Palo Alto and asked him if the company had any spare parts lying around. The president of Hewlett-Packard was so impressed by the boy's tone of brash self-confidence that he arranged for Jobs to work as an apprentice in one of his factories during the following summer vacation.

Carnation Software

John Brockman, who became a super agent for software authors and computer-book writers in the early 1980s, claims to have learned his business acumen from his father, who was in the flower business in Boston. Brockman, Sr., was known as the "Carnation King of America," representing the chief growers of the Boston area. What's the difference between selling carnations and representing software authors? Not much, according to his son, "except that carnations smell better and don't talk back."

Deals

So as not to spoil his son, John D. Rockefeller paid him one cent for finding each fence post that needed repairs on the family estate. That day the child made thirteen cents. Later on, he paid his son fifteen cents an hour for repairing those fences. Junior also collected five cents from his mother for every hour he practiced the violin.

This example seems to have spread among the puritanical rich. Gerald Bronfman, one of Sam Bronfman's nephews, gave his daughters a weekly allowance of thirty-seven and a half cents. To make sure he didn't overpay, he alternated between thirty-seven and thirty-eight cents each week.

Mom Speaks Out

Lulu May Perot remained the closest advisor to H. Ross Perot, founder of Electronic Data Systems, (EDS) one of the greatest success stories of our time. She served on its board of directors and worked for her son as a bookkeeper. When Perot was struggling with the decision of rescuing some Americans from Vietnam in 1969 (as decribed in Ken Follet's bestseller *On Wings of Eagles)*, his business associates warned him that such a dangerous mission might make the price of EDS stock fall. But his mother counseled Perot to press ahead, saying, "Let them sell their shares."

Father Knows Best

Max Palevsky, founder of Scientific Data Systems, the first company to make small computers, enrolled at the University of Chicago to study philosophy. His father was disappointed. As one of those immigrants who came to America because he believed that the streets were paved with gold, he was not too happy having to work as a housepainter. Now his son wanted to study philosophy. "How can you make a dime from philosophy?" Max did not know, but went on to study logic in graduate school. Later he got a job as a logician at Bendix, to teach computers how to think logically. After a stint with Packard-Bell, Max Palevsky raised $1 million worth of venture capital and started building small computers on his own. When it went public, the philosopher was suddenly worth $50 million. Interviewing him one day, financial writer "Adam Smith" asked him whether the money had made any difference. Palevsky thought for a minute, but could not think of any difference. He had the same house and the same friends. Then he realized that his money had helped in one respect: "It made my father happy. My father said, 'I did the right thing. I was right after all.'" And when the son asked right about what, the father replied: "I was right what I thought before I came, about the streets, and the gold."

SOB

"Family business—talk about Greek tragedies revisited," Leon A. Danco of the Center for Family Business in Cleveland was quoted as saying in *INC*. magazine. "I swear, the typical founder of a family business would have no problems whatsoever if he could be immortal and celibate." There is another organization to help sons and son-in-laws in conflict with the boss. Called Sons of Bosses, or SOB for short, it was founded by Gerry Slavin in 1969, and has chapters throughout the United States. Later, the national organization renamed itself to the more respectable but less exciting National Family Business Council, but some chapters retain the more descriptive epithet.

Childhood Lessons

Ralph Nader, the consumer advocate, summed up the problem with American consumers in an interview with *INC*. magazine: "Almost 99 percent of what comes in on a person every day comes in with the message, 'Don't create. Obey. Trust. Believe.' When I was ten years old I came home from school. My parents were in the backyard, reading, and my father looked up at me. He said, 'Ralph, what did you do today? Think or believe?' I didn't quite get it, you know. I went up to my room and was trying to figure it out. A little later I got it, with some help. It's true."

Paper Route

The earliest business experience outside the home for generations of American children has been the delivery of the local newspaper, and many later executives learned some useful lessons. Benjamin F. Fairless, president of U.S. Steel after World War II, remembered: "I started at the age of five, selling papers for the *Cleveland Penny Press*. Each afternoon I met the train and grabbed my precious bundle: 12 copies for regular customers and 6 or 7 extras that I peddled around town. The papers cost me half-a-cent apiece; I sold them for a penny. It was, I often think, the best business I was ever in—no overhead, no taxes, and I netted 50 percent of my gross. All I lacked was volume."

STARTING OUT

Eureka

The idea of the cotton gin came by chance to Eli Whitney. He had been trying to find an easier method of extracting the seeds out of cotton bolls, when he noticed through the window that a fox was trying to raid his chicken coop. Although the fox could not get inside the coop, it managed to get most of the feathers from his prey through the mesh. Whitney then began experimenting with a claw or rake that could pull cotton fibers through a grid and leave the seeds behind.

A Showman

H. W. Johns, one of the founders of the asbestos giant Johns-Manville, which filed for bankruptcy in the wake of a wave of liability suits, already was in the roofing business in Brooklyn when he was 21. In the middle of the last century, he had patented something he called "portable roofing", a blend of rag felt and coal tar. Johns had tried all kinds of different materials, including flour and sawdust, to improve roofing, and it was this search that led him to read about the indestructible and fireproof qualities of asbestos fiber. The mineral had few commercial uses and was imported at a high price from Italy. But Johns had heard about some deposits on Staten Island, and he easily persuaded a farmer to give him a wagonload from what was considered a useless outcropping of rock.

Johns spent many a long night in his improvised "laboratory" to figure out a way of making asbestos shingles suitable for roofing. He was making progress when the Civil War intervened. Finally, in 1868, he began to market asbestos roofing. Asbestos cloth was so scarce that he rarely had more than a few yards on hand, and he sold it at a dollar a square inch. He employed great showmanship in demonstrating the unusual qualities of asbestos by donning a glove he had made of asbestos and dramatically pulling a handful of red-hot coals from the potbelly stove in his office.

Pong

Nolan Bushnell, the founder of Atari and other enterprises, is usually described as the quintessential Silicon Valley entrepreneur. His interest in electronics goes back to his days as a ham radio operator when he was 10 years old. While attending the University of Utah, he spent his time running the games at the Lagoon Amusement Park in Salt Lake City. He soon had an army of 100 kids under his management. Despite his obvious talent, Bushnell was so distracted that he graduated at the bottom of his engineering class. His basic ambition at that time was to work for Walt Disney's amusement empire. He failed to get a job with Disney, however, and that is how he ended up with Ampex in Redwood City.

It was the boredom of his job that drove Bushnell's active mind to tinker. The video game craze began with his invention of Pong, an electronic version of table tennis, in the early 1970s. Bushnell installed a coin-operated game at Andy Capp's Tavern in Sunnyvale. Not long afterward he received a call from the owner asking him to take away his machine, which seemed to have broken down. In fact, Bushnell simply had to empty the quarters so that the patrons could put more in. Knowing he had a winner, Bushnell quit his job with Ampex and founded Atari when he was 29. He took the name from the Japanese game *go*—it means "I'm going to attack you."

Godot

The world's first electronic game was built by a Viennese refugee in Canada. Josef Kates escaped from the Nazis in 1938, and spent most of the war years in a refugee internment camp in Quebec. It was from there that he won a scholarship to McGill University for placing first among all the high school students who wrote the exam. Later Kates became an engineer, and while working for the computer center at the University of Toronto, he built "Bertie the Brain," which played tic-tac-toe with visitors to the 1951 Canadian National Exhibition. Kates made a number of serious inventions that could have made Canada a leader in computer engineering had he found government or private backing. But the university chose to buy a British-made computer instead.

Seeing his invention shelved, Kates designed—as far back as 1953—the first computerized reservation system for Transcanada Airlines. Then Kates founded his own company Teleride, which coordinates mass transit in a number of cities both in Canada and the United States. Customers can telephone and get the precise time a bus is scheduled to arrive at their stop. This is made possible by electronic odometers that report the precise location of the bus every thirty seconds to a central computer. "The reason people don't like the bus," Kates discovered, "is not the bus. It's the wait."

Quality

According to Paul Luongo's guide to *America's Best!* the Rolls Royce of the kite business is a typical mom-and-pop operation. Bill and Betty Hartig founded their company, called Nantucket Kiteman and Lady, because of the way they made their first sale in New York's Central Park. A well-dressed woman grabbed an orange kite from Betty's hand, pressed a ten dollar bill into her hand, and took off "like the dickens." The kite cost one dollar to make. As their cottage industry grew, Betty and Al quit their jobs in New York City and moved to Nantucket Island, Massachusetts, where a toy store offered them a home in exchange for kites. They make about 5,000 kites according to their patented designs, which they market largely by mail order. The secret of their success is the quality. They have turned down mass orders. Each of the kites is had-sewn by Betty and test-flown by Al. One of their early kites, the Warlock, is now at the Smithsonian Institution in Washington, D.C.

Business Genius

Recently there were centenary celebrations for the automobile, the quintessential industrial product of the twentieth century. In fact, all the basic ideas needed to manufacture a mechanically propelled wagon were known before 1840: the automobile is actually older than the railroad. In the 1830s and 1840s, steam stagecoaches made regular trips between certain cities in England, and, in the words of Burton Hendrick (*The Age of Big Business*):

> Occasionally a much resounding power-driven carriage would come careering through New York and Philadelphia, scaring all the horses and precipitating the intervention of the authorities. . . . The French apparently led all nations in the manufacture of motor vehicles, and in the early 1890s their products began to make occasional appearances on American roads. The type of American who owned this imported machine was the same that owned steam yachts and a box at the opera. Hardly any new development has aroused greater hostility. It not only frightened horses, and so disturbed the popular traffic of the time, but its speed, its glamor, its arrogance, and the haughty behavior of its proprietor, had apparently transformed it into a new badge of social cleavage. It thus immediately took its place as a new gew-gaw of the rich; that it had any other purpose to serve had occurred to few people.

The person who found a general purpose for the automobile more than anybody else was Henry Ford. Born in Michigan, in 1863, the son of an English farmer and a Dutch mother, Ford was mainly interested in mechanical devices on his parents' farm. He liked getting in the crops, because of the McCormick harvesters, and he became enthralled with the machinery in the dairy. Already as a boy he had developed a destructive curiosity to take everything apart. Young Henry horrified one of his rich playmates when he reduced his brand-new watch into pieces; he amazed him by putting it back together again. As the industrialist remembered those days: "Every clock in the house shuddered when it saw me coming."

Henry Ford's business genius also manifested itself early. At 16 he ran away from the farm to get a job in a machine shop. He immediately noticed an anomaly: no two machines in the shop were alike. From his weekly savings he bought a $3 watch and took it apart. He calculated that if thousands of watches could be made, all exactly the same, they would only cost thirty-seven cents a piece. "Then everybody could have one," was his conclusion. Later he formulated it as his philosophy for manufacturing automobiles: "Anything that isn't good for everybody is no good at all." It was this idea that took the automobile from being merely a plaything of the rich and created a new age.

Profane Cows

Young Henry Ford hated working on his parents' farm so much that he retained a lifelong hatred for cows. To him they symbolized laziness, and he once described the cow as "the crudest machine in the world." Scientists at the Ford labs were instructed to find substitutes for dairy products, because the boss believed earnestly, if somewhat irrationally, that if all cows were destroyed, there would be no more war in the world.

He Got His Hands Dirty

When starting out, Henry Ford received much encouragement for his automobile contraption from his hero, the great Thomas Edison. The two met at a convention, and after listening to the young man's answers to his pointed questions, Edison urged him on: "Young man, that's the thing! You have it—the self-contained unit carrying its own fuel with it! Keep at it!"

Ford never forgot. Many years later, when he built his museum of technology at Dearborn, he had the whole of Edison's laboratory moved brick by brick from Menlo Park, New Jersey. After the opening ceremonies (which happened to be on October 29, 1929, until very recently the worst day in the history of the New York Stock Exchange), Ford asked his former employer what he thought of his reconstructed workplace. Thomas Edison, who enjoyed getting his hands dirty, looked at the spotlessly clean laboratory, and answered his protégé diplomatically: "It's 99-1/2 percent perfect."

Obstacles

Not all the great business tycoons were inventors of proprietary technology. On the contrary, many of them saw scientists flounder for lack of marketing know-how. It takes a special kind of person to overcome the public's resistance to a product. Henry Ford did not invent the automobile, but he emerged as one of the few winners from among hundreds of early car manufacturers simply because he made it easier for people to buy his product. His mass-production methods enabled him to lower the price of his automobile, which in turn attracted vast numbers of new customers, who made him successful.

Similarly, Powel Crosley, Jr., did not invent radio, but practically founded the radio business. In 1919 his son heard a radio and asked Dad to buy him one. But the cheapest set cost $119. Although he knew nothing about radio, Crosley bought a manual for a quarter and hired a couple of engineering students from the University of Cincinnati, who put together a smaller one-tube set that Crosley could sell for $20. However, there were still other obstacles that discouraged the public from buying radio sets even at the much lower price. The box had nothing coming out of it that was worth listening to. Crosley got another two amateurs to build a twenty-watt transmitter, which later led to the first commercial broadcasting station. For a while Powel Crosley was the world's largest manufacturer of radios.

Ministry

Cyrus Eaton was preparing to become a Baptist minister, when a chance introduction to John D. Rockefeller, the richest Baptist in the world, changed the course of his life. Born in Pugwash, Nova Scotia, the 17-year-old Cyrus was spending the summer of 1900 with his uncle, a Baptist pastor in Cleveland, Ohio. Rockefeller was visiting the church and immediately offered to help the boy: he could study for the ministry at McMaster College in Toronto and work for Rockefeller during the summers. But Cyrus found it difficult to serve two masters and went to work for the oil tycoon full time. At 24, the future mining magnate got his chance to prove his mettle. In 1907, he was sent by a group of Rockefeller associates to the recently established province of Manitoba in central Canada. His mission was to obtain a franchise to build and operate an electric light plant. The financial panic on Wall Street scared off investors, and Eaton decided to borrow the money and build the plant himself. After operating it successfully for two years, he sold it at a handsome profit. He was on his way.

Turtle Oil

Actress Polly Bergen panicked when she was suddenly offered three grandmother roles in a row. She was 32, but still thought of herself as 18. She went to a chemist and tried out a dozen rejuvenation creams until she got him to mix one for her. Soon she was sharing her secret with fifty other women, and that's how she and a woman friend thought of starting a mail-order business. They each put up $1,500 and first advertised in throwaway papers in Hollywood: "Then we ran our first ad in the *Los Angeles Times* magazine section and they put it on the pet page because I had drawn a little turtle in the ad, and they thought I was selling turtles."

The big break came on the "Merv Griffin Show," when Merv finally asked her what she was doing. Polly couldn't think of anything she was doing in show business: "So I said, well, I make this oil that's incredible. From turtles. And I kidded around about it." Griffin then asked where women could buy it. Bergen said that it wasn't available anywhere, unless the ladies wrote her. The following week she received 2,700 letters, each one containing a check ranging from fifty cents to $20.

Cream

The Estée Lauder cosmetics firm remained a close-knit family business for decades. When Leonard Lauder, as older son, became president, he said that members of the family look upon themselves as "winders of the clock or directors of the symphony orchestra who try to stimulate our group of talented and brilliant people to do the best they can."

There has always been a vague mystery about Estée Lauder's origins in Budapest or Vienna, with nobility or dermatology lurking in the lineage, depending on whether she was pursuing clients in the shop or in Palm Beach. As a Hungarian myself, I found several pieces of corroborating evidence in some of the anecdotes Marilyn Bender relates in her book, *At the Top*. First, in the earliest days, Mrs. Lauder would go up to complete strangers, criticize their make-up and offer suggestions. She often ended up selling them several bottles of her home-made cosmetics. (People often criticize strangers on a bus or tram in Budapest.) In her more mature years, Estée Lauder was fond of telling about a stranger accosting her at the hairdresser. The woman pulled her hair back to look for any sign of a facelift, and accused her of impersonation, by shouting: "I've known Estée Lauder for years, and she must have had her face lifted!" (I have known many Hungarian ladies, including my mother, with such youthful skin.) And, finally, there was that opinionated, self-confident common sense. From the earliest days, she has produced something called a "Super-Rich All-Purpose Creme." She once observed: "It's all-purpose because I don't believe in night cream. How does a cream know it's dark outside?"

More Cream

Sir James Goldsmith began to build one of the largest fortunes in Britain at the age of 20, when he spent his entire fortune of £100 on purchasing the French rights to a British cream to treat rheumatism. Three years later he sold out his interests for £250,000.

Jet-Setter

W. E. Boeing, a timber trader was also a hobbyist aviator. He got into the business of building airplanes when his own broke down and he couldn't get parts to fix it. Boeing had a friend in naval engineering, and the two of them built the first Boeing aircraft in 1916. In the beginning, business was slow, so the company also manufactured furniture and early prototypes of speedboats, which they called "sea sleds."

Airlift

Freddie Laker, the enfant terrible of the transatlantic air wars, got into the no-frills airline business during the Berlin airlifts of 1948 and 1951. He had been buying old planes and parts after World War II, and during the Berlin crisis he chartered these to the Allies to fly cargo in and people out. His planes were responsible for ferrying 250,000 refugees out of the divided city.

Only a Heartbeat Away

Sam Cummings became a successful international arms dealer because that was the only business he knew. He had been a weapons expert with the CIA during the Korean War. He named his new business the International Arms Corporation and operated it out of a post office box in Washington, D.C. His letterhead described him as the vice president so that "anyone I dealt with would think there was at least one other person working in the company."

Automaniac

Dave Schwartz, while growing up in Los Angeles, was always interested in cars. When other kids were on their paper routes, he washed cars. Later, he earned his way through college by buying and selling used cars. His only losing venture came about when he departed from his mania. While still in his teens he invested in some plastic fishing rods that were supposed to be unbreakable. When young Dave tried to sell them to Sears, he told the buyer to try and bend one. The rod broke, but Sears offered to take them anyway. The young entrepreneur lost thirty-five cents on each rod and went back to cars.

Car dealing absorbed Dave Schwartz more than his studies, so he left UCLA and opened a used car lot with capital he borrowed from his mother. This was in the Nixon era, and the laid-back entrepreneur still has the famous poster of the president with the caption: "Would You Buy a Used Car from This Guy?" The answer blowing in the wind was mainly negative: Schwartz was losing all his mother's money and a lot more besides. One day, after having a lemon towed back to his lot, the customer asked him to rent her a car instead of giving her a replacement. After three months he had both her check and the car, so Schwartz decided to try leasing on a bigger scale. An actor friend joked that the new business should be called "Rent-A-Wreck." Schwartz put out a sign, and the following morning CBS phoned wanting to do a story. Fifteen years later, the little used car lot that began renting old cars as a sideline has 300 franchises and grosses more than $40 million a year.

Legend

The garage is almost as mandatory for the birth of a high-tech business as a manger for a Nativity scene. Apple I, as everybody must know, was created in the garage of Steve Jobs' parents' home in Los Altos,

California. It ran on a $20 chip. First Jobs and Steve Wozniak assembed computers for fellow members of the Homebrew Computer Club at Stanford University. Their first commercial order was for fifty computers from the Byte Shop in Mountain View, and, in order to pay for the parts, Jobs sold his old Volkswagen bus and Wozniak his Hewlett-Packard calculator. That was in 1976. The following year Apple had sales of $800,000, and in seven years $1.5 billion. Apple became a Fortune 500 company in a record five years.

Pranks

What brought Steve Wozniak and Steve Jobs together wasn't just their mutual interest in electronics but their common bond in pranks. Wozniak was an early telephone hacker who used the "blue box" invented by John Draper (a.k.a. Captain Crunch) to make free calls anywhere in the world. But the different talents of the future founders of Apple Computer also showed up early: whereas Woz enjoyed calling the Vatican, demanding that the Pope be woken, Jobs was already thinking of how to market the illegal boxes to other hackers who did not like paying Ma Bell.

Model Entrepreneur

Tom Bradley, Mayor of Los Angeles, declared May 27, 1986, "Nina Blanchard Day" to commemorate the twenty-fifth anniversary of the founding of the largest modeling agency on the West Coast. Just before founding the agency, Ms. Blanchard had gone bankrupt as owner of a franchised modeling school. She tried to find work and failed. In desperation she decided to invest her last $300 in a new business. Because of her experience with the school, Nina Blanchard knew a lot of models who needed work. But when photographers began calling her, Nina was afraid to tell fashion photographers that her models might not be ready yet for prime time. Instead she said that they were unavailable. Soon word got around that all of the Blanchard Agency's models were always booked. This in turn attracted the established models, who wanted to be represented by the hottest agency in town. And when they signed on, their prophecy became self-fulfilling.

Mama Never Cooked Like This

Susan Mendelson began making snacks, cookies, and cakes, to supplement her income, while working at the Vancouver East Cultural Centre. Very quickly her food became the main attraction at the theater and her future career: "People began calling to reserve cheesecake for intermission, and critics began to review my baking," she told Allan Gould, author of *The New Entrepreneurs: 80 Canadian Success Stories*. As the fame of her concoctions spread, she was asked one day to come into the studios of CBC radio to talk about her cheesecake. Listener response was so strong that she became a regular, first on radio, and then on local television. In 1979, she and a friend, Deborah Roitberg, opened a take-out catering firm called "The Lazy Gourmet." It was ideally suited to the emerging Yuppie generation: people could bring their own dishes, fill them with the Lazy Gourmet's custom-made creations, and pretend that they did it themselves. As the catering grew to a staff of twenty-five and began to serve restaurants, bar-mitzvahs, board meetings, office parties, and weddings (including this author's), Susan Mendelson found time to write a number of best-selling cookbooks with titles such as *Mama Never Cooked Like This* and *Let Me in the Kitchen! (a Cook Book for Kids and Other First-Timers)*; she was also commissioned to prepare *The Official Expo 86 Souvenir Cookbook*. She even goes back to her roots in theater at the Cultural Centre, where she produced a sell-out *Song and Dance Cooking Show* for children. Mendelson thinks her secret is simple: "Believe it or not, it's simply paying attention to the customers. They must feel that they are the most important person in the world and responsible for my success. They must be looked after all the time. In a service-oriented business, you lose touch with that and you're lost. And keeping the staff happy, so they'll be loyal and want to be here."

Family Feud

Early in the computer revolution the phenomenon of the computer widow was recognized. Wives who before would lose their husbands to TV football found a much more serious threat in the computer. It is not uncommon, especially for those who get into programming, to stay up all night or to disappear for weeks on end. Mrs. Alexis Adams was one computer widow who planned revenge on her husband Scott.

At the same time that Scott Adams began to spend endless hours programming a game called "Adventureland" on his TRS-80 Model I, Mrs. Adams found out that she was pregnant. To get his attention, Alexis took all his disks, including the only copy of the game, and put them in the oven. When Scott started on a frantic search, she told him that his programming days were over until he spent more time with her. Fortunately, she had not turned on the gas, and the husband and wife jointly founded Adventure International, makers of highly successful

computer games and educational software. The company was soon gross-
ing $10 million a year, and the Adamses built a castle surrounded by their
own 2,000 acre wilderness park, near Disney World in Florida. When last
heard from, they were living there happily and harmoniously ever after.

Cookies

When Tara and Gayle Hallgreen, sisters and ex-waitresses, started
Cookies by George in Vancouver, they wanted a bank loan. The loan
officer was incredulous: "Cookies? we won't loan you money for *that*!"

After reaching a million dollars in sales within a couple of years, Tara
claims the banks have changed their mind: "They are saying: 'Ahhh,
cookies!' "

As two arts graduates, they might have been prepared for the initial
rejection. After all, Gayle received her degree from the University of
British Columbia in an envelope stamped, "No Commercial Value."

DOING BUSINESS

The Landlord of New York

John Jacob Astor made his first couple of million in the fur and tea trade,
but it was New York real estate that made him the richest American of his
time. Some of his methods have survived the test of time. According to a
panegyric written soon after Astor's death in 1848:

> He had a firm faith in the magnificent future of New York as the greatest city
> of the continent, and as fast as his gains from his business came in, they
> were regularly invested in real estate. A part was expended in leasing for a
> long period property which the owners would not sell, and the rest in buying
> property in fee simple. In his purchases of land Mr. Astor was very
> fortunate. He pursued a regular system of making them. Whenever a
> favorable purchase could be made in the heart of the city, he availed
> himself of the opportunity, but as a rule he bought his lands in what was
> then the suburb of the city, and which few besides himself expected to see
> built up during their lifetime. His sagacity and foresight have been more
> than justified by the course of events. His estate now lies principally in the
> heart of New York, and has yielded an increase greater even than he had

ventured to hope for. Seventy hundred and twenty houses are said to figure on the rent roll of the Astor estate at present, and besides these are a number of lots not yet built upon, but which are every day increasing in value. When Mr. Astor bought Richmond Hill, the estate of Aaron Burr, he gave one thousand dollars an acre for the hundred and sixty acres. Twelve years later, the land was valued at fifteen hundred dollars per lot.

In 1810, he sold a lot near Wall Street for eight thousand dollars. The price was so low that a purchaser for cash was found at once, and this gentleman, after the sale, expressed his surprise that Mr. Astor should ask only eight thousand for a lot which in a few years would sell for twelve thousand.

"That is true," said Mr. Astor, "but see what I intend doing with these eight thousand dollars. I shall buy eighty lots above Canal Street, and by the time your one lot is worth twelve thousand dollars, my eighty lots will be worth eighty thousand."

Condescension

In 1830, after John Jacob Astor had made the bulk of his fortune, he set about realizing a dream he had long cherished. When he had first come as a poor stranger to New York, he had once stopped on Broadway to notice a row of buildings that had just been erected and were considered the finest in the street, and had then made a vow that he would one day build a larger and finer house than any on Broadway. He now set to work to carry out the plan he had cherished ever since. He owned the entire block on Broadway between Vesey and Barclay streets, with the exception of one house, which was the property of a Mr. Coster, a merchant who had amassed a large fortune and retired from business. Mr. Astor made him many offers for his house, but the old gentleman was unwilling to move. Astor offered him the full value of his house, which was $30,000 and increased the bid to $40,000 but Mr. Coster was obstinate. At length Mr. Astor, in despair, was compelled to reveal his plan to his neighbor.

"I want to build a hotel," he said. "I've got all the other lots. Now name your price."

Mr. Coster replied that he would sell for $60,000 if his wife would consent, and that Mr. Astor could see her the next morning. Astor was punctual for his appointment, and his offer was accepted by the good lady, who said to him condescendingly, "I don't want to sell the house, but we are such old friends that I am willing for your sake."

Mr. Astor used to remark with great glee that anyone could afford to exhibit such condescension after receiving double the value of a piece of property.

Promoter

Jeno Paulucci, the founder of Chun King, Jeno's, Inc., and a number of other enormously successful businesses, is the quintessential entrepreneur: promoter, ideas man, salesman. He began in the grocery business, while still in high school, as a fruit-stand barker in Duluth, Minnesota. One day a shipment of bananas came in that had been damaged during refrigeration, causing an unusual discoloration of the peel. Jeno was told by his boss to try and get rid of the bananas by discounting them from the normal twenty-five cents per four pounds. Instead, the young man hit upon the idea of exploiting the fact that these browned bananas looked different. So he set up a big pile of crates and started barking: "Argentine bananas!" Of course there was never such a thing as Argentine bananas, but, as Max Gunther wrote (in *The Very, Very Rich and How They Got That Way*), "the name had an exotic lilt to it, a sound of value. A crowd gathered to look at Paulucci's speckled brown pile. He convinced his listeners that these loathsome looking objects were a new type of fruit, never before imported into the United States. Being of generous heart, he was prepared to let them go at the astonishingly low price of 10 cents a pound (nearly twice what they would have cost as ordinary, undamaged, non-Argentine bananas). He sold eighteen crates in three hours."

Wholesaler

As Jeno Paulucci graduated to becoming a commissioned salesman for a grocery wholesaler, he invented new techniques. Rather than calling on individual stores and selling in small amounts, Paulucci convinced grocers to form cooperatives and buy from him at a discounted rate for very large bulk purchases. Another way he increased sales was to convince the buyers that they had to buy without delay to avoid higher prices later. He had his sales pitch interrupted by telegrams that he had arranged beforehand, in which his employers wanted him to warn customers of an imminent rise in the price of peas.

Paulucci was soon making more money on commission than the company president was on salary. It was time to move on, and Paulucci became fascinated with hydroponics and bean sprouts, which led him to Chun King, an unpromising canned food business that brought him notoriety and ultimately $63 million from Reynolds Tobacco. In the early days of trying to sell his strange combination of Cantonese food mixed with his mother's Italian spices, Paulucci wanted the chief buyer of the national chain Food Fair to taste his concoction. As Max Gunther tells it:

Paulucci pulled out a can opener and pried the lid off a can of chop suey vegetables. Lying right on top of the vegetables, hidden from the buyer's view by the raised can lid, was a cooked grasshopper. It was the kind of accident that can happen to any food processing company once in a while, even the biggest. Chun King's kitchens, though housed in a Quonset hut, were in fact as clean as anybody else's. But Paulucci was strongly aware, as he gazed horrified at the grasshopper, that his company's grand image was in mortal danger.

He hesitated for half a second. Then he picked up a spoon, smiled broadly and said: "This looks so good that I'm going to take the first mouthful myself." He ate the spoonful, including the grasshopper, with apparent relish.

Paulucci got the order.

Imitation

Japan is not often thought of in terms of entrepreneurial spirit or promotional flair. But according to *Forbes* magazine, Den Fujita, who has coventured more than 500 McDonald's franchises throughout Japan, used to promote this foreign food as something that would turn your hair blond if you kept eating it. Now his approach is to say that it will make kids grow into larger adults. He thinks that the Japanese diet of rice and fish may account for the generally smaller size of his compatriots, and that if he could serve enough hamburgers to kids before they reach 12 they might not only grow but also remain addicted customers. Fujita himself sticks to noodles, but in imitation of the late Ray Kroc, he is looking to buy a professional baseball team.

Fair Bidding

When Benjamin Franklin was trying to get a piece of the government printing business, he found that a competitor, Andrew Bradford, had it pretty well sewn up within the State of Pennsylvania. What riled Ben most was Bradford's sloppy work. So, after a speech by the governor had been published by Bradford according to his usual low standard, Franklin reprinted it on fine paper, composed in the most elegant type. He then mailed a copy to the governor and to each member of the assembly. Soon afterward, Ben Franklin got all the government's printing business in Pennsylvania.

Sensible Bidding

During the War of 1812, there were fears that the British would attack America's Atlantic harbors. In the spring of 1814 the commissary general of the U.S. Army invited bids from boatmen for conveying provisions from New York to various military forts in the vicinity. The labor was to be performed during the three months that the militia was called out, and the successful contractor would be exempted from military duty. Bids poured in from the boatmen, offering to do the work at ridiculously low figures, mainly to secure this exemption.

Cornelius Vanderbilt, barely 20, was reluctant to bid at first, because he knew that the work could not be performed at the prices his colleagues offered. He was also something of a patriot, having helped his country's cause the previous year by bringing an urgent message for reinforcements from Fort Richmond to New York. Finally, as much to please his father, he offered to transport the provisions at a price he calculated he would need to do the job well. He so little expected to succeed that he did not go to the commissary's office on the day of the awarding of the contract; he only heard from various other boatmen about their own lack of success. Then he called on the commissary, merely through curiosity, to learn the name of the fortunate man, and to his utter astonishment was told that he had won the contract. The government was satisfied, from his sensible offer, that he would do the business thoroughly, and this, the commissary assured him, was the reason for his selection.

Handshake

The Reichmann brothers of Canada — Albert, Paul, and Ralph — have built one of the largest real-estate development companies in North America. Considered by the press as highly reclusive, the brothers made their presence known in 1977 when they bought eight Manhattan skyscrapers in a single deal for $320 million. Commercial properties were depressed following New York's brush with bankruptcy, and in hindsight the transaction is sometimes ranked a close second to the $24 paid for the whole island.

The Reichmann family are Orthodox Jews who fled to Canada from Hitler's Germany via Morocco, where they became bankers and acquired their business methods. The Reichmann brothers commit themselves verbally, and often they have built the actual office tower before the written contracts for the land have been negotiated and signed. They learned to do business on a handshake in Morocco, where "the first time you don't honor a handshake is the last time anyone will shake hands with you."

Timing

Sir James Goldsmith's failure to take over Goodyear in late 1986 netted him an estimated $90 million in profits. One of the best-known international financiers and so-called greenmailers today, his motto is: "If you see a bandwagon, it is too late."

Luck

Gerald Ronson, one of the new breed of British entrepreneurs (voted Businessman of the year in 1984 in England), believes that luck played perhaps as much as 50 percent in helping him build his fortune. He cites the time he bought up some of the most valuable land around Tucson, Arizona. Ronson happened to be in Tucson, buying a savings and loan association, when he heard that a part of Howard Hughes's estate, 12,500 acres of prime land, was up for quick sale for $75 million—in cash. Ronson knew where the land was—between the airport and the city center—and needed no time to figure out which direction Tucson was going to sprawl. However, in the early 1980s, interest rates were going through the roof, and one could wait for a long time for the land to accumulate. Ronson called a few friends and presold about $40 million worth before clinching the deal. Soon thereafter, he sold another $80 million worth of land, getting himself well into profit, which he estimates will in the end be at least twice the original purchase price. And all because he happened to be visiting from London to buy a small savings and loan institution. It was also his luck to have rich friends.

Knowledge

Thayer Lindsley's chance to build one of the great mining fortunes in Canada came because Thomas Edison gave up too soon. In 1901, the famous inventor was searching for a reliable supply of the nickel he needed for building storage batteries. Edison staked out claims around the small township of Falconbridge, near Sudbury, Ontario. When the exploratory drilling encountered quicksand, he turned to other sources and the claims lay idle until the 1920s, when Lindsley came along. As founder of a company appropriately named Ventures, Thayer Lindsley was so sure of finding ore that he bought the old Edison claims for the seemingly enormous sum of $2.5 million. It turned out to be a puny investment in what became Falconbridge, one of the largest mining concerns in the world.

A modest man completely absorbed in mining, Lindsley was so shy that he once spent several hours patiently arguing with a magazine writer why he would make a poor subject for an article.

Facts

Howard Hughes, in his Hollywood days, was busy producing a historical epic, when a newly hired assistant pointed out that a particular scene could become ludicrous because of the inaccuracy of some historical detail. When the young man suggested that he should go to the library to check it, Hughes shouted at him: "Never check an interesting fact!"

DOWN AND UP

Wildcatter

Columbus Marion Joiner was the wildcatter who started the Texas oil bonanza in October 1930, drilling a gusher after three long years of frustration. The effort exhausted all his resources, and immediately his creditors began to sue. "Dad" Joiner, as he was known, was too ill to attend the preliminary hearing for putting his assets into receivership. But he had the sympathy of Judge Robert Brown at the Rusk County District Court, who declared: "Personally, I feel that a man who has been three years getting a baby is entitled to nurse it awhile."

The Original J.R.

The man who bought out the leases of the bankrupt Joiner was the legendary H. L. Hunt, Jr. "June" Hunt (as he was nicknamed for junior) had gained his experience in the oil fields of Arkansas and Louisiana. He also had a reputation for acquiring leases for nothing and paying for them when he sold them to the next buyer, at a great profit. When he made his deal with Dad Joiner, Hunt is said to have had only $109 in the bank. Other legends had him paying his drilling crews with winnings he made in all-weekend poker games. During the El Dorado oil boom in the early 1920s, Hunt had an opportunity to beat most of the high-stakes gamblers who converged there. As he told *Esquire* magazine, he was accused by them of cheating, but, in fact, he had merely exercised his photographic memory.

The tycoon who built one of the great Texas fortunes and sired a number of famous offspring played his cards close to his chest. A man of few words, he told a friend that he learned most of what he knew by listening. And he set careful limits to his gambling. According to one of his less flamboyant children, Ray Hunt, who is the present head of Hunt Oil, his dad told him that he never took a risk that, if everything turned out the worst possible way, would prevent him from going right ahead with his life and plans.

Giant

About twelve miles from the original gusher that Dad Joiner found and June Hunt bought, Malcolm Crim ran the general store in Kilgore, a village of 700. A good many of them were poor cotton growers who had run up several years' worth of debts at the store. One day Crim had his fortune read and was told that some day oil would be found under his farm. The storekeeper believed it and spent what little cash he had on buying leases on adjoining lands. Then came Joiner's find, but it seemed too far away, and Crim had no money left to drill. A promoter persuaded him to allow a well to be drilled in partnership. The result was a well that produced 22,000 barrels a day. In a scene straight out of the movie *Giant*, Malcolm Crim drove into Kilgore to tell his mother. Spattered all over with oil, he found her on the way to church. Malcolm Crim took his religion seriously. As soon as he sold his leases to Humble Oil, the first thing he did was cancel every debt owed to him, mailing a receipt stamped "paid" to each of his less fortunate customers.

Starting Again

"My name is Opportunity and I am paging Canada." Despite the fact that the year was 1933, the nadir of the Great Depression, former stockbroker, speculator, and self-made Brooklyn millionaire Joe Hirshhorn was announcing his entry into the roller coaster world of Canadian mining. The advertisement in the *Northern Miner* continued: "Canada, your day has come. The world is at your feet, begging you to release your riches cramped in Mother Earth. Carry on until the pick strikes the hard, firm, yellow metal, until the cry 'Gold!' resounds through the virgin forest . . ."

As anybody who has lived in Canada knows, such flamboyance is received there with about the same enthusiasm as the withdrawal of money from a Zurich bank. But Hirshhorn, who had won and lost and won again a fortune on Wall Street, now applied his hard-won lessons to the relatively virgin territory of Canadian mining. His first investment of $1,700 in McLeod-Cockshutt Mines quickly turned into $200,000. In 1936 he paid $25,000 to drill for gold at the Preston East Dome Mines, which had been abandoned and thought to have been exhausted. The stock had sunk to five cents, and when it began to rise, Hirshhorn bought. Then speculators tried to sell short, as often happens with penny stocks, but Hirshhorn kept on buying until he owned enough shares to control the market. The stock reached $2 and Hirshhorn bought mineral claims to 500 square miles in Northern Saskatchewan, where Rix Athabasca became the first uranium mine financed with private capital. Meanwhile, he kept searching in northern Ontario and hired Franc Joubin as his geological consultant. Joubin told him that discouraging reports about the Algoma district were wrong and that deep diamond drilling would find enormous deposits of uranium ore. Joubin asked for $30,000 to test his idea. Hirshhorn provided it, because: "I bought on my faith in the man talking to me. That's what counts with me."

Joubin was proven right. After two months of drilling in the Blind River area, he came upon the largest find of uranium outside of Africa. The time came for Hirshhorn's expertise in securing his claim. In total secrecy he flew up into the northern wilderness a 100 men, including geologists, engineers, and lawyers, who came with claims already filled in.

Credit

Atari was started in 1972 with Nolan Bushnell's own capital of about $500. He bought parts on thirty days' credit, but demanded immediate payment for his games so that he could pay his suppliers. The first year Atari sold more than 10,000 coin-operated machines at $1,200 each. Three years later he sold the company to Warner Communications for $28 million.

Homeric

Mitch Kapor, the founder of Lotus Development, was teaching Transcendental Meditation in the mid-1970s. Although he gave up the Maharishi ("there's less there than meets the eye") for more conventional psychological counseling and software programming, his TM background was useful when he needed to find a name for his company in 1982. The lotus is a symbol of "perfect enlightenment" in India, and this mantra helped to make Kapor not only relaxed but also perfectly rich. Unfortunately, the flower has a different connotation in the West. When the company's stock began to flounder, Wall Street analysts compared the first rush of investors to the sailors in the *Odyssey*, who became so intoxicated with eating lotus that they became the unwary victims of the monster Cyclops.

Vacillation

Many small businesses fail because they cannot raise relatively small amounts of venture capital. In hindsight, many investors wonder whether they would have had the perspicacity to get in on the ground floor of a great enterprise, such as Ford or IBM. Chauncey M. Depew, the great orator and political figure of the 19th century, described his greatest commercial mistake:

> Gardner Hubbard, father-in-law of Alexander Graham Bell, came to me one day and said he thought he could put a promising investment in my path. His son-in-law had perfected what he called the "talking telegraph." Hubbard had joined in the enterprise after actually hearing it work, and was giving Bell a hand. Money was needed. If I would invest $10,000 in the company they were forming, they would give me a paid-up one-sixth of the enterprise, and Hubbard was sure I would make money by it.
>
> I wanted to think it over. When Hubbard left I posted down to see my friend William Orton, then president of the Western Union Telegraph Company. He told me in good faith to drop the matter at once. He said the invention was a toy, that Bell could not perfect anything with commercial possibilities, and that above all, if there was anything of merit in the thing, Western Union owned the Gray patents and would simply step in, superseding Bell, and take the whole thing away from him.
>
> That cooled me off, and I felt that I was out of the deal when I left Orton's office. But the same afternoon Hubbard dropped in again to find out if I had made a decision. I told him what Orton had said, and that I had better drop out of the matter.
>
> Hubbard ridiculed the idea that Western Union could win a patent suit with the Gray patents, which he said he knew all about. He told me more about Bell's work and his prospects, and I seemed to be weaned away from Orton and back to Hubbard's side again. I told him to call and see me again the next day, and went home that night resolved to risk the $10,000 in Bell's device. But Orton dropped in to see me after the evening meal, and argued again against my investing with Bell. He said the Western Union would take his device away from him, and finally I was convinced. It was my most expensive chat. Next day I told Hubbard I had decided not to invest any

money with Bell, and although we argued some more, I stuck to this last decision and Hubbard went away. Bell won a victory against the Western Union in the courts, and had a clear field; and the telephone invention has resulted in the development of a corporation of such size and capitalization as to eclipse anything to be found in the business world. Because I was a bit weak and vacillating, and could not seem to make up my own mind and stick to it, I lost a cool two hundred million dollars.

Over the Barrel

Jim Warren founded the West Coast Computer Fair in 1977, and one of the people working for him at the time was Jim Egan, whose job was to help customers decorate their booths. Industry shows are the cheapest way to reach customers within the trade, but some undercapitalized entrepreneurs hardly have enough to rent a booth, let alone pay for the decorations. Egan was approached by a couple of long-haired kids who wanted some chrome displays to make their "stuff look flashy." Egan said he had the displays for rent. The kids said they were short of cash, but perhaps Egan might like some stock in their new company. Egan, who had seen them come and go in his twenty years in the business, said he would accept only hard cash. So Steve Wozniak and Steve Jobs did without the chrome, fixed up their booth, and kept the stock in Apple to themselves. Presumably, Jim Egan is still decorating booths for hard cash.

Win Some, Lose Some

Nolan Bushnell started a whole host of ventures, many of which have failed. He freely admits to being better at starting companies than at running them. He likes to invest his money in other people's ventures, although he missed out on perhaps his greatest opportunity in 1976, just when he was riding high with Atari. A very young man came to pitch him on the idea of a personal computer that he was putting together in a garage. Bushnell dismissed the idea and the young man, who happened to be Steve Jobs, co-founder of Apple Computer. Whenever reminded of his prospecting talent, Bushnell replies: "I never claimed to be perfect."

Hidden Talent

Many women inherit a business when their husbands die and face the choice of selling or running it. But sometimes they take a small business and make it into a big one. Leah Hertz describes the poignant case of a widow who knew nothing about her husband's hardware business, though they had been married for thirty-two years.

"My place, he always told me, was at home with the children." She was vaguely aware, however, that the business was losing money during the decade that her husband was dying of cancer. After his death, the 57-year-old widow could have sold out "and gone down to Florida and sat there with all the rich wives and got bored to death. I could have become an alcoholic and I could have felt sorry for myself." Instead, Jennifer Kinnock Trafford fired some of the feuding managers and rescued her husband's company from the verge of bankruptcy. In five years she turned it around into a profitable proposition. When asked why, with all her hidden talent for management, she did not help her husband out in the business during those downhill years when he was sick, she replied: "I did not want to interfere, because it would have meant that I knew he could not run it any longer. His state of mind was more important to me than the business."

Finishing Up

Bill Lear made a childhood resolution to make enough money so that he could not be stopped from finishing anything. A typical American tinkerer, inventor, self-made millionaire, Lear made a fortune with the Learoscope and other navigational aids for aviation. He later branched out into stereo systems and communications satellites. He was in his sixties when he launched the first Learjet, producing the ultimate personal aircraft at a price that most top executives could not resist. At 65, Lear sold the business, but did not like the life-style of a Beverly Hills millionaire. So he established a laboratory in Reno, Nevada, where he worked on developing a better steam engine and improving his jet aircraft. Lear kept working, even when he knew he was dying of leukemia, and his last words to one of his colleagues were: "Finish it, you bet we'll finish it."

· 10 ·

POLITICS

GOVERNMENT

Public Service

The first act of the Continental Congress after the Declaration of Independence was to organize the Department of the Treasury. Michael Hilligas and George Clymer, merchants, were appointed joint-treasurers of the United Colonies. They were each to receive a salary of $500, but first they had to give the strapped Congress bonds of $100,000 each.

Rewards of Public Life

During the Revolutionary War, George Washington depended on his friend, Robert Morris, for financial advice. The Philadelphia merchant kept the credit of the struggling colonies afloat and unstintingly gave from his private fortune. When even Washington was ready to give up in despair because he had no money to pay his troops, who were ready to surrender or disband, Morris applied "to the purser of our allies, the French," and saved the perishing army. In 1781 Congress unanimously elected him as superintendent of public finances. The public-spirited merchant struggled to save the infant republic from being crushed under a mountain of debt. Meanwhile, he neglected his own business affairs, "which finally resulted in those great embarrassments of mind and circumstances which weighed upon his declining years. In his old age, Mr. Morris embarked in vast land speculations, which proved fatal to his fortune. The man to whose financial operations our country is said to owe as much as to the negotiations of Franklin, or even the arms of Washington, passed the latter years of his life in prison, confined for debt."

Personal Finances

One of Robert Morris's protégés was the young Alexander Hamilton, who became the first secretary of the treasury. He had already accomplished more than enough to be president of the junior chamber of commerce, having started at the age of 12 to run a large shipping company by day and studying and writing commercial articles at night. After he entered public life, Hamilton, like Morris, allowed the country's affairs to consume him. He was

> harrassed by the abuse of personal and political enemies, and suffering for the adequate means to support his family. While building up the financial system which was to redeem his country, the state of his own finances may be judged by the following letter to a personal friend:
>
> Dear Sir:—
>
> If you can conveniently let me have twenty dollars for a few days, send it by bearer. A. H.

The amount of personal toil he performed for the government was enormous. Talleyrand, who was at this time a refugee in Philadelphia, after his return to France spoke thus of Hamilton: "I have seen in that country one of the wonders of the world—a man, who has made the future of the Nation, laboring all night to support his family."

Executive Decision

After the third time the Treasury Building burned down, in 1833, there was a great deal of controversy about where to rebuild it. Worn out with the arguments of the rival factions, President Jackson one morning strode out of the White House and thrust his cane in the ground: "Put the building right here!" he exclaimed. The spot his cane made became the northeast corner of the present-day Treasury Building.

Harassing Mr. Lincoln

During the darkest days of the Civil War, a committee was appointed by the chamber of commerce in Boston to visit President Lincoln and suggest that he hurry up and finish the war, since business was hurting. A Mr. Pierce was the chairman of the delegation, who is the source for what happened:

> We found a man who looked as if he had lost all the friends he ever had in the world. He invited us to take seats and inquired our business. As I was the spokesman I opened the case, and as I proceeded the President's face relaxed. By and by he smiled and betrayed actual interest and by the time I concluded he was almost in a broad grin. After I had finished he inquired if that was all I had to say, and on my saying that I thought it was, he asked if some of the other gentlemen wouldn't like to say something. They replied that they thought I had fully covered the ground. And then what do you suppose this solemn man did? Well, he just moved his chair over to mine, smoothed his trousers over his knee, then reached over and smoothed mine down, too, and then with a queer look, which none of us will ever forget, he said: "Mr. Pierce, did you ever notice what a difference there is in legs?" What did we do? We grabbed our hats, and took the first train for Boston—and we never dared to make our report!

Slave Auction

Abraham Lincoln's abhorrence of slavery went back to an incident in his youth in New Orleans, where the Great Emancipator first saw the complete degradation of a human being. He was rambling over the city with a couple of companions, when they happened upon a slave auction. A vigorous, attractive mulatto girl was undergoing a thorough examination at the hands of the bidders: they pinched her flesh and made her trot up and down the room like a horse to show how she moved and to satisfy prospective buyers about the soundness of the merchandise. Lincoln was so revolted by the spectacle that he left the scene with a deep feeling of unconquerable hate. He asked his friends to leave with him and made a prophetic remark: "If ever I get a chance to hit that thing, I'll hit it hard!" One of those companions later remarked that "slavery ran the iron into Abraham Lincoln then and there."

Self-Made

Abraham Lincoln used to tell how, soon after his nomination for the presidency by the Illinois Republicans, he was approached in Decatur by an old Democrat.

"So you're Abe Lincoln." The future president nodded and waited for the other to make his point.

"They say you're a self-made man."

"Well, yes; what there is of me is self-made."

"Well, I must say," the Democrat observed after making a careful survey of the Republican candidate, "it was a damned poor job!"

Politics

Following the enormous speculations in Erie railroad stocks that led to the panic of 1873, there was a congressional investigation. Jay Gould, who bought politicians wherever he needed to build the railroad, was frank about where his own loyalties lay: "In a Republican district," he told the panel, "I was a Republican; in a Democratic district, a Democrat; in a doubtful district I was doubtful; but I was always for Erie."

Can Do

Bernard Baruch, one of the greatest of Wall Street speculators, entered public service at almost the same moment as America entered World War I. President Wilson appointed him to the Council of National Defense, with $10 billion to marshal ammunition and food supplies. He was not a popular choice, and just the year before he was accused of making a killing when Wilson's peace note caused a break in stock prices. It troubled the press that Baruch had built no companies and produced nothing, except vast profits. Furthermore, he seemed unashamed of it. "I am a speculator," he told a congressional committee that asked his occupation. When Baruch described how he had made $500,000 in one afternoon, a Congressman sighed: "I wish you could teach me how to do it."

Baruch naturally took charge in Washington, D.C. As an outsider he did not know the meaning of the bureaucratic phrase that something cannot be done. When it took too long to get some expenditure approved, he simply used his own money. And when his secretary complained that they needed more space, Baruch instructed: "Buy the building."

Ouch

Bernard Baruch, when he went into government, devised a program to help raise the standard of living for farmers. It was given then to an endless succession of bureaucrats, was debated by a presidential panel, and, finally, the politicians went at it. When Baruch saw again the revised farm bill, he could barely recognize his own offspring. Asked by a friend whether he would like to see his program put into effect, the man from Wall Street replied: "I never did like porcupines."

Representation

It has been a long tradition for business leaders to serve in public life. Calvin Coolidge was considering a certain businessman for a cabinet appointment, when one of his advisers objected: "Mr. President, that fellow's a son of a bitch."

"Well," replied the laissez-faire chief executive, "don't you think they ought to be represented, too?"

Bribe

In the nineteenth century, the bread dealers of Lyons, France tried to raise the price of bread beyond the regulated tarrif. They thought that they could prevail on M. Dugas, the provost of the merchants in that city, to befriend them at the expense of the public. M. Dugas told their delegation that he would examine their petition and give them an early answer. The bakers then retired, having first left upon the table a fat purse of 200 louis d'or, intended as private inducement for the provost. In a few days the bakers called upon the magistrate for an answer, not in the least doubting that their gift had effectively pleaded their cause. M. Dugas addressed them:

> I have weighed your reasons in the balance of justice, and I find them light. I do not think the people ought to suffer under a pretence of the dearness of corn, which I know to be unfounded; and as to the purse of money left with me, I am sure that I have made such a generous and noble use of it, as you yourself intended: I have distributed it among the poor in our two hospitals. As you are opulent enough to make such large donations, I cannot possibly think you are incurring any losses in your business; and I shall, therefore, continue the price of bread as it was before I received your petition.

The Finest that Money Could Buy

Big city politics in the America of the late nineteenth century offered tremendous opportunities for corrupt entrepreneurs and politicians. At stake were the public utilities and transit systems. One of the men who started these enterprises in Philadelphia, William H. Kemble, had been indicted for attempting to bribe the Pennsylvania Legislature. He had been convicted and sentenced to one year in the county jail and had escaped imprisonment only by virtue of a pardon he obtained through political influence. Charles T. Yerkes, one of his partners in politics and street railway enterprises, had been less fortunate, for he had served seven months for assisting in the embezzlement of Philadelphia funds in

1873. It was this incident in Yerkes's career that drove him to leave Philadelphia and settle in Chicago. There, starting as a small broker, he ultimately acquired sufficient resources and influence to embark in the street railway business, at which he had already served an extensive apprenticeship. Under his domination, the Chicago aldermen attained a depravity that made them notorious all over the world. They openly sold Yerkes the use of the streets for cash and constantly blocked the efforts that an infuriated populace made for reform. Yerkes purchased the old city railway lines, lined his pockets by making contracts for their reconstruction, issued large flotations of watered stock, heaped securities upon securities and reorganization upon reorganization, and diverted their assets to business in a hundred ingenious ways. Despite the crimes that Yerkes perpetrated on American cities, one contemporary historian found "something refreshing and ingratiating about the man. Possibly this is because he did not associate any hypocrisy with his depredations. 'The secret of success in my business,' he once said frankly, 'is to buy old junk, fix it up a little, and unload it upon other fellows.' Certain of his epigrams—such as, 'It is the strap-hanger who pays the dividends'—have likewise given him a genial immortality."

Boss

Peter Widener, the son of a poor immigrant bricklayer, began as a butcher at Philadelphia's Spring Garden Market in the 1880s. A butcher shop at that time was a political institution, a center for all-night poker games, and a meeting place for a political clique to exchange gossip. It was inevitable that Widener rose rapidly in the machinery of the twentieth ward. Soon he went into municipal politics, and because of his business experience he was entrusted with the city treasury. Through such public service, and by advocating the building of the Metropolitan railway system, he became enormously rich and powerful in the state and even nationally. He built several great art galleries and became a philanthropist. One contemporary historian described him as "a born speculator, emphatically a 'boomer.' His sympathies were generous, at times emotional; it is said that he has even been known to weep when discussing his fine collection of Madonnas."

What he learned in government, the ex-butcher gave back to business. Once Widener had to preside over a turbulent meeting of shareholders of the Metropolitan railway, during which it was proposed that all the company's visible assets be turned over to a company the stockholders knew absolutely nothing about. When several of these stockholders demanded that they be given an opportunity to discuss the projected lease, Widener turned to them and said in his politest and blandest manner: "You can vote first and discuss afterward."

Image

When Robert Kennedy was running for senator in New York, he was discussing an election pamphlet with the advertising people in charge of the campaign. He came upon a picture showing him shaking hands with a prominent union official.

"There must be a better picture we can use," Kennedy said.

"Why, what's wrong with this one?" asked the ad man.

"The fellow is in jail," said Kennedy, who was U.S. Attorney-General at the time.

Dress

Barry Goldwater's family owns one of the oldest department stores in Phoenix, Arizona. The senator once turned up at a Washington D.C. party in a fancy tuxedo with watered-silk lapels that displayed a flowery pattern.

"One thing about owning a store," said Goldwater, "you've got to wear whatever doesn't sell."

They Check In, but They Don't Check Out

For years, the seemingly indestructible German cockroach has overrun Congress with impunity, until Californian Gary W. Short walked in with the solution to the problem. Short, with a varied entrepreneurial background, discovered that roaches have this in common with some members of Congress: sex will lure them to their doom. He developed a trap with a male sexual scent that attracts female roaches. Understandably curious, they enter the trap, where they and their eggs are consigned to a pit full of nondrying glue. The females, of course, exude their own scent, whicn in turn lures males to their death. According to *California Business* magazine, Short made a bid to become the official roach buster to Congress, which could more than double his annual profit to $18 million. It is rare, of course, that a businessman can actually profit from service in Washington, D.C. It is still more rare to eliminate the incumbents.

Self-Incriminating

Sonny Liston, the boxing champ, once walking about in Washington, D.C. referred to the Capitol as the Seagram Building, "because everybody who goes there takes the Fifth."

PATRONAGE

Honor

Georges Clemenceau, the journalist who became prime minister of France both before and at the end of World War I, awarded the Legion of Honor to a rich businessman who had contributed heavily to his election. As he pinned France's highest decoration on the tycoon's chest, Clemenceau said: "This is the honor, Sir, that you wanted. All you have to do now is deserve it."

Perks

"Please give my friend Mr. Perkins a good position in your Department, and oblige yours truly, — A. Lincoln."

The message was written on a card to the Secretary of the Treasury Chase, the signature apparently that of the president, and the bearer was duly installed into a clerkship at $1,600 a year. Three months had passed when Eli Perkins appeared at the secretary's desk with another card: "Please promote my friend, the bearer, and oblige yours truly, — A. Lincoln."

Eli was content with being rated at $2,000 a year for three months longer, when a similar card to the foregoing procured him a raise of $400 more. The other clerks were beginning to be astonished at the rapid promotion of the most strictly ornamental loafer in the department.

About this time the secretary of the Treasury, while riding with the president, remarked that he had attended to his wishes regarding Mr. Perkins and trusted that he was pleased with his action in the matter. The surprised president replied in return that he could remember no such man. An investigation being started, the alert Eli promptly hurried to the White House, and, after waiting patiently in the anterooms for several hours, was finally admitted to the presidential presence. He confessed to Mr. Lincoln that, animated by a sincere desire to benefit the nation, he had used his name on the cards aforesaid, but he pleaded in extenuation that the signatures were excellent imitations and that he had only done the whole thing "for a little flyer."

"Now, Mr. President," he said winningly, producing a card from his pocket, "do me the favor to glance at this, and you will see at once what an odd knack I have at these little imitations." The card read: "Mr. Secretary, please have Mr. Perkins furnished with champagne cocktails every two hours while on duty and charge the same to the Stationery Fund. Yours truly — A. Lincoln."

The president read the card, his lips twitched nervously for a moment or two, and something like a cough-suppressed chuckle was heard under his vest as he tried unsuccessfully to frown on the unabashed Eli. At last he said: "You may go, Mr. Perkins."

Eli bowed and made for the door. With his hand on the knob he suddenly remembered something, and, smiling sweetly, he turned and murmured: "Mr. President, my position— shall I . . . ?"

"You may keep it for the present, sir," Lincoln replied, and Eli Perkins slid down to the national money factory and told the boys how he had refused the appointment of minister to Austria, though the president had begged him to take it on his knees.

(The only certainty about the authenticity of the anecdote above is that Eli Perkins was a renowned humorist and practical jokester of the nineteenth century.)

The Wisdom of Solomon

Postmasterships have been traditionally among the federal patronage plums to reward political support, and many presidents have been bedevilled about awarding them. There was a dispute in Lincoln's time about the post office in Dayton, Ohio, which had two Republican applicants, splitting the local party organization. Petition after petition in favor of one or the other poured in upon the president, and delegation after delegation hastened to Washington, D.C. to argue the case. Mr. Lincoln was a long-suffering man, but his patience gave out at last. He could not determine that one applicant was in the slightest degree more competent, or more patriotic, or better supported, than the other. Finally, after being bored by a fresh delegation, he instructed his secretary:

"This matter has got to end somehow. Bring me a pair of scales." The scales were brought.

"Now, put in all the petitions and letters in favor of one man, and see how much they weigh, and then weigh the other fellow's pile."

It was found that one bundle was three-quarters of a pound heavier than the other.

"Make out an appointment at once for the man who has the heavier papers," said Mr. Lincoln; and it was done.

Trustee

In 1833 Abraham Lincoln was made postmaster at New Salem, a job he held until it was abolished. When the office was closed down, there remained a balance of less than $18, a sum so small that the government overlooked it for several years. Finally, an agent of the Post Office Department paid a visit to Springfield, Illinois, where Lincoln shared an office with Mr. Henry, who later related that knowing his partner's chronic poverty he

> did not believe he had the funds on hand to meet the draft, and was about to call him aside and loan it to him, when he asked the agent to be seated a moment. He then went over to his boarding house and returned with an old blue sock with a quantity of silver and copper coin tied up in it. Untying the sock, he poured out the contents on the table and proceeded to count it, and the exact sum (and the identical coin) was found which years before he had received for postage-stamps from his friends in Salem.

No matter how much he needed money during the intervening years, Lincoln never thought of using funds that he held in trust for the government.

Condition

When the pretzel lobbyist approached the postmaster-general about issuing a special stamp to honor the pretzel industry, J. Edward Day replied: "We will do it, but only if you develop a glue on the back that tastes like beer."

INTERFERENCE

Savoir-faire

The postal service, as a government enterprise, dates back to 1683, when the Twopenny Post Office was established in Britain. It actually began a little earlier as a private enterprise; the brainchild of a certain Mr. Povey, who also wrote a pamphlet entitled "The Virgin of Eden, with the Eternity of Hell Torments." He had the idea of sending letters by messengers to different parts of London and surrounding areas. He called the service the "Halfpenny Carrier," the amount he charged for each letter. Despite the low fee, the business thrived and attracted the attention of the government. According to one account, "The ministers finding the plan too lucrative for a private subject, laid an injunction on the inventor, restraining him from carrying it on any longer; and without giving him any compensation, took it into their own hands."

Of course, they also quadrupled the cost of the service to the consumer. Today the losses incurred by the Post Office is one of the greatest drains on the British treasury.

Gratitude

Lyndon Johnson liked to tell a story about a little boy who had addressed a letter to God, telling how his father had died and how his mom was having financial difficulties. He prayed that the Lord might send her $100 to help out. Unable to deliver the letter to the addressee, the Post Office forwarded it to the closest equivalent it knew: J. Edward Day, postmaster-general. Day was touched enough to put a $20 bill from his own wallet into an official government envelope and sent it to the boy. Two weeks passed, and the postmaster-general got another letter:

> Dear God:
> Much obliged for all you have done, but we need another hundred dollars. But please, when you send it to Mom, don't do it through Washington, because the last time they deducted eighty percent of it there.

Deliveries

Perhaps the best sampling of the wit of J. Edward Day was on the occasion of Willard Wirtz being appointed secretary of Labor. Day recalled the fact that his own father, Dr. James Day, had brought Wirtz's wife Jane into the world.

"The Day family has been making deliveries a long time, and the Wirtzes understand what labor is all about," quipped the postmaster-general.

Laissez-faire

When Colbert took over managing the finances of France, he sent for the principal merchants of the kingdom. In order to ingratiate himself with them, and to acquire their confidence, he asked: "Gentlemen, what can I do for you? They answered unanimously:

"Pray, sir, do nothing! *Laissez nous faire*—let us do for ourselves."

Final Word

Christopher Wren, who rebuilt St. Paul's Cathedral and much of London after the Great Fire of 1666, was invited to design a new town hall in Windsor. When he submitted his plans, a member of the corporation, or town council, insisted that the roof required better support and wanted extra pillars to be added. In vain did Wren, the greatest architect in the realm, argue that his planned structure was perfectly safe; the politician knew better. He also managed to spread alarm throughout the community and succeeded in pressuring Wren to add the supports.

Many years later, when both the artist and his patron were dead, some repairs and cleaning were performed on the hall. The workmen were surprised to find that, invisible from the floor below, the extra columns Wren put in were two inches short of touching the roof. Thus had Wren both satisfied his critics and found his vindication as an artist.

Ask What You Can Do for Your Country

Soon after America entered World War II, the government introduced selective rent controls, including for hotels. The price for each room was to be fixed at the highest rate it rented during March 1942. The Sheraton flagship hotel in Boston had a bridal suite where the regular double rate was $24 and the single $20. In fact, a businessman had occupied it alone for most of the month, checking out on the morning of the thirty-first. That evening, a poor sailor arrived with his new bride at the hotel. He could barely afford the hotel's minimum rate of $7, but the next day he would be off to the war to fight for his country, and the manager, whose son had also enlisted, let the young couple have the bridal suite at the minimum rate.

It was one of the more expensive gestures in the hotel's history. Several years later, an audit investigating possible infractions of wartime regulations turned up the fact that the Sheraton had been charging more than the rate established on that fateful day in March. The government exacted several thousand dollars in fines based on trebling the difference of $13 between the two rates. It also forced the manager to display a card in the bridal suite with the following schedule:

Single occupancy $20

Double occupancy $ 7

Evil Empire

Winston Churchill had a lifelong contempt of communism, bolshevism and socialism. During the Revolution of November 1917, he declared to the House of Commons: "There is not a single social or economic principle or concept in the philosophy of the Russian Bolshevik which has not been realized, carried into action, and enshrined in immutable laws a million years ago by the white ant."

When Lenin returned from Zurich to Russia in a German train to start the Bolshevik Revolution, Churchill described the event in terms of germ warfare: "The Germans turned upon Russia the most grisly of all weapons. They transported Lenin in a sealed truck like a plague bacillus."

Churchill elaborated on the image in the Commons: "Lenin was sent into Russia by the Germans in the same way that you might send a phial containing a culture of typhoid or of cholera to be poured into the water supply of a great city, and it worked with amazing accuracy."

Socialism

Following the next world war, no sooner had Churchill saved Britain from Hitler, than he was defeated in parliamentary elections by the Labour Party under the leadership of Clement Attlee. While Sir Winston became Leader of Her Majesty's loyal opposition, the new government began a massive process of nationalization. One day, Churchill encountered Attlee in the men's room of the House of Commons and chose a urinal distant from the one where the prime minister was taking care of his business.

"A bit stand-offish today, Winston?" remarked Attlee.

"That's right," Churchill shot back, "because every time you see something big you want to nationalize it."

TAXES

He Moves in Mysterious Ways

During the Dark Ages the exorbitant taxes exacted by a ruler were also the main connection he had with his subjects. Gregory, bishop of Tours, described in his *History of the Franks* the relationship between death and taxes in the late sixth century A.D.:

King Chilperic became very sick. When he got well his younger son, who was not yet reborn of water and the Holy Spirit, fell ill, and when they saw he was in danger they baptized him. He was doing a little better when his older brother named Clodobert was attacked by the same business. Their mother Fredegunda saw they were in danger of death and she repented too late, and said to the king: "The divine goodness has long borne with our bad actions; it has often rebuked us with fevers and other evils but repentance did not follow and now we are losing our sons. It is the tears of the poor, the outcries of widows and the sigh of orphans that are destroying them. We have no hope left now in gathering wealth. We get riches and we do not know for whom. Our treasures will be left without an owner, full of violence and curses. Our storehouses are full of wine and our barns of grain, and our treasuries are full of gold, silver, precious stones, necklaces, and all the wealth of rulers. But we are losing what we held more dear. Come, please, let us burn all the wicked tax lists." Then the king repented and burned all the tax books and when they were burned he sent men to stop future taxes. After this the younger child wasted away in great pain and died.

Liberty or Taxes

Henry David Thoreau, the author of *Walden*, found himself in jail once for not paying his taxes. Ralph Waldo Emerson visited him in his cell: "Well, what in heaven's name are you doing in jail?" he asked.

"What are you doing out of it?" Thoreau replied.

Audited

A common, unfounded belief is that the income tax was introduced only as a consequence of World War I. In fact, tax collecting is one of the world's oldest professions, and I found two amusing examples from England showing that most modern aspects of taxation—including the dreaded audit—were fully developed more than a century before. The first victim was a typical self-employed, free-lance artist struggling to make ends meet. It is the most difficult condition to explain—then and now—to the auditors.

Michael Kelly in 1806 appears to have upset the commissioners of the Income Tax in making his return of "pursuits and emoluments." In the pride of his heart, he declared his income at 500 pounds yearly. But the commissioners were not contented and urged that his various employments must bring him in twice or thrice that annual sum. This is Kelley's account of his interview:

"Sir," said I, "I am free to confess I have erred in my return; but vanity was the cause, and vanity is the badge of all my tribe. I have returned myself as having 500 pounds per annum, when in fact, I have not five hundred pence of certain income."

"Pray, sir," said the Commissioner, "are you not a stage-manager of the Opera House?"

"Yes, sir," said I, "but there is not even a nominal salary attached to that office. I perform its duties to gratify my love of music."

"Well, but Mr. Kelly," continued my examiner, "you teach?"

"I do, sir" answered I, "but I have no pupils."

"I think," observed another gentleman who had not spoken before, "that you are an oratorio and concert singer?"

"You are quite right," said I to my new antagonist, "but I have no engagement."

"Well, at all events," observed my first inquisitor, "you have a very good salary at Drury Lane?"

"A very good one, indeed, sir," answered I, "but, then, it is never paid."

"But you have always a fine benefit, sir?" said the other, who seemed to know something of theatricals.

"Always, sir," was my reply; "but the expenses attending it are very great; and whatever profit remains after defraying them is mortgaged to liquidate debts incurred by building my saloon. The fact is I am at present very like St. George's Hospital—supported by voluntary contributions—and have even less certain income than I felt sufficiently vain to return."

Enigma

There is another story of an audit of property tax in a book first published in London in 1824. Again, the victim's reaction sounds thoroughly modern:

Horne Tooke is said to have given in his return under the property-tax, as having an income of only sixty pounds a year. Being, in consequence, summoned before the Commissioners, who found fault with his return, and desired him to explain how he could live in the style he did, with so small an income; he replied that he had much more reason to be dissatisfied with the smallness of his income than they had; that as to their enquiry, there were three ways in which people contrived to live above their income, namely, by begging, borrowing and stealing, and he left it to their sagacity, which of these methods he employed.

The Tax Collector Cometh

Theodore Hook, the English poet and wit, was entertaining some friends
with some of his improvised songs, when a servant entered to announce:
"Excuse me, sir, but Mr. Winter, the tax-collector, is here to collect payment." Hook remained at the piano, and without missing a beat began to
sing the following verses:

> Here comes Mr. Winter, collector of taxes.
> I advise you to pay him whatever he axes:
> Excuses won't do; he stands no sort of flummery.
> Though Winter his name is, his presence is summary.

Lament

Following World War I, a businessman wrote this lament to the Commissioner of Potter County (Pennsylvania) when asked to pay yet another
tax:

> I have been held up, held down, sand-bagged, walked-on, sat on, flattened
> out and squeezed. First by the United States government for federal war tax,
> excess profits tax, Liberty Loan bonds, thrift stamps, War Savings stamps;
> for the state, county and city taxes, for capital stock tax, merchants' license
> and auto tax, and by every organization that inventive mind can invent to
> extract that which I may or may not possess.
>
> The government has so governed my business that I don't know who owns
> it. I am inspected, suspected, examined and reexamined, informed,
> reinquired and commanded, so I don't know who I am, where I am or why I
> am here.
>
> All I know is, I am supposed to be an inexhaustible supply of money for
> every known need, desire or hope of the human race, and because I will not
> sell, I have to go out and beg, borrow or steal money to give away. I have
> been cussed, discussed, boycotted, talked to, talked about, lied to and lied
> about, held up, hung up, robbed and nearly ruined, and the only reason
> that I am clinging to life is to see what in Hell is coming next.

Easy Enough for Him to Say

Mortimer Caplin was commissioner of the Internal Revenue Service in
the 1960s. Explaining his occupation, he once said: "The one difference
between a tax collector and a taxidermist is—the taxidermist leaves the
hide."

Love Boat

The 1986 overhaul of the U.S. tax code swept away some of the more arcane distinctions and exemptions under which people could deduct business expenses. For example, in 1983, a new regulation allowed cruises to be deducted if they were taken for the purpose of corporate seminars and conventions. For the deduction to be legal, the cruise ship had to fly under an American flag and be traveling between approved ports. The IRS also required the schedule of meetings and programs—at least, of what went on above board. Despite all of these businesslike safeguards, the new tax law immediately became known as the "Loveboat Bill."

Is Anybody Listening?

John Randolph, the eccentric congressman from Virginia at the beginning of the nineteenth century, once informed Congress: "Mr. Speaker, I have discovered the philosopher's stone: pay as you go."

ECONOMICS

Out on a Limb

Senator Alben Barkely of Kentucky once described an economist as a "guy with a Phi Beta Kappa key on one end of his watch chain and no watch on the other."

President Truman was growing frustrated with the contradictory and ambiguous advice he received from his economic advisors.

"Get me a one-handed economist," he once ordered. "All my economists say: 'on one hand . . . but, on the other.' "

Progress

Somebody had estimated that if Christopher Columbus had established a business the very day he first discovered America, and had proceeded, through poor management, to lose $1,000 a day, he would have to keep going until the year 4232 just to pile up the first billion in losses. Today, however, there are businesses that lose a billion in a year, not to mention the U.S. government, which manages to do it every single working day.

Capital Financing

These days government finances capital projects usually through issuing bonds. Here is an alternative from the nineteenth century:

> The principal market in Guernsey, one of the Channel Islands, was built without money. The governor issued four thousand market notes, and with these paid the workmen who built it. These notes circulated through the island, until the market was built and occupied; and when the rents came in, these notes were received in payment of the rents, and were canceled. In the course of a few years, the notes, being all paid in, were publicly burned in the market.

(According to the same source, the Water Works in Upper Canada were constructed by a similar method.)

Pay Day

A few days after Calvin Coolidge moved into the White House, a special messenger from the Treasury Department brought the new head of government his first paycheck. The president received him graciously, looked at the check, and said: "Call again."

Depression

After three years of economic slump and four years of Herbert Hoover, actor Otis Skinner did not look forward to the 1932 elections. Talking to Calvin Coolidge, he hoped that the former president might be persuaded to run again: "It would be the end of this horrible depression." "It would surely be the beginning of mine," said Coolidge.

Recession

During the 1980 election, Ronald Reagan was mainly campaigning on economic issues. He talked of the coming of another depression, which President Carter was unwise to correct: "That shows how much he knows. This is a recession." It gave Reagan his punchline: "If the President wants a definition, I'll give him one. Recession is when your neighbor loses his job, depression is when you lose yours. And recovery will be when Jimmy Carter loses his."

Music

During the famous 100 days that created the New Deal, Franklin Delano Roosevelt often worked through the night with his economic advisers. One night he asked his secretary of the treasury, Will Woodin, an amateur musician, to bring his violin with him. According to the president's son, James Roosevelt:

> About two o'clock in the morning, every one was getting a little punchy with fatigue but there was still so much work to be finished. Father called for a breather, sent for refreshments, and said to the Secretary: "Will, get out that violin of yours and play it for us." So the secretary, a delightful fellow, uncased his fiddle, tuned it, and with no accompaniment, ran through some pieces by Debussy, and if my memory is correct, a number or two that he himself composed.

Over the Top

Following World War II, many consumer products were under price control, which made the Democratic administration of Harry Truman increasingly unpopular. One day, President Truman was looking at a list of suggestions submitted by Paul Porter, his price control czar, about items that could be safely removed from regulation, when his eyes fell upon Hawaiian sleigh bells. The chief executive scribbled a note against it: "It's decisions like this, Paul, that will will get us over the top."

So What's New?

Arthur Burns served as chairman of the Council of Economic Advisers during President Eisenhower's first term. During their first meeting, Dr. Burns proposed a plan for reorganizing the way economic information and advice would flow to the president.

"Should I put it into a memo?" asked Burns.

"Keep it short," said Ike, "I can't read."

"Then we'll get along fine," replied the economist, "I can't write."

That's Why

President Kennedy appointed Elizabeth Rudel Smith as the first woman to the post of treasurer of the United States. In trying to explain to her daughter what that meant, she said: "From now on, every banknote in the country will have my signature on it."

The child was amazed: "But, mommy, you could never even keep your checkbook straight."

Language

Two of the economists advising Harold Wilson's Labour government were the Hungarian-born Cambridge dons Nicholas Kaldor and Thomas Balogh. Balogh especially was difficult to follow, holding forth on complicated economic theories in an impenetrable Central European accent. After being forced to listen to Lord Balogh through dinner at High Table, a fellow don remarked: "There are three forms of conversation: dialogue, monologue and Balogh."

Bull

Milton Friedman is certainly one of the best-known and probably the most influential economist today. A favorite of the Reaganites, free-enterprisers, and Libertarians, he has most of his time taken up with politics. "People's capacities to do scientific work decline with age," the 74-year-old Nobel Prize winner told *Los Angeles Times* reporter Jonathan Peterson, "while their capacities to throw the bull increase."

Economics Lesson

As a young father, Milton Friedman believed that his children should receive a practical education in economics. Once when the family was taking a long train journey, the future author of *Free to Choose* gave young Janet and David the choice of enjoying a good sleep in the Pullman berths or sitting up in coach and receiving the extra cash that their father saved. The children were forced to perform their own cost-benefit analysis, and, like most hard-nosed children, took the money over their comfort.

Nixon, the Disciple

Milton Friedman, the apostle of capitalism and freedom (some wags called his book on the subject *Capitalism and Friedman*), managed to influence President Nixon in some areas of social policy, such as ending the draft, but the president listened to others when it came to economics. The final rift came in 1971, when Nixon imposed wage and price controls as anti-inflationary measures. And almost as if to rub salt into Friedman's wound, the president declared: "We are all Keynesians," referring to the great English economist who had been the apostle of the New Deal and the welfare state. Writing to John Kenneth Galbraith, the chief American Keynesian economist and his ideological foe, Friedman remarked ruefully: "You must be as chagrined as I am to have Nixon for your disciple."

· 11 ·

BUSINESS
AND
THE MUSES

ARTISTS AT WORK

Going to Work

Many literary men of genius worked, sometimes in lowly positions, at banks and insurance offices: Charles Lamb, H. G. Wells, Franz Kafka, T. S. Eliot, Wallace Stevens, among many others. Here are descriptions of two of them going to work. First, a portrait of the American poet Wallace Stevens, who worked at the legal department of an insurance company in Hartford, Connecticut, as described by Brendan Gill of the *New Yorker*:

> Morning and evening he walked the mile or so between his house and his office and even in rain or snow would never accept a ride; people learned to leave the forbidding pedestrian alone. His solitary walking had a purpose: he composed as he walked. . . . Stevens was as obviously engaged in putting one foot of verse in front of the other as he was in putting one physical foot in front of the other. Once, my sister, glancing out of a window, saw Stevens going by her house. As she watched, he slowed down, came to a stop, rocked in place for a moment or two, took a step backward, hesitated, then

strode confidently forward—left, right, left, right—on his way to work. It was obvious to her that Stevens had gone back over a phrase, dropped an unsatisfactory word, inserted a superior one, and proceeded to the next line of the poem he was making.

And a verbal snapshot of Charles Lamb from the year 1817: the essayist and friend of Coleridge spent thirty-three years as a clerk in the accountants' office of the East India Company:

> Persons who had been in the habit of traversing Covent Garden at that time might, by extending their walk a few yards into Russell Street, have noticed a small, spare man, clothed in black, who went out every morning, and returned every afternoon as the hands of the clock moved towards certain hours. You could not mistake him. He was somewhat stiff in his manner, and almost clerical in dress, which indicated much wear. He had a long, melancholy face, with keen, penetrating eyes; and he walked with a short, resolute step city-wards. He looked not one in the face for more than a moment, yet contrived to see everything as he went on. No one who ever studied the human features could pass him by without recollecting his countenance: it was full of sensibility, and it came upon you like new thought, which you could not help dwelling upon afterwards; it gave rise to meditation, and did you good. This small, half-clerical man was—Charles Lamb.

While this description implies that one could almost set one's watch by Mr. Lamb's comings and goings, the anecdotes preserved about his punctuality attest otherwise. Once he was summoned into the presence of the directors of the East India Company and was gently reprimanded for his habitual lateness.

"But if I d-d-do come late, gentlemen," stuttered Lamb in self-defense, "you should c-c-consider how early I leave."

Retirement

Few people had minds less cut out to be an accountant than Charles Lamb, especially since Lamb hated facts. He proclaimed himself to be "a matter-of-lie" man. He described his retirement: "It was like passing from life into eternity. I wandered about, thinking I was happy, but feeling that I was not. When all is holiday there are no holidays. Think of this, thou man of sudden wealth, and if it shall so chance that thou hast been tallow chandler in thy days of usefulness, make a clause in thy bill of sale that shall reserve to thee the right of still assisting at the factory on 'melting days.'"

The East India Company seemed to treat the author with tolerance during his working life and generously after his retirement, settling upon him a pension of £450 pounds a year. After Lamb's death (he was a life-long bachelor), his sister Mary received a "Widow's Portion" of £120.

The Hundred Dollar Kiss

Edwin Booth, the great American tragedian of the last century, was traveling with his family by rail. In the same parlor car was a lady more remarkable for the loudness of her style and the oppressive gorgeousness of her jewelry than for her refinement. She not only conceived the most intense passion for the stage star, but took special pains to manifest it—an interest that seemed to be only the more inflamed by the profound indifference of the actor to her presence. She would repeatedly say to her companion, loud enough to be overheard: "Oh, I'd give a hundred dollars to kiss that divine Booth just once."

At Omaha, a poor emigrant attracted the attention of the travelers as they returned to the car after dinner. He had set out for California, but had been robbed while asleep, and lacked the funds to go on or even to eat. Booth, whose generosity in his palmy days was proverbial, put his hand in his pocket through sheer force of habit, and without a word handed the poor man a hundred-dollar note. And as he did this, his eye fell upon his decked-out admirer standing near. With the sweeping stride of a Shakespearean hero he abruptly went up to her: "Did you say, Madam, that you would give a hundred dollars to kiss me?" The lady was staggered for a moment, but having her bluff called she responded with an "I did," and opened her huge purse defiantly. With deliberation, the star passed his arm around her neck, and giving her a sound smack, held out his hand for the fee. Having received it, Booth wheeled around, forced it into the emigrant's hand, saying simply: "There's another," and without changing his countenance, or taking any further notice of the kissed donor, went back to his seat.

Prospects

During World War I, T. S. Eliot was working as a junior clerk with Lloyd's Bank in London. By chance, a friend of his, the literary critic I. A. Richards, ran into one of Eliot's superiors during a Swiss vacation, and they started to discuss their mutual acquaintance. As Clifton Fadiman tells the story,

> the senior banker was a pleasant man who seemed unable to frame a question that he obviously wanted to put to Richards. Eventually it came out:

did Richards think that Eliot was a *good poet?* Richards replied that in his opinion, which would not be shared by everyone, Eliot was a good poet. The other man was pleased to hear it. Some of his colleagues considered that banking and poetry did not go together, but in his view if a man had a hobby and did it well it helped him in his work. He ended by telling Richards that he could tell Eliot that if he continued to do as well as he was doing at the bank, "I don't see why—in time, of course, in time—he mightn't even become a branch manager."

Donation

Dumas père was once asked by a committee of Parisian artists to give a donation toward the burial of a man.

"Was he a writer, or an artist?" Dumas inquired.

"Not exactly," came the reply, "but he was known to many of us. He was our local bailiff."

"How much is the burial?" asked Dumas.

"Twenty-five francs."

The writer pulled fifty francs from his pocket.

"Here. Go bury two bailiffs."

Battle of the Books

Ezra Pound took violent objection to an essay by the British critic Lascelles Abercrombie and, being something of a swordsman, actually challenged him to a duel. At which point Abercrombie recalled that it is the man challenged who has the choice of weapons, and suggested that the two writers bombard each other with unsold copies of their own books. Pound could have won easily, since his avant-garde poetry had a very small audience, but the barb from the more popular writer found its mark and the challenge was withdrawn.

Another episode involving slow-selling books: Franklin Pierce Adams and Alexander Woollcott were friends and knights of the Algonquin Round Table. Woollcott was signing his newly minted book of essays, *Shouts and Murmurs*, and asked only half-rhetorically: "What is so rare as a Woollcott first edition?" Adams, who happened to be standing by, murmured: "A Woollcott second edition."

Where the Money Goes in the Book Trade

The peculiarities of discounting in the book trade are illustrated in this anecdote about Mark Twain. Browsing one day in a bookstore, he picked up one of his books and asked for the price. He then suggested that since he was a publisher, he was entitled to a 50 percent discount. The clerk agreed.

"As I am also an author," Twain went on, "it would appear that I am again entitled to 50 percent discount." The clerk bowed.

"And as a personal friend of the proprietor," the author continued, "I presume that you will allow me the usual 25 percent discount." Another bow from the salesman.

"Well," drawled the unblushing humorist, "under these conditions I think I may as well take the book. What's the tax?" The clerk took out his pencil and figured industriously. Then he said with the greatest of obsequiousness: "As near as I can calculate, sir, we owe you the book and about 37 and a half cents."

Gift Horse

Authors like to sign books in bookstores only partly because it makes them briefly the center of attention. A more practical reason is that none of the new books in a bookstore are really sold yet, because the bookseller can return them to the publisher for credit against other purchases. And authors know, of course, that signed books are unlikely to be accepted back by the publisher if they remain unsold. Some booksellers fear more than book thieves the obscure author lurking in a hidden nook of the bookshop and leaving his signature on a few miserable copies of his work.

The late Salvador Dali was not much given to lurking. He once sailed into a New York bookstore and demanded a copy of his *Secret Life of Salvador Dali*. The clerk began to wrap the book, when Dali asked him: "Have you read the book?" The young man, who recognized the flamboyant artist, had to admit he had not.

"Take it," said Dali, handing him back the package, "it is my gift to you. Here, I'll even autograph it for you."

Signing the copy of his book with a flourish, Dali left the store, and the clerk was too stunned to realize that he might end up having to pay for his gift.

Gift Monkey

The Monkees rock group was a "made-for-television" idea to capitalize on Beatlemania. In 1965, a British TV company wanted to create a program based on a fictional rock group. It auditioned 500 applicants, and picked two musicians and two actors with no musical performance background. The venture was so successful that the group crossed from fiction into the real world of concerts and touring and screaming fans. Despite their popularity, the Monkees quit in 1968 while they were ahead. When they got together for a twentieth-anniversary tour, the fans were waiting in a hundred cities and in larger numbers than ever. Asked about the group's future, Mickey Dolenz, now a successful TV producer, expressed his inner conflict with the appropriate animal metaphors: "I'm certainly not going to look a gift Monkee in the mouth. But we're not going to flog a dead horse, either."

First Things First

Mischa Elman's father was also his manager, looking after the box office receipts, which were often handed over directly. One night, the violin prodigy was playing Bach's "Chaconne" at Carnegie Hall while the old man was standing nervously in the wings, looking at his watch. Finally he could stand it no longer and whispered to his son on stage: "Mischa, can you hear me?" Play a bit quicker, the bank is closing any moment!"

ART AND BUSINESS

Understatement

On March 30, 1987, Christie's, the London auction house, sold one of Vincent van Gogh's paintings of sunflowers for $40 million, three times the previous record for any single work of art. Recalling van Gogh's futile attempts to sell the painting at any price a few months before his suicide, auctioneer Charles Allsop commented: "He was not very good at marketing it."

Penance

Samuel Johnson was born in Lichfield, a bookseller's son, and during his childhood he felt an aversion to his father's occupation. Toward the end of his life, the learned Doctor made his last visit to Lichfield, staying with friends, who were rather alarmed when Johnson disappeared early one morning and did not return until supper. When he appeared, the Doctor stood pensively for a few moments, before giving his explanation to the lady of the house:

Madam, I beg your pardon for the abruptness of my departure from your house this morning, but I was constrained to it by my conscience. Fifty years ago, Madam, on this day, I committed a breach of filial piety, which has ever since lain heavy on my mind, and has not till this day been expiated. My father, you recollect, was a bookseller, and had long been in the habit of attending Uttoxeter market, and opening a stall for the sale of his books during that day. Confined to his bed by indisposition, he requested me, this time fifty years ago, to visit the market, and attend the stall in his place. But, Madam, my pride prevented me from doing my duty, and I gave my father a refusal. To do away the sin of this disobedience, I this day went in postchaise to Uttoxeter, and going into the market at the time of high business, uncovered my head, and stood there with barely an hour before the stall which my father had formerly used, exposed to the sneers of the standersby and the inclemency of the weather; a penance by which I trust I have propitiated heaven for this only instance, I believe, of contumacy towards my father.

Publishers

The relationship between publishers and authors has long held a particular fascination for anecdotists, both in its commercial and human aspects. Against the usual stereotype of the greedy publisher (or booksellers, as they were called well into the nineteenth century) and the starving author, one might want to read Isaac D'Israeli's essay on the *Secret History of Authors Who Have Ruined Their Booksellers*. As he wrote:

The copiousness and the multiplicity of the writings of many authors have shown that too many find a pleasure in the act of composition which they do not communicate to others.   . . .We see one venting his mania in scrawling on his prison walls; another persisting in writing folios, while the booksellers, who were once caught, like Reynard who had lost his tail, and whom no arts could any longer practise on, turn away from the new trap; and a third, who can acquire no readers but by giving his books away, growing grey in scourging the sacred genius of antiquity. . .

Mutual Ruin

Much of what D'Israeli says still applies to academic books churned out by the university presses, except that in the old days the booksellers published such books without any subsidy. Among other cases, he cites Theophilus Raynaud, a Jesuit whose "collected works fill twenty folios, an edition which finally sent the publisher to the poor-house." And there is Nicholas de Lyra, an Italian theologian of the Renaissance, who managed to bankrupt two printers after he "had inveigled them to print his interminable commentary on the Bible. Their luckless star prevailed and their warehouse groaned with eleven hundred ponderous folios, as immovable as the shelves on which they for ever reposed!" Only a direct petition to the pope saved the hapless publishers from debtor's jail.

Irrepressible

D'Israeli's reference to the prison graffiti is to William Prynne, an insufferable Puritan and contemporary of Ben Jonson, who wrote a book against the theater, called *Histriomastix*. Unfortunately, he included an attack on Queen Henrietta Maria, the consort of Charles I, for occasionally acting in court masques. He was fined and sentenced to sit in a pillory at Westminster and Cheapside, and in each location had one ear cut off. It is not clear how this operation would have affected his ability to write, and the authorities tried other means to discourage him. One eyewitness who saw Prynne sitting in the pillory at Cheapside says that they were also burning "his huge volumes under his nose, which had almost suffocated him." To no avail, because soon after his release from imprisonment, Prynne published a volume of "Comfortable Cordials against discomfortable Fears of Imprisonment, containing some Latin Verses, and Texts of Scripture, written by Mr. Wm. Prynne, on his Chamber Walls."

Unloading

Andrew Millar bought the copyright to Fielding's novel *Amelia*, paying £800, which was a huge price in the eighteenth century. (Milton's *Paradise Lost* was bought by Jacob Tonson for £5; Dr. Johnson sold *Rasselas* for £10 so he could bury his mother.) After making the purchase, Millar showed the manuscript to Sir Andrew Mitchell, requesting to have his opinion of the work. Sir Andrew told him that it bore the indelible marks of Fielding's genius and was a fine performance. Nevertheless, he also said it was far beneath *Tom Jones*, and he advised Millar to get rid of his printed copies as soon as he could. The publisher took the advice, but devised a stratagem to sell advance orders to the book trade. At the beginning of the auction, Millar announced: "Gentlemen, I have several works to put up, for which I shall be glad if you will bid, but as to *Amelia*, every copy is spoken for." This maneuver had its effect, because the booksellers were anxious to put down their names for copies, and the edition, though very large, was immediately sold out.

Revenge

Lord Byron once presented his publisher, John Murray, with a richly bound copy of the Bible, which the latter proudly displayed in his home for all to see. One of Murray's guests was leafing through the book when he noticed that there had been an alteration in the Gospel of John. In the sentence "Now Barabbas was a robber," Byron had changed the last word to "publisher." (In 1964 William Jovanovich, the American publisher, issued his memoirs under the title, *Now Barabbas*.)

The Check Is in the Mail

O. Henry was experiencing the not unusual delay of his publishers' advance and wrote several queries about the promised payment. Finally, the short-story writer decided to call in person on his publishers.

"I'm sorry," explained the cashier, "but the officer who signs the checks is laid up with a sprained ankle."

"But my dear sir," exploded the frustrated author, "does he sign them with his feet?"

Keeping the Author Happy

During their careers most successful authors come up with a terrible book that a publisher probably will bring out just to keep the writer happy, even against the publisher's business judgment. A story circulating in New York a few years ago had a well-known writer of several best-sellers strong-arming his publisher into bringing out just such a misbegotten novel. When the book predictably failed the author asked for a meeting with his publisher. During lunch he complained that not enough money was being spent to promote his book. The publisher finally had enough. He is said to have reached into his pocket and pulled out a bunch of keys: "Here," he said as he threw the keys in front of the author, "why don't you drive a truck to my house, take whatever you want, and rob me that way."

Sweeney Todd

Bantam Books was threatened with a lawsuit by Lee Iacocca's barber, Gio Hernandez, the Cuban-born hairdresser at the Hotel Pierre. According to *People* magazine, Hernandez claims to have brought together two of his clients, Bantam Vice-President Stuart Applebaum and the chairman of

Chrysler Corporation. The barber of Pierre is in fact a kind of powerbroker since a great number of celebrities line up for his $45 haircut.

After *Iacocca* became a publishing phenomenon, Bantam gave Hernandez a check for $5,000, as a finder's fee. Gio promptly sent it back and hired the late Roy Cohn, who knew how to give back an insult. In his letter to Bantam, Cohn called the $5,000 more a tip for the haircut than compensation for his client's services as agent, powerbroker, and possibly writer.

In late 1987 the case was still pending.

The Art of Negotiating

Samuel Goldwyn wanted to gain the upper hand early in a negotiation. He needed to borrow an actor from Darryl Zanuck, but was told by the secretary that Zanuck was in a meeting. The impatient mogul insisted that Zanuck nevertheless be told of the urgency of his call. When finally the producer came to the phone, Goldwyn began the conversation with: "Darryl! What can I do for you today?"

Opener

After David Selznick had established his separate studio, he received a midnight phone call.

"David, you and I are in terrible trouble," Samuel Goldwyn said ominously at the other end of the line.

"Why, Mr. Goldwyn?" Selznick asked, thinking that Hollywood must have burned down.

"You've got Gable, and I want him," Goldwyn explained.

You Lose Some

Sam Goldwyn did not always get his own way. After the success of *The Secret Life of Walter Mitty*, the mogul tried to lure its author, James Thurber, to come and work at his studio. As an opener he offered the humorist $500 a week. Thurber was quite content to be working for Harold Ross at the *New Yorker*, so he declined in a polite letter, saying that "Mr. Ross has met the increase." Goldwyn raised the offer to a $1,000, and when he did not hear back, to $1,500 a week. Thurber declined again, so Goldwyn went to $2,500, but with no success. The matter rested there for a while, when Goldwyn decided to write again.

Whether he had forgotten the previous offer, or upon reconsideration thought it too high, this time he proposed a salary of $1,500 a week. Thurber was ready with his reply: "I am sorry, but Mr. Ross has met the decrease."

Hard Work

Igor Stravinsky was once offered $4,000 to do the score for a film. He told the Hollywood producer that he found the fee inadequate.

"It's what we paid the previous guy," the producer explained.

"Ah, but my predecessor had talent," replied the composer, "and I have not, which makes the work for me that much more difficult."

Argument

Lord Grade, head of Britain's Associated Television, in a heated argument once made reference to something being as obvious as "the answer to two plus two."

"What *is* two and two?" his antagonist insisted.

"Buying or selling?" Grade asked.

When criticized about some of his programming, Lord Grade said: "All my shows are great. Some of them are bad. But they are all great."

Disaster Movie

Lord Grade decided to expand from television into motion pictures and put a lot of money into Dino de Laurentiis's epic *The Sinking of the Titanic*. After he lost most of his investment, the mogul observed: "It might have been cheaper to raise the Atlantic."

Eulogy

Noel Coward heard the news that a rather dumb producer had blown his brains out. There had been no love lost between the playwright and the impresario: "He must have been a terrific shot," marveled Coward.

PATRONS

Patron

When Edmund Spenser finished his masterpiece *The Fairie Queen*, he carried it to the earl of Southampton, the great Elizabethan patron of several poets. As the earl read a few pages in his study, he sent his servant to Spenser, who was anxiously waiting downstairs, with twenty pounds. Reading further, he cried in a rapture: "Give that man another twenty pounds!"

Proceeding still further, he said, "Give him twenty pounds more."

But finally losing patience, he instructed his servant: "Go, turn that fellow out of the house, for if I read more I shall be ruined."

Too Little Too Late

Samuel Johnson struggled for years in dire poverty while working on his great English Dictionary, the first of its kind in the language. He had prepared a prospectus and asked, among others, the earl of Chesterfield, for his patronage. The earl sent £10 but was too busy to see Dr. Johnson. As the work neared completion, Chesterfield heard of its merits and wrote two flattering essays about it in the hope that it may yet be dedicated to him—a standard acknowledgment of patronage in those days. Johnson's rejection is one of the gems of the English language:

My Lord,

I have been lately informed, by the proprietor of the World, that two papers, in which my Dictionary is recommended to the publick, were written by your Lordship. To be so distinguished is an honour, which, being very little accustomed to favours from the great, I know not well how to receive, or in what terms to acknowledge. When, upon some slight encouragement, I first visited your Lordship, I was overpowered, like the rest of mankind, by the enchantment of your address; and could not forbear to wish that I might boast myself *Le vainqueur du vainqueur de la terre*;—that I might obtain that regard for which I saw the world contending; but I found my attendance so little encouraged, that neither pride nor modesty would suffer me to continue it. When I had once addressed your Lordship in publick, I had exhausted all the art of pleasing which a retired and uncourtly scholar can possess. I had done all that I could; and no man is well pleased to have his all neglected, be it ever so little.

Seven years, my Lord, have now past, since I waited in your outward rooms, or was repulsed from your door; during which time I have been pushing on my work through difficulties, of which it is useless to complain, and have brought it, at last, to the verge of publication, without one act of assistance, one word of encouragement, or one smile of favour. Such treatment I did not expect, for I never had a Patron before.

Is not a Patron, my Lord, one who looks with unconcern on a man struggling for life in the water, and, when he has reached ground, encumbers him with help? The notice which you have been pleased to take of my labours, had it been early, had been kind; but it has been delayed till I am indifferent, and cannot enjoy it; till I am solitary, and cannot impart it; till I am known, and do not want it. I hope it is no very cynical asperity not to confess obligations where no benefit has been received, or to be unwilling that the Publick should consider me as owing that to a Patron, which Providence has enabled me to do for myself.

Having carried on my work thus far with so little obligation to any favourer of learning, I shall not be disappointed though I should conclude it, if less be possible, with less; for I have been long wakened from that dream of hope, in which I once boasted myself with so much exultation,

> My Lord,
> your Lordship's most humble,
> Most obedient servant,
> Sam Johnson

Lord Chesterfield never replied to the letter. When someone asked him about it, his lordship replied that it was "very well written."

Starving Artist

Samuel Morse, inventor of telegraphy, was also a painter. In fact, one of his works recently set an auction record for an American painting. But, as is often the case, when he was creating those works of art, he was starving and looking for commissions. In 1832 he came back from Europe and heard that Congress had voted money for murals to be painted in the rotunda of the Capitol. The artists were to be selected by a committee headed by John Quincy Adams. Morse thought he would stand a good chance to get some work, because of his growing reputation and his recommendations from other painters. Adams, on the other hand, did not think that any American artist would be good enough and wanted to hire talent from Europe—an attitude that has not altogether disappeared today. When James Fennimore Cooper, who was a friend of Morse's, heard about Adams's stand, he wrote a scathing anonymous attack in the

New York Evening Post. Adams assumed it had been written by Morse himself and struck his name from the list of artists to be considered.

Samuel Morse's poverty at this time was later described by General Strother of Virginia:

> I engaged to become Morse's pupil and subsequently went to New York and found him in a room in University Place. He had three or four other pupils and I soon found that our professor had very little patronage. I paid my fifty dollars for one-quarter's instruction. Morse was a faithful teacher and took as much interest in our progress as—more indeed than—we did ourselves. But he was very poor. I remember that, when my second quarter's pay was due, my remittance did not come as expected, and one day the professor came in and said, courteously:
>
> "Well, Strother, my boy, how are we off for money?"
>
> "Why, professor," I answered, "I am sorry to say that I have been disappointed, but I expect a remittance next week."
>
> "Next week," he repeated sadly, "I shall be dead by that time."
>
> "Dead, sir?"
>
> "Yes, dead by starvation."
>
> I was distressed and astonished. I said hurriedly:
>
> "Would ten dollars be of any service?"
>
> "Ten dollars would save my life. That is all it would do."
>
> I paid the money, all that I had, and we dined together. It was a modest meal, but good, and after he had finished, he said:
>
> "This is my first meal for twenty-four hours. Strother, don't be an artist. It means beggary. Your life depends upon people who know nothing of your art and care nothing for you. A house dog lives better, and the very sensitiveness that stimulates an artist to work keeps him alive to suffering."

Music

Thomas Britton was a coal dealer with such passion for music that he was known as the "musical small-coal-man." He purchased every book on music that he could find; he also found time to gain a high proficiency in chemistry. This unusual man met an abrupt fate in 1714, according to Maunder's *Biographical Treasury*: "His harmless life was put to an end by a silly trick of a ventriloquist, which frightened him so much that he never recovered."

Itch

Giacomo Puccini came to New York in 1910 to attend the rehearsals of his *Girl of the Golden West* at the Metropolitan Opera. The management arranged for a tea party where the benefactors of the opera house could meet the great composer. Puccini was working the crowd of admiring Vanderbilts, Astors, and Rockefellers, when his agent and publisher, Tito Ricordi, grabbed him by the arm and made an announcement:

"Ladies and gentlemen, we have not come to New York to drink tea but to work and to rehearse. Thank you very much, and come along Giacomo!" He then dragged Puccini from the room.

"For heaven's sake, Tito, why did you do that?" the composer asked when they were outside in the street.

"To restrain myself," Ricordi shouted, "I was getting a burning itch to smack a billion dollars right in the face!"

Connoisseur

Henry Clay Frick, the steel magnate, used to carry back and forth his collection of paintings and other fabulous art objects between his New York townhouse and his country estate in Massachusetts, where he spent the summer. The treasures, packed in specially made railroad cars, were nevertheless exposed to considerable hazards by being transported back and forth twice a year. The journalist Oswald Garrison Villard once asked Frick whether he was ever worried about his paintings being damaged or stolen. "Not at all," replied the art-loving tycoon, "they are insured."

How to Start a Collection

Armand Hammer, the octogenarian chairman of Occidental Petroleum, recently donated a large part of his art collection to the Los Angeles County Museum of Art. He became a collector by accident. In 1921 he went to Russia as a young doctor to help out following the civil war and during the typhoid epidemic. But the famine that ensued was even worse, and Hammer ended up selling wheat to the Russians. Since the government had no money to pay him with, he received concessions in asbestos mining and foreign trade. Hammer went back to America and signed up Henry Ford and thirty-seven other companies on an exclusive basis. As he revealed in an interview in *ARTnews*, when he returned to the Soviet Union:

> The Russians gave me a big house to live in, but there were no furnishings. So I sent for my brother, Victor, who had studied art at Princeton, to come over and help me furnish my house. Victor went out and found he could buy works of art and antiques for the price of ordinary furnishings. And that's how I became interested in art. Our house became a museum filled with paintings, French furniture, 18th century furniture—Louis XIV, XV, XVI

furniture, tapestries, Aubusson rugs, Sèvres china, beautiful silver, all of which Victor paid a pittance for, because they were sold at commission stores mostly in Moscow. People didn't have money; they would bring their things in and put them on sale for whatever they would bring. There were very few buyers; the only buyers were the embassies and Armand Hammer.

Over the years, Armand Hammer became a passionate collector. Asked for his favorite work of art, he was said to admit that he did not own it: Renoir's *The Luncheon of the Boating Party* at the Phillips Collection in Washington.

"I never envied anybody as much as I do the Phillips. If that picture came up at auction today, I think I'd hock my shares in Occidental Petroleum."

Calvary

When Henry Huntington, the railroad tycoon and art collector, was in the hospital about to undergo surgery, he solemnly summoned his agent for buying rare books, Dr. A. S. W. Rosenbach, and his art dealer, Sir Joseph Duveen. He asked them to sit on either side of his bed, where he lay with his arms outstretched. After some small talk, during which the dealers muttered encouraging hopes for the health of their biggest customer, Huntington turned to the art dealer and asked: "Sir Joseph, do I remind you of anyone?" Duveen looked startled but could not think of an answer. Then the patient turned to his book dealer, and asked the same question: "Doctor Rosenbach, do I remind you of anyone?" The good doctor could not think what his patron meant. Henry Huntington stretched his arms out a little wider and said with a wicked smile: "Well, I remind myself of Jesus Christ on the cross between the two thieves."

· 12 ·

REWARDS

BEING RICH

It's All Relative

John Jacob Astor, then the richest man in America, explained to Julia Ward Howe: "A man who has a million dollars is as well off as if he were rich."

When a reporter asked J. Paul Getty if his wealth exceeded a billion dollars, the oilman thought for a minute and said: "Probably," and after another pause added: "But remember, a billion dollars doesn't go as far as it used to."

Small Change

Nubar Gulbenkian was filling out a form sent by a market research company, and one of the questions asked what his position was. "Enviable," he wrote.

Once when he bought a new Rolls-Royce, Gulbenkian was excited by the automobile's perfect steering. "It can turn on a sixpence," he tried to explain to a friend, "—whatever that is."

Envy

Andrew Carnegie, at the height of his fame, arrived in Paris at the end of a European tour. Hundreds of journalists mobbed him as he descended from his private train at the Gare de l'Est.

"Which city in Europe did you like most?"

"What's the difference between the old and the new world?"

"What do you intend to do in Paris?"

The industrialist tried to answer one or two questions, but found himself unable to satisfy the rapid-fire reporters. Se he tried another approach.

"What a wonderful profession you have," enthused Carnegie, "You want to discover all that is to know about life; you keep track of everything that goes on; you notice every new phenomenon. I deeply regret that I did not become, like you, a journalist." This confession was first received in momentary silence. Then one of the reporters piped up:

"You can rest assured, Mr. Carnegie, that we regret even more deeply that we did not become, like you, billionaires!"

This brings to mind the story of the man who obviously envied Carnegie's wealth and was telling Mark Twain how, in his opinion, the money was tainted.

"Certainly," Twain agreed, "'taint yours, and 'taint mine."

The Rothschilds

No family has been associated with financial astuteness and wealth so long and in so many countries as the Rothschilds. Although their wealth was eclipsed by the large numbers of nouveau riche created by industrial America, the Rothschild family's political influence has been without parallel. It would be simply impossible to write a history of modern Europe without the Rothschilds. Several events during the Napoleonic Wars helped raise the family to legendary status.

As often told, Meyer Amschel Rothschild was a cloth merchant and coin dealer in the German town of Frankfurt am Main during the second part of the eighteenth century. He originally lived in a house with a "red shield" sign, hence the family name. As Meyer's money-changing business grew, so did his five sons. He sent Jakob to Paris, Salomon to Vienna, Kalmann to Naples, and Nathan to England, while Amschel helped his papa at home. The various branches pooled and exchanged information, skills, and resources.

When Prince Wilhelm of Hesse-Cassel had to flee his principality in a hurry from Napoléon's army, he had twelve million silver florins in his palace vaults. Unwilling to trust any of his courtiers, the prince sent for Meyer and offered him free use of the money if he could take it away. On these terms the elder Rothschild undertook the trust, and by the assistance of some local Jewish bankers, who were his friends, the treasure was smuggled out of Cassel. Then it was shipped to London, where Nathan Rothschild carefully invested it and made a handsome profit. After the fall of Napoléon, the old Prince was astonished and grateful to receive back not only his original treasure but a healthy profit as well.

Similar cooperation was used when the British government was desperate to supply Wellington's army in Spain with gold with which to buy provisions. Nathan in London shipped gold to his brother Jakob in Paris, who smuggled it across the Pyrenees. But the one coup most often told about the Rothschilds's sense of timing concerns the Waterloo campaign. According to one legend, Nathan Rothschild received, by a special family messenger, news of Wellington's decisive victory eight hours before the British government did. Another story has him watching the battle in person and then galloping back to London, where he immediately went to the stock exchange. There he stood, in his favorite place, leaning against a pillar, a study of utter gloom, which made everybody stampede to sell. When the stocks were sufficiently depressed, Rothschild and his agents started buying. And when the good news about Waterloo finally became universally known, the share prices went up, making Rothschild an enormous fortune.

As with most legends, modern historians have been skeptical about the details. According to Reginald Colby's article, "The Waterloo Despatch," Nathan Rothschild arrived back from the Continent a few days before the battle, and he was informed of its outcome by one of his agents, called Roworth, on the evening of June 20, 1815, or twenty-four hours before Wellington's own aide-de-camp brought the news. However, Rothschild informed the British government of what he knew early on the morning of June 21, *before* going to the Royal Exchange. Details of the victory did not become generally known or were not believed in London until the following day. As for the first tumbling and then sharply rising stocks, research has shown that the week before the battle 4 percent consols were quoted at 70-1/2, which dropped to 69-1/16 two days before the battle, because of the pessimism that gripped London. On the morning of June 21, when Rothschild employed his privileged information to sell, the consols stood at 70 and three days later they rose to 71-1/2 —hardly a killing. However, the Rothschilds were to perfect their sense of political timing, and this famous incident probably gave rise to the adage that one should sell on good news.

The Works

The head of the Austrian branch of the Rothschild family invited to a banquet Julius Bauer, the Hungarian-born humorist who was a favorite with the Viennese in the early part of this century. After the formal toasts, a general cry went up for Bauer to speak. He complied with exactly the kind of witty, light, and pointed speech that the guests wanted. Afterward, Count Rothschild himself rushed up to his guest in a state of rapture: "Ah, Herr Bauer, I wish I could be as witty as you!" he gushed. The humorist fixed him with a mournful stare: "What, that too?"

Lucky

On top of their immense wealth, the Rothschilds were also proverbially lucky. Another story from the days of the Austro-Hungarian monarchy has a poor vendor of lottery tickets selling Count Rothschild a ticket, which then won the top prize of 600,000 gold crowns. Next day the seller called on Rothschild: "In addition to your uncounted wealth, you have won, sir, the top prize in the lottery. I had the great honor of selling the ticket to you myself. Here is the number . . ."

"My dear man, no need to go on," said the banker graciously, "I'm most happy that you came to see me and that I can express my gratitude. I am going to give you an annuity of six thousand gold crowns for life; you will start receiving 500 crowns at the beginning of each month."

The lottery vendor would not hear of such an arrangement: "Sir, be kind enough to give me six thousand crowns once and for all."

"But why would you want only six thousand just once," asked the astonished count, "when I'm offering you that much each and every year for the rest of your life?"

The poor man had a ready explanation: "Because with *your* luck, sir, I doubt if I'd live to the first of next month."

Plutocrats

During the 1890s, the age called "gilded" by Mark Twain, the gulf between the rich and poor became more like a Grand Canyon. While the poor were reeling from one depression to another, and their armies were marching on Washington, D.C., the nouveau riche achieved new levels of extravagance reminiscent of the decline of Rome. Charles and Mary Beard described some of these excesses in their book *The Rise of American Civilization:*

At a dinner eaten on horseback, the favorite steed was fed flowers and champagne; to a small black-and-tan dog wearing a diamond collar worth $15,000 a lavish banquet was tendered; at one function, the cigarettes were wrapped in hundred dollar bills; at another, fine black pearls were given to the diners in their oysters; at a third, an elaborate feast was served to boon companions in a mine from which came the fortune of the host. Then weary of such limited diversions, the plutocracy contrived more freakish occasions—with monkeys seated between guests, human gold fish swimming about in pools, or chorus girls hopping out of pies.

The Working Rich

Most people have heard F. Scott Fitzgerald's famous dictum that "the rich are different from you and me," and also Ernest Hemingway's retort: "Yes, they have more money." Sometimes they also work harder.

H.L. Hunt, whom *Life* magazine in 1948 called the richest man in America, remained a shy, hard-working recluse who would rather leave his modest automobile a few blocks from his skyscraper in Dallas than pay what he considered a stiff parking fee. During World War II, Hunt Oil produced more oil than the German Reich (including the Rumanian oil fields), yet Hunt, who spent much of his money on conservative causes, did not care that much for wealth. "Money as money is nothing," he would say, "it is just something to make book-keeping convenient."

In the 1950s, Hunt had to fly from Dallas to New York at a moment's notice and called the Waldorf-Astoria to have his regular suite ready. The king and queen of the Hellenes happened to be staying in the suite, and the embarrassed management hurriedly moved them into another. When Hunt arrived, he noticed that the Greek royal couple had left large bouquets of flowers. "Isn't it nice of the king and queen," the tycoon remarked to his entourage, "to leave us all their flowers."

Little Gloria, Happy at Last

One of the wealthiest women in America, Gloria Vanderbilt is also one of the working rich. Asked which felt better—inherited or earned money—she replied without hesitation: "Oh, darling, the money you make is better."

Ancestors

William Gladstone, prime minister to Queen Victoria, once saw an old painting in a dusty antique shop. It was the portrait of an aristocrat, dressed in velvet and lace in the fashion of the sixteenth century. Although Gladstone liked the painting a great deal, he did not want to pay the price the dealer was asking. Not long afterward he was invited to the house of a rich merchant and noticed the same painting. While he stood in front of it and admiring it afresh, his host came up and said: "I'm glad you like him. He is one of my Elizabethan ancestors. Actually, he was a minister to the Queen."

"Three guineas less," replied Gladstone, "and he would have been my ancestor."

Heirs

At a White House dinner given by Theodore Roosevelt, Mrs. Nancy Astor was seated ahead of Mrs. Grace Vanderbilt. "The Astors skinned skunks a hundred years before the Vanderbilts worked ferries," Mrs. Astor explained.

Memory

Toward the end of his life, Cornelius Vanderbilt was staying at a Saratoga hotel with his family. In the lobby, a somewhat overdressed lady approached the old man and reminded him of their acquaintance. The Commodore spent some time chatting affably with her, while his wife and daughter sat stonily and sniffed the air with scorn. Afterward, his daughter reproached him: "Father, don't you remember her as that vulgar woman who used to sell us poultry back at home?"

"I certainly do," the old man replied, "and I remember your mother when she used to sell root-beer at three cents a glass over in Jersey, when I went up there from Staten Island peddling oysters out of my boat."

Definition of a Yacht

Cornelius Vanderbilt was attending dinner at Bar Harbor, Maine, to celebrate the victory of his sloop *Aurora* in the squadron run from Portland to Rockland. In an after-dinner speech, he declared: "Yachts like these don't come under the cynical definition I once heard a Camden lobsterman give. 'What exactly is a yacht?' a lady said to this old lobsterman. He plugged a lobster's claws and mocked: 'What's a yacht? Oh, ye just take an old tub or craft, and' fill her up with whiskey an' chicken an' cigars, an' thet's a yacht.'"

Cruising

Franklin Roosevelt was a frequent guest aboard Vincent Astor's yacht the *Nourmahal*. Once when he received an invitation for a winter cruise, he said: "I hope you aren't putting that big boat in commission just for me."

"The *Nourmahal* is commissioned all year round, Mr. President," Astor replied.

"In that case, I guess we'll have to raise the taxes on the rich again," laughed F.D.R.

History

Among the many properties William Randolph Hearst bought was St. Donat's castle in Wales. When his wife heard that the castle was Norman, she asked: "Norman who?"

Closed Doors

J. P. Morgan heard through the grapevine that his protegé, Charles Schwab, was going out with a chorus girl.

"I'm really disappointed in you," the financier called him on the carpet.

"But, Mr. Morgan," protested Schwab, "at least I'm not a hypocrite. All I did was what other young men in my position, or you yourself have been doing behind closed doors, for years."

"And that's what doors are for," replied Morgan.

Room Service

Thomas Du Pont, industrialist and Delaware politician in the 1920s, once found a sexy feminine nightgown in the Chicago suite where he was staying. He rang for the manager and handed the garment to him with the order: "Fill it, and bring it back."

They Are Playing My Tune

The man who parlayed $1,000 into the worldwide Sheraton hotel chain also enjoyed photography and writing songs. It was a tradition that whenever Ernest Henderson walked past a Sheraton bandstand, the orchestra would strike up one of his tunes.

Such Stuff as Dreams Are Made Of

According to another hotelman, when Conrad Hilton was having the first night of his honeymoon with Zsa Zsa Gabor, he was also deep into negotiations about adding another hotel to his chain. His chief competitor was Ernest Henderson, founder of the rival Sheraton chain. Hilton was waiting in the bridal suite while his movie-star bride was delaying her entrance from the lavish bathroom. When she finally came into the bedroom, Zsa Zsa saw Conrad's eyes dreamily abstracted, seemingly filled with anticipation and lust. Just to make sure, Zsa Zsa wrapped her soft arms around her latest husband, sat herself comfortably in his lap, and in a very sexy voice purred into his ears: "Vat are you teenkink, my beeg, handsome dahlink?"

And Hilton was supposed to have replied equally softly and sexily: "I'm thinking . . . I am dreaming of how I'm going to grab the Blackstone away from under Ernie Henderson's nose."

Naps

Despite the constant controversies swirling around him, the hatred inspired by his acquisitiveness, and the death threats, John D. Rockefeller lived to be almost 100, reputedly with all his original teeth intact. There is no word that he ever did push-ups, jogged, or pedaled an executive bicycle. He had a placid disposition. He never got excited and was never rushed. He did have a secret: he always took a half hour nap at noon. Later in life he would take as many as five naps in his simple office on 26 Broadway. It was of that room that a disappointed visitor once asked:

"How can you hope to impress anybody in an office like this?"

"Who do I have to impress?" Rockefeller replied.

Protocol

Society columnist Igor Cassini once asked Bernard Baruch how he arranged the seating at his dinner tables so as not to offend any of the numerous notables.

"I never bother about that," Baruch replied. "Those who matter don't mind, and those who mind don't matter."

Turkey

Baruch himself was guest of honor at a Thanksgiving night banquet, at which Jimmie Walker was the toastmaster. He introduced the Sage of

Wall Street: "You have been giving your attention to turkey stuffed with sage. I now present to you a sage stuffed with turkey."

Conversation Partner

Robert Lacey, in preparing research for his recent biography of the reclusive Henry Ford II, was given every discouragement. One assistant told the biographer: "Mr. Ford has learnt from experience never to trust writers." And, "Mr. Ford feels like a monkey who has put his hand through the bars of the cage too many times for a banana, while journalist after journalist stubbed their cigarettes out on him."

Unfazed, Lacey moved his family from England to Detroit, and stormed Motown's social bastions to get close to his quarry. At the first dinner party where the Laceys met Kathy and Henry Ford, the writer's wife found herself seated next to the industrialist. Without any preamble, Ford asked her: "Tell me, would you rather have AIDS or a Third World War?"

Mrs. Lacey was somewhat lost for words, but finally managed to mumble her preference for AIDS.

"Oh, I'd rather have another war," Henry Ford begged to differ, "I had a good war last time round, I enjoyed that war."

And he went back to his meal.

Yes, Virginia, There Are Free Lunches

The 1986 Christmas season saw big-ticket giveaways as inducements for the rich to buy even bigger ticket items. Antonio Martinez-Monfort found it difficult to sell luxury condos in Tampa, Florida, until he offered to throw in a $30,000 BMW "for free." Chicago jeweler Lester Lampert wanted to give away a Rolls-Royce Silver Shadow to the purchaser of his $425,000 diamond baubles. And another jeweler, Fred Joailler of Fifth Avenue, tried to lure customers by offering a free trip to Paris where one would stay at the top luxury hotel and eat at top restaurants. "We think that no one," Mr. Joailler told *Newsweek*, "should be exempt from getting something for nothing." The rich must have decided otherwise, because no one had claimed the trip by the week before Christmas. *Newsweek* thought it may have had something to do with the free ticket to Paris: it was only coach class.

Gluttony

At about the time of Queen Victoria's accession to the throne, a wealthy London merchant who had lately retired from business consulted Sir

Astley Cooper, a famous physician, about the state of his health. After a few questions, the doctor discovered that the merchant was excessively fond of the good things in life and decided to diagnose him in his own language: "You are a merchant, sir, and therefore must possess an extensive knowledge of trade; but did you ever know of an instance in which the imports exceeded the exports that there was not a glut in the market? That's the case with you, sir; take more physic, and eat less."

Principles

"It's easy to have principles when you're rich," said Ray Kroc, the McDonald's hamburger magnate. "The important thing is to have principles when you're poor."

MISERS

School for Misers

"Plum Turner" and "Vulture Hopkins," two noted misers, were immortalized in Pope's *Moral Essays* (Epistle 3). Richard Turner had been a Turkey merchant (meaning he traded in the Levant, not in turkeys), and he died in 1733. When possessed of £300,000 he gave up his coach because interest was reduced from 5 to 4 percent. He then put £70,000 into the Charitable Corporation for better interest. When he lost this sum, he took it so much to heart that he kept to his chamber ever after.

John Hopkins was generally known by the name of "Vulture," perhaps after Voltore, a character in Ben Jonson's celebrated play, *Volpone*. He lived worthless, but died wealthy: he would give to no person living, but bequeath his riches, also around £300,000 with the proviso that it could not be touched until after the second generation. A wealthy London merchant who resided in Old Broad Street, Hopkins was the architect of almost all his wealth, which originated in some highly fortunate speculations in stocks, and was considerably increased at the explosion of the South Sea Bubble in 1720. On one occasion he paid an evening visit to Guy, the founder of the hospital named after him in Southwark, who was also as remarkable for his private parsimony as his public munificence. As Hopkins entered the room, Mr. Guy lighted a farthing candle that lay ready on the table and desired to know the purport of the gentleman's visit.

"I have been told," said Hopkins, "that you, sir, are better versed in the prudent and necessary art of saving than any man now living, and therefore I wait upon you for a lesson of frugality; an art in which I used to think I excelled, but am told by all who know you, that you are greatly my superior."

"And is that all you came about?" replied Guy; "why, then, we can talk this matter over in the dark." Upon this, with great deliberation, he extinguished the farthing candle. Struck with this example of economy, Hopkins rose up, acknowledged himself convinced of the other's superior thrift, and took his leave.

The Witch

Hetty Green, known as the "Witch of Wall Street," was the richest woman in America when she died in 1916, aged over 80. She made her fortune herself, through shrewd investments, mainly in real estate and through, in the words of one biographer, "forgery, perjury, penury, ruthlessness and stamina." Her meanness, though legendary, was all too real. She dressed in rags, fashioning newspaper into underwear, sleeping in cold-water apartments, and using for office space a free desk and corner given by her bankers or brokers. One would expect them to have been happy with her business, but, in fact, Mrs. Green's poor hygiene turned other customers away; and the bank could not use her millions, because she insisted on having her money available to her upon demand at all times.

Hetty Green spent a good deal of her life fighting taxes and using high-priced lawyers to prove to the government that she did not own anything. She lived at boarding houses and hotels under different aliases and insisted upon paying rent when she stayed with acquaintances to avoid any obligation. At one of her tax hearings she was asked:

"Where did you stay last night?"

"At the Hotel St. George in Brooklyn," replied Mrs. Green. "I have paid my bill there and I don't know where I shall go to-night."

Then, as the assistant corporation counsel was about to put his next question, she asked sweetly: "Couldn't you find me a place, Mr. Dean?"

The Successors

Hetty Green was haunted by the question of who would inherit her wealth. In her biography, *The Witch of Wall Street*, her haunted existence is described:

Conjured out of her fancy there were apparitions among those pursuers from whom Mrs. Green was constantly fleeing. There were poisoners, garroters, and men with daggers. Sometimes she professed to believe these enemies had been hired by the ever-swelling tide of her poor relations who would inherit her fortune when she died. At other times she would confide a belief that she was being hunted by men who had choked her father to death. One time she told her friend Mrs. Whelpley that the marks of assassins' fingers were on her father's throat as he lay in his coffin. "Like this," she said, and seized her own throat with fingers flexed as talons. Livid lines remained on her waxy flesh when she ended this curious attack on herself.

Hetty Green did in fact have two children. But she had denied her only son medical aid, so he became a cripple for life. Colonel E. H. Green and his sister took their revenge when their mother died by squandering her fortune on patent medicines and buying yachts that they then neglected and left to sink. And they derived as little happiness from the money as their mother had.

Mongrel Love

Hetty Green showed the most warmth toward her dogs. At one time she had a mongrel that liked to bite visitors. One of them suggested that she should get rid of the dog. Mrs. Green refused, saying: "The dog loves me—and he doesn't even know how rich I am."

Values

The world was shocked when J. Paul Getty paid the ransom to his grandson's Italian kidnapers only after they had mailed the boy's ear to him. In 1956 his 12-year-old son, Timmy, was dying of a brain tumor, but Getty could not find the time to leave Britain and visit him in California. Yet the billionaire was not entirely heartless. When his dogs got sick, he spared no expense and he reportedly cried for three days when one of them died.

Lost Appetite

Ostervald, a Parisian banker, left three million francs when he died in 1790. He began accumulating money early. He was accustomed to drink a pint of beer at a local tavern where he had his daily supper. After each meal he would collect as many bottle corks as he could find, and in the end he sold these for twelve louis d'or. This became the foundation of

Ostervald's splendid fortune, gained for the most part by stockjobbing. A few days before his death, a servant importuned him to purchase some meat to make a little soup for his master.

"True, I should like the soup," said the dying millionaire, "but I have no appetite for the meat—and what is to become of that? It would be a sad waste."

Cheap Coffin

There are several stories about misers carrying their penury close to their graves. In England, at the turn of the nineteenth century, there was Edward Nokes who, according to a contemporary account, gave a strict charge that his coffin should not have a nail in it. This was actually adhered to, the lid being made fast with hinges of cord, and minus a coffin-plate, for which the initials E. N. cut upon the wood were substituted. His shroud was made of a pound of wool. The coffin was covered with a sheet in place of a pall.

The same source describes Thomas Pitt of Warwickshire, who "some weeks prior to the sickness which terminated his despicable career, went to several undertakers in quest of a cheap coffin."

Life Imitates Art

And finally a portrait worthy of Molière painted by the antiquarian John Timbs:

Thomas Cooke, of Pentonville, who died in 1811, leaving great wealth, was known to put on ragged clothes and apply as a pauper at gentlemen's houses for a dispensary letter, for the cure of his eyes. In his latter days, when wearing a well-powdered wig and long ruffles, he would pretend to fall in a fit at a door, and if assistance was offered, would ask for water; and if pressed to take wine, would appear reluctantly to consent, and then drink two glasses. Meanwhile he was discovered to be the rich Mr. Cooke, the sugar-baker, worth a hundred thousand pounds. In a few days he paid a second visit about dinner time, under the pretence of thanking the gentleman for saving his life the other day; he stayed to dinner, caressed all the children and took their names in writing, and the parents thus believed he would leave them legacies. They then poured upon Cooke presents of provisions, most of which he sold. . . . Among other meanness, the miser, who was ceremoniously religious, used to take the sacrament at home; "it saves my pocket," said he, "at church I must put a shilling into the plate."

At length death came for the miser. He sent for medical men—some would not attend; but a surgeon who came was turned out of the house for cheating Cooke by sending medicine, when the medical man told him he could only live six days. Cooke's executors gave him what he would have called an extravagant funeral, but the mob pelted with cabbage-stalks the procession from the miser's house at Pentonville to his grave.

PHILANTHROPISTS

The Discount Philanthropist

Taylor was the name of a successful stockjobber in London in the early part of the nineteenth century. He lived as a miser, barely surviving on the necessities of life. John Timbs describes his last days:

On his death-bed the officers of the parish waited upon him at his request, and found the old man on a wretched bed in a garret, dining on a thin slice of bacon and a potato, of which he asked them to partake. One of them accepting, the miser desired the cook to broil him another; but, finding the larder totally empty, Taylor rebuked her harshly for not having it well supplied with a quarter of a pound to cut out in slices for company. He then informed the overseers of the poor that he had left, by his will, one thousand pounds sterling for their relief, and eagerly inquired if they would not allow him a five percent discount for prompt payment! This being assented to, Taylor, apparently much delighted, immediately gave them a cheque for nine hundred and fifty pounds, and soon after breathed his last.

An Incurable Giver

At the age of 40, Edward Colston was an eminent East Indian merchant, with forty ships and immense riches flowing to him. He distributed many thousands of pounds to various charities in and about London, besides private gifts in many parts of the kingdom. In the year 1708 he instituted a magnificent school in Bristol that cost him an immense sum and endowed the same with a large annuity. He likewise gave £10 for apprenticing every boy in that place, and for twelve years after his death the same amount to put them into business. And his private charities were believed to have far exceeded the public. One of Mr. Colston's ships, which had been missing from the East Indies for three years and was presumed lost, at length arrived richly laden. When his principal clerk brought him the report of her arrival, and of the riches on board, he said that since she had been totally given up for lost, he would not claim any right to her. He ordered the ship and merchandise to be sold and the proceeds to be applied toward the relief of the needy.

At one time Colston entertained thoughts of marriage, as chronicled in a near contemporary account:

> He paid his addresses to a lady with whose attractions he had become somewhat smitten, but being somewhat timorous lest he should be hindered in his favorite charitable designs, he thought he would make a trial of her temper and disposition. Therefore, one morning, he filled his pockets with gold and silver, in order that, if any object presented itself in the course of their tour over London Bridge, he might satisfy his intentions. While they were walking near St. Magnus' church, a woman in extreme misery, with twins in her lap, sat begging; and as he and his interested lady were arm in arm, he beheld the wretched object, put his hand into his pocket, and took out a handful of gold and silver, casting it unhesitatingly into the poor woman's lap. The lady being greatly alarmed at the profuse generosity, colored prodigiously; so that when they had gone a little further toward the bridge, she turned to him and said:
>
> "Sir, do you know what you did a few minutes ago?"
>
> "Madam," replied Mr. Colston, "I never let my left hand know what my right hand doeth."
>
> He then took his leave of her, and for this reason he never married to the day of his death at the age of four score and five.

Ritual

Long before the great American philanthropic foundations, there was Muria Kimata of Tokyo, who formed a company to lend money to the poor at low interest. It proved a failure, for though there were enough poor people anxious to borrow, few of them could repay their loans. Muria Kimata had to abandon his project, having lost heavily himself and having involved many of his friends with him. He still had, however, a large fortune, and on the anniversary of his father's death, he called his stockholders together, and out of his private means paid to each the amount of his loss. Then, placing their receipts, with all the obligations and securities given to the company by the poor borrowers, in a brazier with incense, he burned them before the shrine of Hotoke Sama.

A Speculator's Conscience

In 1720, the year celebrated for the bursting of the South Sea Bubble, a gentleman called late one evening at the banking house of Hankey & Company. He was in a coach but refused to get out, but desired that one of the partners of the house would come to him. Into the hands of this banker, when he appeared, he put a parcel, very carefully sealed up, and desired that it might be taken care of till he should return again. A few days passed, a few weeks, a few months, but the stranger never returned. At the end of the second or third year, the partners agreed to open this mysterious parcel. They found the large sum of £115,000, with a letter stating that it had been obtained by the South Sea speculation, and directing that it should be put in the hands of three trustees, whose names were mentioned, and the interest to be appropriated to the relief of the poor.

Stewardship

Richard Reynolds was an English merchant in Bristol who amassed a fortune in the early part of the nineteenth century. A deeply religious Quaker, he used to refer to himself as merely a steward of the Almighty. According to a contemporary,

> he devoted his entire income, after deducting the moderate expenses of his family, to charitable purposes, and he thought his round of duty still incomplete, unless he devoted his time likewise. He often deprived himself of slumber to watch beside the bed of sickness and pain and to administer consolation to those in trouble. On one occasion he wrote a friend in London, requesting to know what object of charity presented itself, stating that he had not spent the whole of his income. His friend informed him of a number of persons confined in prison for small debts. Reynolds paid the whole sum, and swept that miserable abode of its distressed tenants. Most of his donations were enclosed in blank covers, bearing a modest signature of "A Friend." A lady once applied to him on behalf of an orphan, saying:
>
> "When he is old enough, I will teach him to name and thank his benefactor."
>
> "Nay," replied the Quaker, "thou are wrong. We do not thank the clouds for rain. Teach him to look higher, and thank Him who giveth both the clouds and the rain. My talent is the meanest of all talents—a little sordid dust; but as the man in the parable was accountable for his talent, so I am accountable to the great Lord of all."

Prayer

On a visit to Georgia, Andrew Carnegie went to a small local church. The collection plate was passed around and he placed a $50 bill on it. When the minister counted the collection and saw the bill, he announced to the congregation: "Friends, the Lord has been mighty good to us today. Now let us pray that the bill which the gentleman with the grey hair and beard has given us be a good bill."

Matching Grants

Perhaps the most famous of Andrew Carnegie's philanthropies was to build libraries all over the English-speaking world. But he gave only 90 percent toward the costs, requiring that the community put up 10 percent:

"You cannot push anyone up the ladder unless he is willing to climb a little himself," he said, which became the guiding principle of the Carnegie Foundation.

On another occasion he tried to apply the principle when the treasurer of the New York Philharmonic Society came to make his annual pitch. It was one of Carnegie's favorite charities, and he was about to write a check to wipe out the Society's entire deficit. Suddenly he stopped:

"Surely, there must be other rich, generous music lovers in this town who could help out. Why don't you raise half this amount, and come back to me for the other half," said the great philanthropist, thus inventing the matching grant.

The next day, the treasurer came back and told Carnegie that he had raised $30,000 and would like now to get Carnegie's check. The patron of the arts was immensely pleased at this show of enterprise and immediately handed it over. But he was curious.

"Who, may I ask, contributed the other half?"

"Mrs. Carnegie," came the reply.

A Great Writer

Willy Brandt was given a tour of the newly finished Mann Auditorium in Tel Aviv on his official visit to Israel. He was deeply moved that the Israelis named such an impressive building after Thomas Mann, a great German writer. His host was embarrassed to tell him that the building had been named because of Frederic Mann, a philanthropist in Philadelphia.

"But what did he write?" asked the mayor of Berlin.

"The check," he was told.

Biting the Hand

An unusual method of repaying society is being currently practiced by Patrick Reynolds, grandson of the founder of the R. J. Reynolds Tobacco Company. Patrick, who is an actor, hit the headlines in 1986 when he testified before a congressional committee that was considering legislation banning tobacco advertising from newspapers and magazines. He also starred in a campaign promoting the American Lung Association, claiming that he had quit smoking, and that his father had died of emphysema at the age of 58. Obviously a thorn in the side of his family, Patrick has divested himself of his inherited shares in Nabisco, the parent company of the tobacco giant. Asked if he minded the accusation of biting the hand that feeds him, he replied: "It's the same hand that has killed millions and may kill millions more."

Lawyers

Lord Leverhulme rose from grocery boy to founder of Sunlight Soap in England. After he amassed his fortune, he devoted considerable energy to charitable schemes to improve the conditions of workers. Hearing about the hardships suffered by the fishermen of the island of Harris in the Hebrides, he purchased the whole island, intending to restore the fishing industry and provide better housing for the island's inhabitants. His lawyer drew up a lease for the tenants, full of the usual legal technicalities in language that only lawyers understand. The lawyer then went around the island to get the tenants to sign. On one of these trips he came to a tiny cottage where a very old man lived alone. The lawyer showed him the lease, explaining its terms and provisions and insisting that the fisherman must agree to all its clauses. The old fellow looked at the lease, listened to the lawyer, looked again, and finally he spoke:

"I haven't been able to keep the Ten Commandments for the sake of a mansion in heaven. I'm darned if I'll agree to keep a hundred commandments for the sake of a small cottage on the Isle of Harris."

Lord Leverhulme, who used to enjoy telling this story at his lawyer's expense, gave up his scheme when he realized that the fiercely independent islanders did not want anything savoring of charity.

It Is Easier to Receive

Mother Theresa has said to people who want to support her work in India that "they need to give until it hurts." I doubt if she knows a Scottish story that B. C. Forbes was fond of telling:

A lady called on a businessman to solicit money. She handed him a card that read: "Charity Fair—Give Till It Hurts." The Scotsman read it carefully and genuine tears seemed to well up in his eyes as he handed back her card: "Lady, the verra idea hurts."

My Son Gave at the Office

A charity once approached John Jacob Astor for a donation. The old man took a long look at the list of wealthy people who had already subscribed, then signed his name and wrote a check for fifty dollars. The committee had higher expectations, and one of them ventured to say so: "We did hope for more, Mr. Astor. Your son gave us a hundred dollars."

"Ah," replied the millionaire, "William has a rich father. Mine was very poor."

Moral Fiber

John D. Rockefeller, Jr., gave away millions in various public charities. But he was not a soft touch privately. Once he was asked for a small "tide-over loan" by a member of the Sunday school class he taught regularly at his Baptist church. Rockefeller used the occasion to reproach the young man for coming forth with such a request, explaining to him and the class that he would have to refuse the loan, which might fatally weaken the fiber of his character.

The End of the Day

In setting up the Charles R. Bronfman Foundation in late 1986, the co-chairman of Seagram told *Maclean's* magazine: "It gives me the chance to do what I want for myself, and for the things I so deeply believe in. At the end of the day you cannot ask for more than that."

And That's Final

Somebody once approached Louis B. Mayer for a donation to charity, reminding him of the old saw: "You can't take it with you." The movie mogul seemed surprised and quickly replied: "Then I won't go."

HARD TIMES

Failure

Those who know success are usually familiar with failure. Thomas Edison is well known for his definition of genius as 2 percent inspiration and 98 percent perspiration. He also had something to say about the causes of failure: "Failure is a matter of self-conceit. Men don't work hard be-cause, in their self-conceit, they think they are so clever that they'll succeed without working hard. Most men believe that they'll wake up some day and find themselves rich and famous—and eventually, they do 'wake up.'"

Slow Start

King C. Gillette was working for the Crown Cork & Seal Company as a salesman and dabbling with inventions. His boss William Painter, who had invented the bottle stopper that Gillette went about selling, gave the young man a piece of advice, which is part of the folklore of all inventors: "Why don't you invent something that is thrown away, once used, and customers will have to come back for more?" While Gillette was shaving one morning in 1895, the idea of the disposable razor was born. In those days men used blades that had to be continually sharpened by stropping, and when that failed to renew its edge, they had to be professionally honed by a barber or cutler. Gillette later described how the whole idea of using a much smaller and thinner piece of steel came to him as in a flash:

> the way the blade could be held in a holder; the idea of sharpening the two opposite edges on the thin piece of steel; the clamping plates for the blade, with a handle halfway between the two edges of the blade. All this came more in pictures than in conscious thought, as though the razor were already a finished thing, and held before my eyes. I stood there before that mirror in a trance of joy. My wife was visiting Ohio, and I hurriedly wrote to her. "I've got it! Our fortune is made! Fool that I was, I knew little about razors and nothing about steel, and I could not foresee the trials and tribulations I was to pass through before the razor was a success. But I believed in it with my whole heart.

The Dark Night of the Soul

The early years of the Great Depression hit retailers very hard, and J. C. Penney lost a large part of his fortune and the fruits of thirty years of hard work. Apart from the total financial disaster, Penney suffered a nervous breakdown. In the hospital, which he could ill afford, the 58-year-old businessman confronted his deepest fears and questioned his most dearly held values. He described later the turning point:

> One night I became possessed of the strange idea that the end of life had come for me, and that before morning I would be gone. I took a sedative, and went to sleep at nine o'clock. After an hour I awoke, still with the conviction that this was the last night on earth for me. I got up, wrote farewell letters to my family, returned to bed, and again fell asleep.

To my surprise I was still alive the following morning. Feeling restless and apprehensive, I dressed and went downstairs to the dining room, intending to have breakfast. The place had not yet been opened. I wandered disconsolately down the corridor. Presently the sound of singing led me to the chapel, where a small group of people were engaged in an early morning prayer meeting. They were singing the old, familiar hymn:

> Be not dismayed whate'er betide,
> God will take care of you.

Slipping inside, I sat down in one of the back seats. Someone read a passage of Scripture, which was followed by a prayer. Silently, yet in agony of spirit, I cried: "Lord I can do nothing! Will You take care of me?"

Something I can only explain as a miracle happened to me in that quiet chapel. An appalling weight was lifted from my spirit, and I passed from darkness to light. I had entered the room paralyzed in spirit, and helplessly adrift. I left it with an exhilarating sense of relief from the thought of impending death and a reborn hope in life.

Humor

Myron Cohen, the comedian from the garment trade, told of a meeting of George Becker, the furrier, with his partners, who were depressed after a particularly bad season. Becker tried to put the best face on it: "Let's be optimistic, fellows. After all, the only thing we have to fear is fur itself."

The Life of the Party

Following his suspension as president of Columbia Pictures for forging checks, including one of Cliff Robertson's, David Begelman was reinstated just a couple of days before Christmas of 1977. The occasion gave rise to some gallows' humor, as described by David McClintick in *Indecent Exposure:*

A few of the senior studio executives gathered in Begelman's office just after noon, in effect to escort him to the party and make him feel as welcome as possible. Sitting around the office before going downstairs, they tried hard to talk and act as if nothing had happened, as if there had been no forgery investigation, as if David had just returned from a routine business trip, as if it were just another relaxed, preholiday Friday afternoon.

Then someone decided it would be better to break the tension with a David Begelman "joke." Hollywood contains more amateur comedians per capita than any other community in the world, and the Begelman affair had spawned a number of jokes, none particularly witty but each good for a chuckle.

"Hey, David, I hear they're going to make a movie about your life."

"Oh, really?"

"Yeah, Cliff Robertson is playing the lead."

The laughter was brittle. To the group's surprise, however, it turned out that Begelman, who had not lost his sense of humor, had somehow heard all of the David Begelman jokes and immediately joined the fun.

"How would the Polish government have handled the David Begelman problem?" he asked.

"Just like Columbia Pictures," someone answered.

The laughter was less brittle.

"Free the Beverly Hills One," somebody said.

Louder laughter.

"Well, it looks from now on like Columbia Pictures will be *forging ahead* with David Begelman," somebody else said.

Roaring with laughter, Begelman and the others proceeded down the stairs to the party.

Easy Come, Easy Go

In 1983 Steve Jobs was the largest stockholder in Apple Computer, whose stock was selling at above $60. Still in his twenties, the co-founder of Apple had a mystic streak. Not long before he had wandered about barefoot in India in search of higher truth.

A year later, the stock lost two-thirds of its value, which personally cost Jobs $250 million. Asked how he felt about losing a quarter billion dollars, the young man shrugged and replied: "It's very character-building."

Good News, Bad News

Jack Gallagher, the Calgary oilman who built Dome Petroleum into the largest oil company in Canada, took on enormous risks and debts with Arctic exploration and by buying companies. In 1982, high interest rates had driven the company to the brink of bankruptcy. But for government bailouts, the company would have been completely broke. There was a joke making the rounds at the time that one of the Dome vice presidents came to see Gallagher:

"I've got good news and bad news."

"What's your good news?" asked Gallagher.

"We can buy Gulf Oil for only $200 million."

"Great," Gallagher exclaimed, "but what's the bad news?"

"They want fifty bucks down."

SUCCESS

Maxim

On the occasion of an interview between Sir Thomas Buxton and Nathan
Rothschild, the latter said:

> My success has always turned upon one maxim. I said, I can do what
> another man can, and so I am a match for all the rest of 'em. Another
> advantage I had—I was always an off-hand man; I made a bargain at once.
> When I was settled in London, the East India Company had eight hundred
> thousand pounds in gold to sell. I went to the sale, and bought the whole of
> it. I knew the Duke of Wellington must have it. I had bought a great many
> bills of his at a discount. The government sent for me, and said they must
> have it. When they had got it, they didn't know how to get it to Portugal
> where they wanted it. I undertook all that, and sent it through France; and
> that was the best business I ever did in my life.

Stratagem

James Rothschild once described three different kinds of stratagems to be
used in business: "The first situation is when a man jealously guards his
business secrets and tries his utmost to penetrate those of his competitors. The second approach is more difficult: creating all kinds of false
plans, which have the semblance of complete credibility. The third
method is to be so completely frank about one's true intentions that
nobody believes it."

After a slight pause, James Rothschild said quietly: "I think the third
approach is probably the best; at least that is what I invariably employ
myself."

From Acorns

Salomon, founder of the Austrian branch of the House of Rothschild, was
once walking with a friend in the streets of Vienna. A pickpocket following them tried to lift a red silk handkerchief from the banker's jacket
pocket. The friend noticed and tried to warn Rothschild: "My dear
Count, this fellow is trying to steal your handkerchief!"

"So what? Let him be," Rothschild gestured, "we all started small."

Greed Doesn't Pay

Before Cornelius Vanderbilt had become the undisputed master of the seas, he was anxious to get a piece of the transatlantic traffic, which was dominated at the time by the Collins Line of steamers. Along with the route came fat government subsidies to carry the mail. When one of Collins's ships, the *Arctic*, went down, Vanderbilt saw his opportunity and asked Collins to allow his steamer to run the route. He promised to make no claim for the mail subsidy and to take his steamer off as soon as Collins built another boat. But Collins was afraid to let his competitor get hold of any foreign trade and refused in such a manner as to arouse the Commodore's anger. In response, Vanderbilt told Collins that he would run the latter's line off the ocean if it took his whole life and entire fortune to do it.

Vanderbilt at once offered the government to carry the mail more promptly and regularly than it had ever been done before and to do this without a single cent in subsidy. He was known to carry out his promises, and he pressed his offer on the government so vigorously that he was successful in obtaining the mail route. The subsidy to Collins was withdrawn, and the magnificent line soon fell to pieces in consequence of the bankruptcy of its owner, who might have averted his fate, states a contemporary account, by the exercise of a little liberality.

Self-Made and Proud of It

In the fierce newspaper battles of the nineteenth century, Horace Greeley had a continuing feud with a rival editor in New York. Once, when they were both guests at the same banquet, the editor boasted that Greeley had every advantage from his background, while he himself was "a purely self-made man." Greeley immediately declared: "My worthy colleague has just relieved the Almighty of an awesome responsibility."

This calls to mind another story, when somebody was trying to defend Benjamin Disraeli to John Bright, another English politician. His defender pointed out that Disraeli should at least be given credit for being a self-made man.

"Yes," retorted Bright, "and how he adores his maker."

Faith

Somebody once asked Andrew Carnegie for the main ingredient in his success. "Faith," replied the steel magnate. "Faith in myself, faith in others, and faith in my business."

Incentive

Charles Schwab, the man whom Andrew Carnegie paid one million dollars a year to run his steel empire, said:

> I consider my ability to arouse enthusiasm among men the greatest asset that I possess, and the way to develop the best that is in man is by appreciation and encouragement. There is nothing else that so kills the ambitions of a man as criticism from his superiors. I never criticize anyone. I believe in giving a man incentive to work. So I am anxious to praise but loath to find fault. If I like anything, I am hearty in my appreciation and lavish in my praise.

How to Make a Hundred Million—Legally

When Andrew Carnegie wanted to sell his steel plant, he resorted to bluff. At first, he sold a year's option to his partner, Henry Clay Frick, to buy him out for $100 million. Frick tried to sell the plant to J.P. Morgan, as a basis for setting up a steel trust. But after repeated attempts, he could not interest the financier, so at the end of the year he thought that Carnegie should return the option money. Carnegie wrangled with him, and finally said: "You don't know how to sell a plant. I will not give you back one cent from your option."

As a consequence, Frick dissolved the partnership, forcing Carnegie to buy him out on the basis of the $100 million evaluation.

Carnegie still needed to find a buyer for his steel plant. He went about it indirectly. He began at once to commission a survey for a railroad line from Pittsburgh to New York. He spent about $250,000 in getting rights of way and other things, but this was a bagatelle in the game. Inevitably, his activities came to the notice of A. J. Cassett, president of the Pennsylvania Railroad, who became alarmed. Cassett hurried from Philadelphia to New York to see J. P. Morgan about it.

"Morgan," he said, "if this man Carnegie builds this railroad, and it looks as though he means business, he will put the Pennsylvania Railroad in the hands of a receiver. Do you know what that will mean?"

"What will it mean?" asked Morgan.

"It will mean receiverships for all the trunk lines in America. It must be stopped. I wish you would send for Carnegie and see what can be done."

Morgan did send for Carnegie, who told Morgan that the only way to stop that railroad was to buy out his steel plant, and that he would sell the plant for $200 million and take it all in bonds.

"I will take it," said Morgan at once. He thereupon organized the

United States Steel Trust, and with Carnegie's aid secured several other steel plants. The bonds were put on the market, and they were at once gobbled up by the public. Of course, the railroad never was built, and Carnegie later revealed that he never intended to build it. He simply put up a bluff and carried it through. And that is how U.S. Steel was formed, and Carnegie was canny enough to double the option price he had offered to Frick.

Mathematics

Julius Rosenwald, the Chicago multimillionaire and philanthropist, used to tell the following story about the connection between intelligence and making money:

"A gambler won a million dollars on number 14. When asked how he did it, 'I had a dream,' he said. 'One night I saw in my dream a great big 9, and next I saw the number 6. So I used my brains and figured out that 9 plus 6 is 14.'"

Peanuts

George Washington Carver was responsible for turning the lowly peanut into an industry. He was once approached by a friend who noticed that he was reading the Bible.

"What are you doing?" the friend asked.

"I am studying about peanuts," replied Dr. Carver.

"To me you seem to be reading the Bible."

"I am reading how God reveals Himself to men," explained the agriculturist, "and for me God is revealing Himself through peanuts."

A Way to Look at It

When F. W. Woolworth opened his first store, a merchant on the same street tried to fight the new competition. He hung out a big sign: "Doing business in this same spot for over fifty years." The next day Woolworth also put out a sign. It read: "Established a week ago; no old stock."

Door to the Future

Clarence Francis, who later became chairman of General Foods, originally wanted to get into the oil business. As he planned his career, he targeted Standard Oil as the place where he wanted to get a start. He carefully prepared himself, rehearsed his pitch, pressed his only suit, and went down to Wall Street, where Standard Oil had its skyscraper. Young Francis asked the janitor for the secretary of the company and took the elevator to the designated floor, where he went down the hallway until he found an open door. Adjusting his tie for the tenth time and quickly combing his hair, he once again asked for the secretary of the company. Somewhat to his surprise, he was ushered in to see an old gentleman who listened to his sales pitch and hired the promising young man as a clerical worker on the spot.

"Every day for a long time afterwards," Clarence Francis recalled, "I took a good look at the door that was open. The sign on it read: 'Corn Products Co.'"

And that's how he got into the food business.

How to Make Friends and Money

Despite early successs as a salesman of correspondence courses and of Packard automobiles and a brief career as an actor, Dale Carnegie was slow in finding his route to success. He had a teacher's certificate, but he did not know what to teach. Then he remembered how in his entire education the most important thing he had learned was public speaking. This is what gave him confidence and poise, the ability to deal with people both on the personal level and in business. He proposed to the YMCA schools of New York that he should give courses in public speaking to businessmen. The YMCA had so little confidence in the idea that they refused to pay him the $2 a night he requested as his fee. Instead, they agreed to give him a percentage of the net profits. Within three years, the course proved so popular that Carnegie was receiving $30 a night, and he was besieged with offers to teach in other U.S. cities and in Europe. Out of these courses came the first of many best-sellers, *Public Speaking and Influencing Men in Business* and the Dale Carnegie Institute, which still conducts seminars worldwide.

American Dreams

As far back as he could remember, Tom Monaghan, founder of Domino's Pizza, had been given to big dreams. An orphan from a poor family in rural Michigan, Tom in his teens was dreaming about owning the Detroit Tigers one day. Dropping out of college, he started a tiny pizza store in 1960; today he runs the world's largest pizza delivery company, with annual sales above $2 billion. He owns a franchise of 4,100 stores, still growing, and employing 130,000 people. And, of course, he owns the Detroit Tigers, having paid $53 million for the baseball team in 1983.

"Dreaming is the greatest preparation for wealth," Tom Monaghan told *The Los Angeles Times*. "Because when the opportunity came, I think I was ready for it. A lot of people around me would see me doing things that made no sense to them at all . . . but I had a big jump on them. I was thinking about these things years ago."

The Wright Stuff

A passion that Tom Monaghan had been nursing since adolescence is for the work of Frank Lloyd Wright, another American original. Monaghan has built a collection of Wright furniture and decorative art worth about $13 million. He paid $200,000 for a simple chair designed by Wright, and a record $1.6 million for a dining room set. He is spending millions more on converting a hunting lodge on a private island in Lake Huron into a retreat based on Wright's design concepts. Domino's corporate headquarters outside Ann Arbor is also being built in the Wright style, covering 1 million square feet. Monaghan recently announced his latest tribute to the architect: plans to build an $80 million conference center, with a 435 foot cantilevered tower that will be leaning off center. He wants to call it Domino's Tower, but local wags have already christened it "The Leaning Tower of Pizza."

Last Words

At the age of 77, George Eastman, the founder of Kodak, asked his doctor to show him where his heart was and then shot himself. He explained in a note to his friends: "The work is done. Why wait?"

And Then What

Toward the end of his life Meyer Guggenheim, who made his fortune in mining, was working in his office, when a man burst in, trying to sell him a new smelting process. With his invention, the man claimed in highly excited German, Guggenheim could gain control of all the copper in the world. Meyer listened. The man went on that the next step would be to control all mineral wealth on earth. Old Meyer was unmoved, while the visitor got more excited.

"But, don't you see, that with all that, you would become the richest and most powerful man in the entire world?"

Guggenheim leaned back in his chair, pulled at his whiskers, and finally said: "*Und dann?*"

Exit

Martin Zweig, the investment counselor, has an abstract painting hanging in his office with the motto from Ben Franklin: "The things which hurt instruct."

Zweig also likes to quote one of the stories told about P. T. Barnum when he became a victim of his own success. So many people were crowding into his shows that huge lines were forming outside the tent. To speed up his turnover, Barnum came up with a solution: he put up a big sign inside the tent, which read: "This way to the egress." People, who thought that egress meant another attraction, eagerly filed outside.

It is my hope that the reader will find many new anecdotes outside my tent.

BIBLIOGRAPHY

Adamic, Louis. *Dynamite: The Story of Class Violence in America*. New York: Viking Press, 1934.

Adelman, Joseph. *Famous Women*. New York: John L. Rogers, 1926.

Adler, Bill. *The Washington Wits*. New York: Macmillan, 1967.

After Dinner Stories by Famous Men. New York: Hearst's International Library Co., 1914.

Ames, Mary Clemmer, *Ten Years in Washington: Life and Scenes in the National Capital, as a Woman Sees Them*. Cincinnati, Ohio: 1874.

Anderson, William. *The Popular Scottish Biography; Being Lives of Eminent Natives of Scotland*. Edinburgh: 1842.

Anecdotes of the Hour by Famous Men. New York: Hearst's International Library Co., 1914.

Angell, Norman. *The Story of Money*. Garden City, New York: Garden City Publishing Co., 1929.

Arkell, W. J. *Old Friends and Some Acquaintances*. Los Angeles: Self-published, 1927.

Arnold, Stanley. *Tale of the Blue Horse and Other Million Dollar Adventures*. Englewood Cliffs, New Jersey: Prentice-Hall, 1968.

Asman, David, and Adam Meyerson, eds. *The Wall Street Journal on Management*. Homewood, Illinois: Dow-Jones-Irwin, 1985.

Augustine, Norman R. *Augustine's Laws*. New York: Viking Penguin, 1986.

Barker, Ernest. *The Character of England*. London: Readers Union, Oxford University Press, 1950.

Barmash, Isadore. *The Self-Made Man: Success and Stress American Style*. New York: Macmillan, 1969.

Barnum, P. T. *Struggles and Triumphs: or Forty Years' Recollections of P. T. Barnum.* Buffalo, New York, 1872.

Barrett, Walter. *The Old Merchants of New York City.* New York: 1863.

Bates, William. *The Maclise Portrait Gallery of Illustrious Literary Characters.* London: Chatto & Windus, 1898.

Békés, István. *A Világ Anekdotakincse.* Budapest: Gondolat, 1975.

Bender, Marilyn. *At the Top.* Garden City, New York: Doubleday, 1975.

Bettger, Frank. *How I Raised Myself from Failure to Success in Selling.* New York: Prentice-Hall, 1949.

————. *How I Multiplied My Income & Happiness in Selling.* New York: Prentice-Hall, 1954.

Bird, Caroline. *Enterprising Women.* New York: W. W. Norton, 1976.

Bird, Harry Lewis. *This Fascinating Advertising Business.* Indianapolis: Bobbs-Merrill, 1947.

Birmingham, Stephen. *The Grandes Dames.* New York: Simon & Schuster, 1982.

Bishop, James, Jr., and Henry W. Hubbard. *Let the Seller Beware.* Washington, D.C.: The National Press, 1969.

Black, Hillel. *The Watchdogs of Wall Street.* New York: William Morrow, 1962.

Bloom, Murray Teigh. *Rogues to Riches.* New York: Putnam, 1971.

Boller, Paul F., Jr. *Presidential Anecdotes.* New York: Oxford University Press, 1981.

Bolton, Sarah K. *Lives of Poor Boys Who Became Famous.* New York: Thomas Y. Crowell, 1947.

Bombaugh, Charles C. *Facts and Fancies for the Curious.* Philadelphia: J. B. Lippincott, 1905.

Botkin, B. A. *A Treasury of American Anedotes.* New York: Random House, 1957.

Braude, Jacob M. *Complete Speaker's and Toastmaster's Library.* Englewood Cliffs, New Jersey: Prentice-Hall, 1965.

Bremner, Robert H. *American Philanthropy.* Chicago: The University of Chicago Press, 1960.

Bridges, Constance. *Great Thoughts of Great Americans.* New York: Thomas Y. Crowell, 1951.

Brooks, John. *Business Adventures.* New York: Weybright & Talley, 1969.

————. *The Go-Go Years.* New York: Weybright & Talley, 1973.

Brower, Bill. *The Complete Traveling Salesman's Joke Book.* New York: Stravon Publishers, 1953.

Brower, Charlie. *Me and Other Advertising Geniuses.* Garden City, New York: Doubleday, 1974.

"Brutus." *Confessions of a Stockbroker: A Wall Street Diary.* Boston:

Little, Brown, 1971.

Burruss, William. *Shakespeare the Salesman*. Chicago: The Dartnell Corporation, 1942.

Bursk, Edward C., Donald T. Clark, and Ralph W. Hidy. *The World of Business*. New York: Simon & Schuster, 1962.

Button, Henry, and Andrew Lampert. *The Guinness Book of the Business World*. Enfield: Guiness Superlatives Ltd., 1976.

Campbell, Hannah. *Why Did They Name It . . .?* New York: Fleet Publishing, 1964.

Canney, Margaret, and David Knott, eds. *The University of London Library Catalogue of the Goldsmiths' Library of Economic Literature*. Cambridge University Press, 1970.

Cantor, Eddie. *Caught Short! A Saga of Wailing Wall Street*. New York: Simon and Schuster, 1929 A.C. (After Crash).

Carlston, Douglas. *Software People*. New York: Simon & Schuster, 1985.

Carnegie, Dale. *Five Minute Biographies*. New York: Southern Publishers, 1937.

––––––. *How to Win Friends and Influence People*. New York: Simon & Schuster, 1936.

Cerf, Bennett. *Shake Well Before Using*. New York: Simon and Schuster, 1948.

––––––. *Good for a Laugh*. Garden City, New York: Hanover House, 1952.

––––––. *The Life of the Party*. Garden City, New York: Doubleday, 1956.

––––––.*Laugh Day*. Garden City, New York: Doubleday, 1965.

Chaplin, J. P. *Rumor, Fear and the Madness of Crowds*. New York: Ballantine, 1959.

Chapman, H. S. *1001 One Minute Stories*. Boston: Perry Mason Company, 1927.

Chrysler, Walter P. *Life of an American Workman*. New York: Dodd, Mead, 1950.

Coffman, C. DeWitt, and John Keasler. *Keyhole Inn-Sights: An Uninhibited Peek Into the Hotel World*. Englewood Cliffs, New Jersey: Prentice-Hall, 1972.

Cohen, Myron. *Laughing Out Loud*. New York: The Citadel Press, 1958.

Cohen, Scott. *Meet the Makers: The People Behind the Product*. New York: St. Martin's Press, 1979.

David L. Cohn. *The Good Old Days*. New York: Simon & Schuster, 1940.

Cossman, E. Joseph. *How I Made $1,000,000 in Mail Order*. Englewood Cliffs, New Jersey: Prentice-Hall, 1963.

Cribb, Joe, ed. *Money: From Cowrie Shells to Credit Cards*. London: British Museum Publications, 1986.

Crow, Carl. *The Great American Customer*. New York: Harper & Brothers, 1943.

Cunningham, Mary (with Fran Schumer) *Powerplay: What Really Happened at Bendix*. New York: Linden Press, 1984.

Darvas, Nicolas. *How I Made $2,000,000 in the Stock Market*. New York: Dell, 1961.

———. *Wall Street: The Other Las Vegas*. New York: Ace Publishing Corp., 1964.

Decker, James, ed. *The Good Business Treasure Chest*. New York: Hawthorn Books, 1958.

De Mente, Boye. *Japanese Manners & Ethics in Business*. Tokyo: East Asia Publishing Co., Ltd., 1961.

D'Israeli, Isaac. *Curiosities of Literature*. New York: 1865.

———. *Calamities and Quarrels of Authors*. London: n.d.

Douglass, Paul F. *Six Upon the World*. Boston: Little, Brown, 1954.

Dreier, Thomas. *The Silver Lining; or Sunshine on the Business Trail*. New York: B. C. Forbes Publishing Company, 1923.

Droke, Maxwell. *The Speaker's Handbook of Humor*. New York: Harper & Brothers, 1956.

Drucker, Peter F. *Adventures of a Bystander*. New York: Harper & Row, 1979.

———. *Management Cases*. New York: Harper & Row, 1977.

Elliot, Osborn. *Men at the Top*. New York: Harper & Brothers, 1959.

Ellis, John B. *The Sights and Secrets of the National Capital*. Chicago: 1869.

Fadiman, Clifton. *The Little, Brown Book of Anecdotes*. Boston: Little, Brown, 1985.

Fern, William G. *Lessons from a Self Made Continent*. London: "Modern Salesmanship," n.d.

Firestone, Ross. *The Success Trip*. Chicago: Playboy Press, 1976.

Flexner, Stuart Berg. *Listening to America: An Illustrated History of Words and Phrases from Our Lively and Splendid Past*. New York: Simon & Schuster, 1982.

Forbes, B. C. *Forbes Epigrams: 1000 Thoughts on Life and Business*. New York: B. C. Forbes Publishing Company, 1922.

———. *499 Scottish Stories (for the price of 500)*. New York: B. C. Forbes Publishing Company, 1945.

———. *America's Fifty Foremost Business Leaders*. New York: B. C. Forbes & Sons Publishing Company, 1948.

———. *The Forbes Scrapbook of Thoughts in the Business of Life*. New York: B. C. Forbes & Sons Publishing Company, 1950.

Fortune Magazine. *The Amazing Advertising Business*. New York: Simon and Schuster, 1957.

—————. *The Art of Success*. Philadelphia: J. B. Lippincott, 1955.

—————. *100 Stories of Business Success*. New York: Simon & Schuster, 1954.

Fowler, William Worthington. *Ten Years in Wall Street; or Revelations of Inside Life and Experience on 'Change*. Hartford, Connecticut: 1870.

Friedman, Philip R. *Washington Humor*. New York: The Citadel Press, 1964.

Fucini, Joseph and Suzy Fucini. *Entrepreneurs—the Men and Women behind Famous Brand Names and How They Made It*. Boston: G. K. Hall, 1985.

Fuller, Edmund. *A Thesaurus of Anecdotes*. New York: Crown, 1942.

Fun for the Millions, or The Laughing Philosopher. London: 1824.

Galbraith, John Kenneth. *The Great Crash of 1929*. Boston: Houghton Mifflin Company, 1972.

Gandhi, Mohandas K. *The Story of My Experiments with Truth*. Ahmedabad: Navayivan Press, 1929.

Goldsmith, Walter, and David Clutterbuck. *The Winning Streak*. London: George Weidenfeld & Nicolson, 1984.

Gompers, Samuel. *Seventy Years of Life and Labor*. New York: E. P. Dutton, 1925.

Goodman, Walter. *The Clowns of Commerce*. New York: Sagamore Press, 1957.

Gould, Allan. *The New Entrepreneurs: 80 Canadian Success Stories*. Toronto: Seal Books, 1986.

Green, Abel, and Joe Laurie, Jr. *Show Biz: From Vaude to Video as Seen by VARIETY*. New York: Holt, 1951.

Griffiths, Arthur. *Mysteries of Police and Crime*. London: Cassel and Company, n.d.

Groner, Alex et al. *The American Heritage of American Business and Industry*. New York: American Heritage Publishing Co., 1972.

Das Grosse Buch der Anekdote. München: Bechtle Verlag, 1964.

Grun, Bernard. *Private Lives of the Great Composers, Conductors and Musical Artistes of the World*. London: Rider and Co., 1954.

Gunther, John. *Taken at the Flood*. New York: Harper & Brothers, 1960.

Gunther, Max. *Wall Street and Witchcraft*. New York: Bernard Geis Associates, 1971.

Haas, Albert Jr., and Don D. Jackson, M.D. *Bulls, Bears and Dr. Freud*. Cleveland, Ohio: The World Publishing Company, 1967.

Haden-Guest, Anthony. *The Paradise Program*. New York: William Morrow, 1973.

Halberstam, David. *The Reckoning*. New York: William Morrow, 1986.

Hall, Donald. *The Oxford Book of American Literary Anecdotes*. New York: Oxford University Press, 1981.

Halle, Kay. *The Irrepressible Churchill*. New York and Oxford: Facts On File Publications, 1985.

Harding, Alfred. *The Revolt of the Actors*. New York: William Morrow, 1929.

Harris, Leon A. *The Fine Art of Political Wit*. New York: E. P. Dutton, 1964.

Harris, Leon. *Merchant Princes*. New York: Harper & Row, 1979.

Henderson, Ernest. *The World of "Mr. Sheraton."* New York: David McKay Co., 1960.

Hendrickson, Robert. *The Great American Chewing Gum Book*. Radnor, Pennsylvania: Chilton Book Company, 1976.

Henry, Lewis C. *5000 Quotations for All Occasions*. Garden City, New York: Garden City Books, 1945.

————. *Humorous Anecdotes About Famous People*. Garden City, New York: Halcyon House, 1948.

Hertz, Leah. *The Business Amazons*. London: André Deutsch, 1986.

Higdon, Hal. *The Business Healers*. New York: Random House, 1969.

Hislop, Alexander. *The Book of Scottish Anecdotes*. Glasgow, 1888.

Hoar, William P. *Architects of Conspiracy*. Boston: Western Islands, 1984.

Hoisington, Harland W. Sr. *Wall Street (1920-1970): Five Fabulous Decades*. New York: Vantage Press, 1972.

Holbrook, Stewart H. *Lost Men of American History*. New York: Macmillan, 1946.

————. *The Age of the Moguls*. Garden City, New York: Doubleday & Co., 1953.

————. *Dreamers of the Dream*. Garden City, New York: Doubleday & Co., 1957.

Huck, Virginia. *Brand of the Tartan: The 3M Story*. New York: Appleton-Century-Crofts, 1955.

Iacocca, Lee (with William Novak). *Iacocca: An Autobiography*. New York: Bantam Books, 1984.

Irving, Morgan, and Charles Sopkin. *The Bank Book*. Boston: Little, Brown, 1973.

Johnson, Allen, ed. *The Chronicles of America*. 50 vols. New Haven, Connecticut: Yale University Press, 1921.

Johnston, J. P. *Twenty Years of Hus'ling*. Chicago: 1887.

————. *What Happened to Johnston*. Chicago: 1904.

Kaplan, Gilbert Edmund, and Chris Welles, eds. *The Money Managers* New York: Random House, 1969.

Kent, Robert W. *Money Talk$: the 2500 Greatest Business Quotes from Aristotle to Iacocca*. New York: Facts On File, 1985.

Kieffer, Henry Martyn. *Laugh Again: Short Stories and Amusing Anecdotes for a Dull Hour*. New York: Dodge Publishing, 1913.

Kirkland, Frazar. *Cyclopaedia of Commercial and Business Anecdotes*. New York: 1864.

Kowet, Don. *The Rich Who Own Sports*. New York: Random House, 1977.

Lamott, Kenneth. *The Money-Makers*. Boston: Little, Brown, 1969.

Landon, Melville D. *Wit and Humor of the Age*. Chicago: 1883.

Lanier, Henry Wysham. *A Century of Banking in New York (1822-1922)*. New York: The Gilliss Press, 1922.

Larrabee, C. B. and Henry W. Marks, eds. *Tested Selling Ideas*. New York: McGraw-Hill, 1936.

Learsi, Rufus. *Filled With Laughter: A Fiesta of Jewish Folk Humor*. New York: Thomas Yoseloff, 1961.

Lefevre, Edwin. *Reminiscences of a Stock Operator*. New York: George H. Doran Co., 1923.

Leavitt, Judith A. *American Women Managers and Administrators*. Westport, Connecticut: Greenwood Press, 1985.

Lehr, Lew, Cal Tinney, and Roger Bower. *Stop Me If You've Heard This One*. Garden City, New York: Halcyon House, 1948.

Levering, Robert, Michael Katz, and Milton Moskowitz. *The Computer Entrepreneurs: Who's Making It Big and How in America's Upstart Industry*. New York: New American Library, 1984.

Lieberman, Gerald F. *The Greatest Laughs of All Time*. Garden City, New York: Doubleday, 1961.

Lips, Julius E. *The Origin of Things*. New York: A. A. Wyn, 1947.

Livesay, Harold C. *American Made*. Boston: Little, Brown, 1979.

Lonn, George. *Builders of Fortunes: Portraits and Profiles of Men Who Made Fortunes from the Treasures of the Earth*. Toronto: Pitt Publishing Company, 1963.

Lorimer, George Horace. *Letters from a Self-Made Merchant to His Son*. Boston: Small, Maynard & Company, 1903.

Lundberg, Ferdinand. *The Rich and the Super-Rich*. New York: Lyle Stuart, 1968.

Luongo, C. Paul. *America's Best! 100*. New York: Sterling Publishing, 1980.

McCabe, James D. *Great Fortunes and How They Were Made: or the Struggles and Triumphs of Our Self-made Men*. Philadelphia: 1871.

McClintick, David. *Indecent Exposure: A True Story of Hollywood and Wall Street*. New York: William Morrow, 1982.

MacDougall, Curtis D. *Hoaxes*. New York: Macmillan, 1940.

Madigan, Carol Rosag, and Ann Elwood. *Brainstorms and Thunderbolts: How Creative Genius Works*. New York, Macmillan, 1983.

Mahoney, Tom, and Leonard Sloane. *The Great Merchants: America's Foremost Retail Institutions and the People Who Made Them Great*. New York: Harper & Row, 1974.

Marcosson, Isaac F. *Wherever Men Trade: The Romance of the Cash Register*. New York: Dodd, Mead, 1945.

Marcus, Stanley. *Minding the Store*. Boston: Little, Brown, 1974.

Manchee, Fred. *The Huckster's Revenge*. New York: Thomas Nelson, 1959.

Marks, Sid, and Alban Emley. *The Newspaperboys' Hall of Fame*. Hollywood, California: House-Warven, Publishers, 1953.

Marquard, Ralph. *Jokes and Anecdotes for All Occasions*. New York: Hart Publishing Co., 1977.

Mason, James. *The Great Triumphs of Great Men*. London: 1875.

Maunder, Samuel. *The Biographical Treasury; a Dictionary of Universal Biography*. London: 1842.

Mayer, Martin. *Wall Street: Men and Money*. New York: Harper & Brothers, 1955.

————. *Madison Avenue, U.S.A*. New York: Harper & Brothers, 1958.

Medbery, James K. *Men and Mysteries of Wall Street*. Boston: 1870.

Mendelsohn, S. Felix. *Let Laughter Ring*. Philadelphia: The Jewish Publication Society, 1956.

Menzies, H. Stuart. *Let's Forget Business: The Commentaries of Fortnum & Mason*. London: A. & C. Black, Ltd., 1930.

Meyer, Donald. *The Positive Thinkers*. New York: Pantheon Books, 1980.

Meyers, James. *Eggplants, Elevators, Etc.—An Uncommon History of Common Things*. New York: Hart Publishing Co., 1978.

The Mirrors of Wall Street. New York: Putnam's, 1933.

Moch, Cheryl, and Vincent Varga. *Deals*. New York: Crown Publishers, 1984.

Moore, Dan Tyler. *Wolves, Widows and Orphans*. Cleveland, Ohio: The World Publishing Company, 1966.

de Morgan, John. *In Lighter Vein*. San Francisco and New York: 1907.

Morris, Lloyd. *Incredible New York*. New York: Random House, 1951.

Moskowitz, Milton, Michael Katz, and Robert Levering (eds.) *Everybody's Business Scoreboard*. New York: Harper & Row, 1983.

Murphy, John, ed. *Secrets of Successful Selling*. Englewood Cliffs, New Jersey: Prentice-Hall, 1956.

Newman, Peter C. *Bronfman Dynasty*. Toronto: McClelland & Stewart, 1978.

————. *The Canadian Establishment*. Toronto: McClelland & Stewart, 1975.

Norrie, Ian. ed. *The Book of the City*. London: High Hill Books, 1961.

Norton-Taylor, Duncan. *For Some, The Dream Came True*. Secaucus, New Jersey: Lyle Stuart, 1981.

Von Oech, Roger. *A Whack on the Side of the Head: How to Unlock Your Mind for Innovation*. New York: Warner Books, 1983.

Owen, Robert. *The Life of Robert Owen, written by himself*. London, 1857.

Parker, John F. *The Fun and Laughter of Politics*. Garden City, New York: Doubleday, 1978.

Pascale, Richard Tanner, and Anthony G. Athos. *The Art of Japanese Management*. New York: Simon & Schuster, 1981.

Patten, William. *Among the Humorists and After-Dinner Speakers*. New York: P. F. Collier & Son, 1909.

Pearson, John. and Graham Turner. *The Persuasion Industry*. London: Eyre & Spottiswoode, 1965.

Percy, H. C. *Our Cashier's Scrap-Book—A Portfolio of Bank Anecdotes and Incidents, Queer, Curious, Odd, Ludicrous, Touching*. New York: 1879.

Percy, Reuben, and Sholto Percy. *The Percy Anecdotes*. 20 vols. London, 1821-1823.

Peters, Thomas J., and Robert H. Waterman, Jr. *In Search of Excellence*. New York: Harper & Row, 1982.

Petras, Ross, and Kathryn Petras. *Inside Track*. New York: Vintage Books, 1986.

Porter, Glenn. *The Rise of Big Business, 1860-1910*. New York: Thomas Y. Crowell, 1973.

Pratt, Sereno S. *The Work of Wall Street*. New York: D. Appleton & Co., 1908.

Presley, James. *A Saga of Wealth: The Rise of the Texas Oilmen*. New York: Putnam, 1978.

Rachlis, Eugene, and John E. Marqusee. *The Landlords*. New York: Random House, 1963.

Robinson, Jeffrey. *The Risk-takers: Portraits of Money, Ego & Power*. London: George Allen & Unwin, 1985.

Roosevelt, James, and Sidney Shalett. *Affectionately, F. D.R.* New York: Harcourt, Brace, 1959.

Rosner, Joseph. *The Hater's Handbook*. New York: Delacorte Press, 1965.

Ross, Irwin. *The Image Merchants*. Garden City, New York: Doubleday, 1959.

Roth, Charles B. *How to Make $25,000 a Year Selling*. Englewood Cliffs, New Jersey: Prentice-Hall, 1953.

Russell, Frederic A., Frank H. Beach, and Richard H. Buskirk. *Textbook of Salesmanship*. New York: McGraw-Hill, 1963.

Russell, Oland D. *The House of Mitsui*. Boston: Little, Brown, 1939.

Sachs, Emanie. *The Terrible Siren*. New York: Harper & Brothers, 1928.

Sampson, Anthony. *The Money Lenders*. New York: Viking Press, 1982.

————. *The Seven Sisters: The Great Oil Companies and the World They Shaped*. New York: Viking Press, 1975.

————. *The Sovereign State of ITT*. New York: Stein and Day, 1974.

Scarlatti, Amerigo. *Et Ab Hic Et Ab Hoc: Curiosità del Commercio e della Vita*. Torino: Unione Tipografico-Editrice Torinese, 1927.

Shriner, Charles A. *Wit, Wisdom and Foibles of the Great*. New York: Funk & Wagnalls, 1918.

Schultz Harry D. and Samson Coslow, eds. *A Treasury of Wall Street Wisdom*. Palisades Park: Investors' Press, Inc., 1966.

Schuster, M. Lincoln. *A Treasury of the World's Great Letters*. New York: Simon & Schuster, 1940.

Schwed, Fred, Jr. *Where are the Customers' Yachts? or a Good Hard Look at Wall Street*. New York: Simon & Schuster, 1940.

Schwed, Peter. *God Bless Pawnbrokers*. New York: Dodd, Mead, 1975.

Selfridge, Gordon. *The Romance of Commerce*. London: Bodley Head, 1933.

Silver, A. David. *Entrepreneurial Megabucks*. New York: John Wiley, 1985.

Skinner, Cornelia Otis. *Elegant Wits and Grand Horizontals*. Boston: Houghton Mifflin Company, 1962.

Sloan, Alfred P., Jr. *My Years with General Motors*. Garden City, New York: Doubleday, 1963.

Smiles, Samuel. *Self-Help; with Illustrations of Conduct and Perseverance*. London: 1876.

Smith, Adam, [pseudo]. *The Money Game*. New York: Random House, 1967.

Smith, H. Allen. *The Compleat Practical Joker*. New York: William Morrow, 1980.

Sices, Murray. *Seventh Avenue*. New York: Fairchild Publications, 1953.

Sobel, Robert. *IBM: Colossus in Transition*. New York: Times Books, 1981.

Sopkin, Charles. *Money Talks!* New York: Random House, 1964.

Sparkes, Boyden, and Samuel Taylor Moore. *The Witch of Wall Street: Hetty Green*. Garden City, New York: Doubleday, Doran & Co., 1935.

Stevens, Mark. *The Inside Story of Bloomingdale's*. New York: Thomas Y. Crowell, 1979.

Sutherland, James. *The Oxford Book of Literary Anecdotes*. New York: Oxford University Press, 1975.

Tamarkin, Bob. *The New Gatsbys: Fortunes and Misfortunes of Commodity Traders*. New York: William Morrow, 1985.

Thomas, David. *Knights of the New Technology: The Inside Story of Canada's Computer Elite*. Toronto: Key Porter Books, 1983.

Thomas, Henry, and Dana Lee Thomas. *Fifty Great Americans*. Garden City, New York: Doubleday, 1948.

Thorndike, Ashley H. *Modern Eloquence*. New York: Modern Eloquence Corporation, 1928.

Timbs, John. *A Century of Anecdotes from 1760 to 1860*. London: 1864.

———. *Notable Things of Our Own Time*. London: 1877.

———. *The Romance of London: Strange Stories, Scenes and Remarkable Persons of the Great Town*. London, n.d.

Tobias, Andrew. *Fire and Ice*. New York: William Morrow, 1976.

Towner, Wesley. *The Elegant Auctioneers*. New York: Hill & Wang, 1970.

Townsend, Robert. *Up the Organization: How to Stop the Corporation from Stifling People and Strangling Profits*. New York: Alfred A. Knopf, 1970.

Train John. *The Money Masters*. New York: Harper & Row, 1981.

The Tribune. *Pictured Encyclopaedia of the World's Greatest Newspaper*. Chicago: The Tribune Company, 1928.

Vicker, Ray. *Those Swiss Money Men*. London: Robert Hale, 1973.

Vidám Könyvtár. Budapest: n.p., n.d.

Wall Street Journal. *The New Millionaires and How They Made Their Fortunes*. New York: MacFadden Books, 1962.

Walsh, William S. *Handy-Book of Literary Curiosities*. Philadelphia: J. B. Lippincott, 1892.

Wheeler, Elmer. *Tested Sentences that Sell*. New York: Prentice-Hall, 1937.

White, W. L. *Bernard Baruch: Portrait of A Citizen*. New York: Harcourt, Brace, 1950.

Whiting, Robert Rudd. *Four Hundred Good Stories*. New York: The Baker & Taylor Co., 1910.

Winterich, John T. *Another Day, Another Dollar*. Philadelphia: J. B. Lippincott, 1947.

Wright, J. Patrick. *On a Clear Day You Can See General Motors: John Z.*

De Lorean's Look Inside the Automotive Giant. New York: Avon Books, 1980.

Wright, Richardson. *Hawkers and Walkers In Early America*. Philadelphia: J.B. Lippincott, 1927.

Wood, Robert A., ed. *Cool Millions: Life Among the Super Rich*. Kansas City: Hallmark Editions, 1974.

Zweig, Martin E. *Martin Zweig's Winning on Wall Street*. New York: Warner Books, 1986.

The following periodicals, journals and newspapers were consulted: *Bits & Pieces; Business Week; The Economist; Encounter; Esquire; Financial Times; Fortune; INC.; Los Angeles Times; Maclean's; Manhattan Inc.; Newsweek; New York Times; People; Playboy; Publishers Weekly; Wall Street Journal.*

INDEX